YANKEE SHIPS

An Informal History of the American Merchant Marine

ONE OF THE BEAUTIES THAT LED US ASTRAY

Clipper ship *Lightning*, built by Donald McKay in 1854. She burned in Melbourne in 1869. From a painting by Montague Dawson.

Yankee Ships

An Informal History of the
American Merchant Marine

By

Reese Wolfe

WITH A PREFACE BY
JOHN JENNINGS

THE BOBBS-MERRILL COMPANY, INC.
Publishers
INDIANAPOLIS   NEW YORK

COPYRIGHT, 1953, BY REESE WOLFE

PRINTED IN THE UNITED STATES OF AMERICA

Library of Congress Catalog Card Number: 53-5235

First Edition

To my Mother and Father

from whom I learned the deeper significance
of "the way of the ship."

ACKNOWLEDGMENT

FOR THE inspiration and friendly counsel of Charles Leigh Wheeler, merchant adventurer, I wish to make known my deep appreciation.

To the Honorable Walter B. Beals, Justice of the Supreme Court of the State of Washington, retired, I am indebted in large measure for little-known bits of information and human sidelights on early American history which but for his erudition would not have found their way into this book.

My thanks go also to my brother Cameron Wolfe, scholar and patient critic, and to Jere Quirk, able-bodied seaman, who I hope, if he is alive today, will see here and recognize some old ghosts of whom we talked on many a watch below.

And a special salute to John Forney Rudy, fellow writer, whose interest and encouragement brought the manuscript for this book back from Fiddler's Green.

CONTENTS

PART 1

THE COLONIAL MERCHANT FLEET

PART 2

AMERICA GETS HER SEA LEGS

CONTENTS—*Continued*

PART 3

THE GOLDEN YEARS

PART 4

THE DOLDRUMS

PART 5

BATTLE OF THE SEVEN SEAS

LIST OF ILLUSTRATIONS

PREFACE

OUR WORLD was made and filled out by sailors. The knowledge we would have of it if there had been no ships and no sailors is too fantastic for us to imagine. Let us take for granted ships and men to work them and suppose only that none of the mariners had the boldness to venture out of sight of land and pierce the unknown. What would our world have been like? The result is staggering.

The Phoenicians may actually have felt their way around the Iberian Peninsula and up along the Bay of Biscay into the Channel until they noticed the far-off, misty outlines of the cliffs of Dover and so discovered Britain. Going the other way, the Portuguese might have sighted Africa across the Straits of Gibraltar and coasted down its east coast, turned the Cape of Good Hope and sailed up the west coast to Somaliland and beyond—though in fact they did not. It is conceivable that from there they might have turned and hugged the coast on the other shore of the Red Sea to round the Arabian Peninsula and beyond to the coast of India. Still creeping along the shore, they might have rounded the Malay Peninsula and clawed their way up the coast of China and beyond. The chances are they would have been wrecked or old men before this voyage was completed, but the possibility is conceivable. They might have gone even a little farther, perhaps to Kamchatka, possibly to Japan.

Even so, conceding the utmost to this groping along the visible shore, we can tell by a quick look at the map what great expanses of our civilized world—if I may be excused for calling it that—would have been left unknown and unexplored. The world as we know it we owe to mariners, and bold mariners, who cut across open sea into the unknown. They found the lands and mapped the shore lines.

Columbus had to venture far to the westward, weeks out of sight of land, before he stumbled on America. Others followed his dare and put out to find South America, the Arctic and Antarctica, the East Indies, Australia, New Zealand—to say nothing of a thousand other lands and islands. What a small, incomplete world we would have had if these mariners had had less courage!

What, for instance, would America have become without contact with Europe? How would Europe have developed without America? It is a fascinating speculation.

Speculation or no, the facts remain. And facts are what Reese Wolfe has undertaken to give us here. He takes only a reasonable slice of them, not more than he can handle. In effect, what he offers is a history of the American merchant marine from its very beginning, in the launching of the first seagoing vessel on the Kennebec, down to the present time.

Such histories have been done before, but none of them quite like his, I believe. The story has been told from the angle of the ships involved, from the viewpoint of the owners and of ship captains. Never before has the story been told from the standpoint of the men who had to sail the vessels, and this, I think, is what Reese Wolfe has given us that is new.

Where Columbus and the other celebrated explorers went, sailors had to take them. Sailors, like ships, are at the bottom of the whole history of navigation. For many generations they were at a very uncomfortable bottom. Old sayings, maxims and legal tags testify to their hard lot and uncertain life. According to *Hughes on Admiralty,* the usual view of seamen held by the courts was specific: "They are improvident and wild, easily imposed upon, and the constant prey of designing men." The quarter-deck attitude was expressed by such sayings as "No law off soundings" and "Hard ships make hard men." The sailors themselves said, "We live hard, die hard and go to hell afterwards."

How the conditions underlying such sayings have been modified and made to meet at sea the standards of modern labor is one of the main points Reese Wolfe has given us.

At the risk of being personal, I want to mention an old ghost come to haunt me. Once the Export Line ship *City of Eureka,* home port Portland, Oregon, sailed from the foot of Java Street in Brooklyn. On board was a deck hand who gaped at Brooklyn Bridge as the ship sailed under it and cast a reminiscent eye on Staten Island and the Shore Road as she passed. A dozen days out came the scent of new-turned earth as she came abreast Cape Saint Vincent—a never-to-be-forgotten experience. The next night she passed through the Straits of Gibraltar in a thick fog, with nothing to be seen above or below, and only twenty-four hours later brought up the tumbled mountains of North Africa, far on the southern horizon, like so many distant clouds. It happens I was the novice deck hand, and this was my first voyage. To meet the name of this ship in *Yankee Ships* was like encountering an old friend.

Yet there is a more important point to be made in mentioning the *Eureka* and other ships like her—indeed of ships before her time and since. This is the rise and fall, the fluctuation, of the American merchant marine. The *Eureka* sailed, as I realize now—although I was not aware of it at the time—during one of our low periods. Of some fifty-one in our crew at least two thirds were foreign-born and carried papers to work in an American ship only by purchase or trade. One such period came after the Civil War, another at the close of the clipper-ship era and there have been others since.

It has been a struggle for American seamen to reach a standard that would enable them to compete with foreign crews. Man for man, they have gained it, until today American ships and American sailors have reached a level comparable to any way of life on shore. Reese Wolfe has told how the fight to gain this level was fought and won. I feel this is history from the standpoint of the men who made it. The landlubber as well as the seaman, I think, can read and learn. Is it blasphemous for me to say I hope to God they do?

JOHN JENNINGS

San Francisco
January 1953

PART 1

The Colonial Merchant Fleet

1

HOLDING GROUND

A SEARCHING winter wind sweeps the mouth of the Kennebec River. On the beach a knot of gaunt-faced men are gathered around the crude log ways where a vessel still smelling of fresh-hewn pine and oak rears its bows. The men are silent. The only sounds are the ring of a spike maul or two on soft iron, the *chuck-chuck* of dubbing adzes and the endless talk of the breakers. Their eyes are sullen or defiant, depending on the chemistry of their minds. Some are thinking, perhaps, of the desert of water rolling eastward to meet the sky, but none glances beyond the tumbling surf. It is as if an invisible curtain were there, which by common consent is yet to be drawn.

At last the spike mauls and adzes are quiet. Faces grow tense while the skids are cleared. Free of her blocks, the vessel's bow trembles, and there is a squeal and groan of timbers as she goes slanting down the ways. A thin cheer rises on the wind when their craft safely breasts the surf. She has left her cradle in the New World to forge the first link with the Old. Perhaps her captain senses this. In any event, with understandable pride he scrawls in his canvas-backed journal for the year 1607: *"Virginia* launched this day; a faire pinnace of thirty tons burthen. . . . Geo. Popham, Master."

When the *Virginia* is fitted and readied for the sea her crew shuffles down the beach. One by one, forty-five of them in all, they board their cockleshell. On her two masts they hoist square bits of canvas, and with bitter oaths for the unfriendly shore behind them they sail away with their eyes and hearts on England.

Long before the slab-sided three-masted *Mayflower* lifts her sails over the rim of the Western Ocean the *Virginia,* having made her passage safely, will have weathered the Atlantic in several later voyages until she falls victim, in a lonely stretch of another sea, to the Barbary pirates. A "faire pinnace" indeed, this first oceangoing vessel to be launched in America!

If Captain Popham or any of his gentlemen adventurers had been in the mood to make any such claim when they reached London, however, there would have arisen the inevitable quibbler to challenge them, just as any "first" is always challenged. There is small doubt, for example, that the Dutch, French and Irish fishermen who were on hand to greet the discoverers of Newfoundland years before had built boats, and oceangoing ones at that. But the records, if any, have vanished, except for such vague instances as that of the three hundred-odd vessels which landed their catches for a summer season on the shore of Newfoundland Bay for drying, before the long voyage home.

There are stories, too, about Cortez having built some vessels at the southern extremity of the continent at Zacatula and Acapulco with which to explore the Pacific. But some of these were lost and others were seized by a greedy rival who had got there first, and nothing much came of the enterprise. There was another ambitious gentleman soon after Cortez who, while seeking a kingdom of gold which turned out to be a cluster of clay huts, found himself and his followers deserted among the bogs and poisonous fruits of the Florida coast. His name was Pánfilo de Narváez. He and his men built boats from the hides of their slaughtered horses, made ropes of horsehair, sails from their clothing, and set out for the relative safety of Panuco, in Mexico.

But a storm scattered this doughty band of plunderers, and Narváez himself, while sound asleep, was carried out to sea and oblivion.

All these were dreaming away eternity on Fiddler's Green long before Captain Popham and his crew gave up America as a bad job. The significance of Popham's "faire pinnace" is that his vessel was the first link in an unbroken chain of events, the historical holding ground in which are anchored the beginnings of a fleet that has since sailed forth in every crisis of American history to meet all challenges over the battlegrounds of the world.

It is a truism that in every civilization of the past, bar none, if the greatest possible amount of food had been produced and divided among all who were alive to share it, the result even then would have been a miserable standard of living; but if the world today produced all it could and divided it among the people who are here to share it, we would have for the first time in history a really adequate world-wide standard of living. This potential miracle may be the most important realization for the human race since the discovery of fire and the invention of the wheel.

Since this miracle, or potential miracle, is not yet fully understood by some and is unacceptable to others, the age-old struggle to feed our friends and starve our enemies is still with us. It is not surprising, then, that the story of a nation's ships and sailors inevitably involves the strategy of food. Certainly it was a basic idea in the minds of the earliest colonial sailors of this country. For in war or peace the strategy of food has always been a weapon. It was understood by the American colonists long before the shipbuilders of the Thames district in London first lodged their protests with the Lords of Trade against the Yankee shipwrights. And the colonists in turn, recognizing the weapon for what it was, continued to build their ships and sail them over ever-widening horizons in defiance of the mother country. Finally, it can be fairly stated that the English, overdoing the thing, goaded the Americans into building so many ships that a flourishing commercial rivalry was created which eventually led to war and a new nation.

If ships have thus guided the currents of our history—if, for example, America's first ships brought on her first war as an independent nation—who then are the gallant Argonauts who sailed these fateful vessels and what have been the rewards of their heroic life at sea?

Unfortunately the mariner's lot has been, and to a lesser degree still is, a tough and thankless one. The very phrase by which his career is familiarly described is significant. A doctor practices medicine, a broker plays the market, a farmer works the land. But a sailor? What else could he do, chopping ice from the lines in a driving gale off Cape Stiff, or fighting for his life off a windward shore in a tropical hurricane, what else but follow the sea? Following the sea is a heroic business. It has to be. It is also at times a profitable business. It can even be made to appear a romantic one, depending on how much time and dry land the returned seaman is able to put between himself and his last ship before he begins to talk about it. But any sailor will tell you that following the sea can also be a lonely, monotonous, comfortless, terrifying, dangerous business. The only variation has been one of degree. For in the three or four hundred years since the passing of the galley slaves down to the latest achievements of civilized man as celebrated in the Second World War, the seaman's rise has been slow and painful. Only in the last three decades has the legendary warning printed on salt-beef barrels consigned to sailing ships lost its sting: "Unfit for human consumption but good enough for sailors."

Nor is this to say that the men who built the ships, and more especially the men who owned them, have not had their share of grief and disaster down the years, though admittedly of a less dramatic nature. The fact that not so many years ago shipowners were still being called merchant adventurers gives a hint of the nature of their calling.

By no means, however, do the sailors and shipowners alone flesh out the story. A third element all too often forgotten in the struggle of men against the sea is the American people. Unhappily it cannot be said that the people's part in our maritime affairs has been without drama. The tragic public notion that a merchant marine requires no navy to support it, and then, with a navy built, that a navy needs no merchant marine, has stained salt water with American blood for generations in all the seven seas.

There is more than a little significance in the fact that America's first naval engagements were fought by merchant ships and sailors.

For instance, in a moment of peace when the vagaries of history might lead some to believe that the American colonists were earth-bound landsmen intent only on eking out a peaceful existence ashore, there came pushing over the horizon in Long Island Sound the pinnace of one John Gallop. Elsewhere along the coast in the spring of 1636 others like him were feeling their way in and out of the shallows in homemade bugeyes and pinnaces, swapping corn and tobacco for fish and furs from Monhegan all the way south to Charleston. Gallop's boat was a familiar-looking craft of that day; there were scores of her kind in rivers and coastal waters. In spite of her load of furs and trading goods she handled easily, atilt in the wind of a late-spring day. Half decked over, her cargo was safe from the spray, and her hull was sharp at both ends so that the two full-bellied sails driving before the wind created little danger of her being pooped.

In the lee of an island the wind dropped, but her master remained alert. There was something queer about the boat he was watching in the rough water beyond. He gave a quiet order to his three-man crew. Moving within hailing distance, he recognized the sloop of another trader, a Mr. Oldham. But the decks were deserted, and, getting no answer to his hail, Gallop ran alongside.

Immediately there was a shout from the other vessel. A deckload of Indians leaped from their hiding places behind the bulwarks. Gallop's men fired a volley of musketry as the Indians fended off and attempted to run their stolen boat for Narragansett Bay. Close aboard the enemy once more, he counted fourteen of them. The red men made a brave show with swords, spears and what firearms they had, but another broadside of blunderbusses sent them tumbling below in panic. Gallop's crew were all for boarding and making a quick end of things, but, cautious of the overwhelming odds, he withheld the order. Instead, he put up his helm and ran down on the weather of the drifting sloop full tilt, and rammed. No effect. These were two stout craft built of New England oak. Gallop was forced to haul off and attack again, and yet again. In desperation he ordered the anchor lashed to the bows. At last, with this battering ram, a hole was stove in the enemy's hull, and with a blast of blunderbusses into the hold full of seagoing Indians, surrender was forced.

Aboard the Oldham craft they found the late owner with only a red smear where the top of his head should have been. They tossed the body into the sea as a practical measure and stripped the vessel of her cargo and sails. Then John Gallop and company sailed off into the shadows of history whence they came. Of the ultimate disposition of their prisoners there is no record, leading one to suspect a regrettable sense of delicacy in the original historian.

Already the embryo American merchant navy, eyes straining seaward, was making a discovery. Like so many important discoveries it appeared to be a very simple one: the colonists were merely finding that they could build good ships. Some of them were even better than the English ships. Not only that, they could make them pay at home, and, adding insult to injury, they could sell them at a profit abroad.

Inevitably this set the course toward conflict with a ship-proud mother country. For merchant ships, some of them cock sparrows no bigger than John Gallop's craft, were moving seaward in rapidly growing numbers to join in the Battle of Food.

2

OFF SOUNDINGS

IN JOHN GALLOP's time, in the 1630s, a shipbuilder at Cape Elizabeth (now Portland, Maine), John Winter by name, was building one-masted sloops for English merchants. He had found that in spite of the scarcity of labor and consequent high wages a white-oak vessel could be built for about twenty-five dollars a ton, a live-oak vessel for less than forty dollars, while in Europe no ship could be built for less than fifty dollars a ton. The only wonder is that he and his fellow colonists didn't discover it sooner.

With a lavish supply of first-class materials in the forests at the end of every main street, and with a breed of settlers who had virtually risen out of the sea to become as handy with the spike maul and drawshave as they were with the blunderbuss, it is hardly astonishing, after John Winter had shown the way, to find the ports of Ipswich, Marblehead, Newburyport and Salem falling eagerly to work laying out new shipyards.

As for what kind of dollars they were talking about, and what kind of tons, it is convenient to discuss these things in familiar terms. The truth is that cold, hard cash was almost nonexistent in the colonies and would remain so until clear up to the Revolutionary War and beyond. And of course nobody had even thought of an American dollar yet. Accounts were kept in pounds, shillings and pence.

Every businessman was his own foreign-exchange broker, with a pair of scales and a nice judgment for the fluttering values of the Spanish doubloons, pieces of eight, pistareens, Portuguese moidores, and "joes" in which they actually did business when they could lay their hands on any real money at all. Barter was the rule of the day, since England was careful to maintain an adverse trade balance of generous proportions against the colonies, thus keeping the thin flow of coin of the realm traveling east, not west. But the pound had a definite value, which is easily translated into terms of the dollar.

As for the word "ton" when applied to ships, it can mean almost anything. It is only important to keep in mind that until after the Civil War a ship's weight was *measured* in terms of how much she could carry. A vessel in those days was spoken of as having a capacity to carry so many measured tons, each ton being forty cubic feet. Thus the expression of so many "tons burthen."

Latter-day tonnage figures, scientifically devised though they are, represent a sort of dream weight made popular by the advertising departments of our modern liners. The navy, too, finds these glorified tonnage figures useful. A liner or a warship, for example, is measured by what is called displacement tonnage, which is the highest possible figure that can be quoted since it refers to the actual weight of water displaced by the vessel, including everything aboard her. So it would be a mistake to think of a 1,500-ton destroyer, for instance, as being a colossal craft in comparison with a colonial merchantman.

This is not to say the discrepancy in size is not in favor of the destroyer many times over. For a clearer idea of relative size, consider the fact that before the first battle of the Atlantic in 1775 the entire seagoing American merchant fleet numbering over a thousand ships could, by the simple process of dismasting them, have been comfortably stowed aboard a convoy of a dozen present-day Liberty ships.

To reconstruct an early ship, a crew of close to fifty may be assumed. This seemingly large number was to assure a working crew of twenty-five, since at least half of them could be counted on to be sick at one time or another, and a quarter or more of the crew would probably die, depending on the length of the voyage. The weights to be carried, including food and water for three or four months, and the necessary ship gear, would total about ten thousand pounds. To haul this the hull would need to weigh perhaps twice as much, and the "weight" of the loaded ship—her displacement—would be about 130 modern-day tons. But she would be around a hundred feet long, thirty feet broad, and have a twelve-foot draft.

For these reasons and a good many others it is just as well to forget meaningless tonnage figures and to think of a ship in this story as a sailor would: by her name, the temper of the men of her afterguard, and where bound.

Although colonial passengers had a rough time of it, as will be seen, American shipping was a paying proposition from the start. John Winthrop, governor of the Massachusetts colony, got into the swim early. He caused to be launched on the Mystic River in 1631 a good, sound bark built mainly of locust, rejoicing in the name of *Blessing of the Bay*. This most noteworthy of the early ships, by reason of her long life and fat profits, was built for the announced purpose of keeping open communications with New Amsterdam and to avoid the contingencies of having the governor's constituents scalped by the Indians lurking ashore, or of being lost in the wilderness. That the *Blessing of the Bay* also turned many an honest pistareen by trading on her owner's private account was a happy coincidence.

Freight rates to England were good, too. A passenger paid fifty dollars for the crossing, a horse went for a hundred, and general cargo brought thirty dollars a ton. The "burthen" of the *Blessing of the Bay* was only thirty tons, but even so, as the governor wrote, "Ye charges"—that is, the cost of outfitting the ship, wages for the crew, stores and forty-per-cent interest— "did not exceed 900 pounds in a business that turned a profit of little less than 10,000 pounds. . . . " And, as he was happy to report to his shareholders, "Ye otter skins would pay ye charges."

If the relative fares of a passenger and a horse seem disproportionate, remember that the horse had no choice in the matter. A passenger had to be tempted aboard those floating hells with low rates. Besides, a horse took up more room. On an ocean crossing that took ten or twelve weeks when the weather was good, space was the most valuable item a ship could offer. Most of the early vessels were built with one hold as long and as wide as the ship itself, and decked over so that the headroom was seldom more than five feet. The passengers lived in the hold. A load of sand served the double purpose of ballast and flooring, and on this a fireplace was built, with its chimney thrust up through the deck. Calls of nature were served by buckets which were emptied over the side by the passengers themselves at the change of watch. The only privacy was that afforded by the darkness and smoke that filled the leaky, heaving, noisome quarters.

All in all, and considering the decaying salt horse and biscuit they ate during all but the first few days of the voyage when things were still fresh, fifty dollars seems hardly a bargain price.

At the time of the voyages of the *Blessing of the Bay,* when twenty thousand dollars was considered a fortune, she seems to have justified the faith of those who christened her. So, too, did another American-built vessel launched in the same year, called the *Trial.* The latter's name hints at a less optimistic frame of mind in her sponsors, but both of these ships had long and profitable careers. What is more important, they helped quiet the grave doubts of a land-loving people who had seen more fortunes lost than won in the toils of the sea. For sending a ship to sea in those days was something like betting on a horse race, except that the agony extended over a period of months or, more likely, years. In the case of the horse, however, you could watch him run. You knew also where he was going. These were two advantages unknown to the investor in a sea enterprise, and the odds had to be attractive indeed to induce anybody to risk anything at all on such a gamble.

All of which raises the question of how many of these blind 'Argonauts—and, navigationally speaking, they were indeed blind—how many of them were lost on a lee shore.

Today, with Hydrographic Office charts, fathometers, the miracles of radar and a myriad of other checks and balances reducing navigation to the precise timetable of a seagoing trucking service, it is hard to imagine the actual dangers faced by colonial sailors. The skipper and his bully-boy mates pacing the quarter-deck had a cocksure air about them that was scarcely warranted by the facts. Actually they had only a rough notion of how far they were going and how they would get there.

Their navigating gear consisted of a few highly imaginative maps and charts, a copy of *The Seaman's Secrets* and the Holy Bible. Of these the Bible was undoubtedly the most reliable. There was a magnetic compass, of course, but except for this and a crude way of figuring latitude by the angular distances of the sun from the celestial equator by means of a cross-staff, later slightly improved on by a backstaff, they didn't have anything Jason didn't have several thousand years before when he led the Argonauts on their expedition. Illustrative of the mystery surrounding navigation was the title of a best seller among sea-

men of the day, *Longitude Unveiled.* Even the dullest of them
might guess his latitude by how hot or cold it was getting, but
figuring longitude was in the realm of sorcery.

Eschewing the troublesome business of finding longitude
altogether, one reputable nautical work of the period soberly
advises:

Now there be some that are very inquisitive to have a way to
get the longitude, but that is too tedious for seamen since it re-
quireth a deep knowledge of astronomy, wherefore I would not
have any man think that the longitude is to be found at sea
by any instrument; so let no seamen trouble themselves with
any such rule, but according to their accustomed manner let
them keep a perfect account and reckoning of the way of their
ship.

Such a record of "the way of the ship" was chalked up on a
wooden board, the log board, which folded like a book and from
which each day the position of the ship was deduced. The
main trouble about longitude was that since there were no
chronometers, nobody knew what time it was, while a sight was
being taken at sea, at some such definite point as is now established at Greenwich.

How many of those colonial ships were claimed by the sea
is anybody's guess. But the state of navigation at the turn of
the century may be judged by such recorded cases as Captain
Lanoue's description of several British men-of-war off Plymouth
being wrecked in 1691 through mistaking the Deadman for
Berry Head. And there is the case of Admiral Wheeler's squadron leaving the Mediterranean in 1694 and running aground
on Gibraltar when they thought they had passed the Strait.
Another British fleet—a fleet of transports—was lost near the

mouth of the St. Lawrence in 1711, having erred fifteen leagues in their reckoning during twenty-four hours.

For strictly American losses it is necessary to use a shipping report of the nineteenth century in which a ten-year average shows that thirty-five American vessels a month were being wrecked. At least this is specific, and hints darkly at what sort of fate awaited the shocking majority of seamen in colonial times.

From this it might reasonably be imagined that these groping harvesters of the sea were eager to learn new means of finding their way about. Not at all. These practitioners of the most conservative of all professions continued to guess at longitude by shaky lunar observations for over half a century *after* Thomas Godfrey, an American, invented the sextant in 1730 and John Harrison, an Englishman, perfected his chronometer in 1735. It could be argued, and was, that John Hadley, an Englishman, had devised a quadrant shortly before from which the sextant was developed, but in view of the fact that modern navigation dates from the time of Godfrey's and Harrison's inventions it is astonishing that these two men are so little known.

Before their discoveries numerous rewards had been offered for the solution to the mystery of longitude. In London the Commissioners for the Discovery of Longitude at Sea offered prizes of 10,000 pounds for a method of determining longitude within sixty geographical miles; if within forty miles, 15,000 pounds; and if within thirty miles of the landfall, 20,000 pounds. Lack of education had left John Harrison, a Yorkshire carpenter's son, unable to express his ideas clearly in writing, although his first model won him five hundred pounds for a voyage to Lisbon on a King's ship in 1736, and an improved smaller model won him the Copley medal of the Royal Society in 1749. At last when his son took over the testing of a still later model of his father's chronometer he came within eighteen

A SEVENTEENTH-CENTURY SCHOONER OUT OF MARBLEHEAD

This drawing was made by Frank O. Braynard of the American Merchant Marine Institute from a fine model in the Peabody Museum in Salem, Mass.

Courtesy of the Naval Historical Foundation

THE *HAZARD* OF SALEM

A world trader and privateer. From a painting by George Rotes.

BATTLE OF THE BRIG *CHASSEUR* AND THE SCHOONER *ST. LAWRENCE* IN 1815

miles of the correct landfall in Jamaica in 1762, making John Harrison eligible for the top prize. It was ultimately paid to him after the intercession of the King in 1773, just three years before Harrison died.

Like Harrison, Thomas Godfrey was a poor man, a Philadelphia glazier; and although Benjamin Franklin, who resided in the same house with him, described him as a great mathematician, Godfrey, too, had trouble getting recognition for his sextant. Claims were made, and still are, for Sir Isaac Newton, Hadley and others, whose instruments were tested in 1732. But Tom Godfrey's sextant, described as a common sea quadrant "to which he had fitted two pieces of looking glass in such a manner as brought two stars at almost any distance to coincide," was made in 1730. To settle the disputes that arose, two affidavits sworn before the mayor of Philadelphia proved that Godfrey's sextant was brought aboard the sloop *Truman* by G. Stewart, mate, on November 28, 1730, and was used on a voyage to Jamaica and in the following summer on a voyage to Newfoundland. Perhaps Godfrey's long-drawn-out efforts to collect the prize drove him to drink. Benjamin Franklin found him to be an unpleasant companion much given to argument and hairsplitting over trifles. In any case the Society decided to award him some household furniture valued at two hundred pounds in place of cash, giving as their altruistic motive that the money would be dissipated on alcohol.

If the sextant was too intricate a contraption for popular use by the skeptical mariners of the day, certainly the chronometer was simple enough to earn a place in any skipper's cabin. Since the chronometer offers clockwork precision for determining distances by a comparison with Greenwich time, it is scarcely believable that it had to await two generations of sailors before it could make its way aboard ship as standard equipment. Nevertheless, as late as 1823 the firm of Bryant & Sturgis reprimanded one of their shipmasters for purchasing a chronometer at a cost of $250 and informed him he must pay for it himself. "Could we have anticipated," they wrote him, "that our injunctions respecting economy would have been so totally disregarded we would have set fire to the Ship rather than have sent her to sea."

In spite of the extreme hazards of life at sea, tempting profits and certain other considerations drew the youthful and adventurous from the colonies in growing numbers. The *Trial,* as already suggested, brought great joy to her owners and backers, and she must have been doubly blessed by the womenfolk when she made a voyage from Boston to Malaga, Spain, in 1643 and returned with a cargo which included such household luxuries as olive oil, linens and wool.

When Jack shipped before the mast on the *Trial* and larger ships like her as time went on, he was as likely as not to be your next-door neighbor. And the chances were no more than even that the day he joined his ship would be the last time you would see him alive. Rigged in a leather-lined doublet (which was simply a warm double jacket), leather-lined hose, a red knit cap, a broad leather belt, and affecting a pigtail and ear whiskers or even earrings if he fancied himself a weathered old salt, he would be carrying in his ditty box some sort of good-luck charm. He was certainly going to need it. He would be at sea anywhere from a month to a year, or even two years. During that time he would live with twenty or thirty men in a deckhouse no bigger than your bedroom—provided your ideas of size are modest—but without windows, and half as high. In there he would sleep, eat and spend his "watch below." His lice-ridden bunk would always be occupied either by himself or a shipmate, and his food would similarly be a community proposition, scooped from the "black pan" with his only eating utensil, a sheath knife.

If he wasn't sick half the time with beriberi or scurvy or salt-water boils, then it would probably be because he lay buried in a canvas sack several fathoms under. Of course he might be one of those hardy shellbacks to avoid serious illness, or at least to survive the medical formula for all sickness at sea. Classic in its simplicity, it was a powerful dose of Epsom salts. If that didn't work, then a still more potent dose of jalap—a resin obtained from certain tropical roots—was administered to neutralize the salts. And if neither of these purges turned the trick, and assuming the patient could still swallow, he would then be given a heroic charge of calomel that either killed or cured.

The water with which he washed down his food was drawn from a spigot oozing green slime and crawling with life. As for the food . . . But the weevily biscuit and salt horse called food became a tradition of the fo'c'sle which was to last many, many years beyond Jack's time.

Incidentally, the puzzle of why the so-called fresh water at sea was always universally bad is better understood by realizing that the crude methods of distilling water required more fuel than could be spared for the small amounts of liquid they produced. Endless experiments were made with wood and metal containers to preserve the water's freshness, but no voyage was more than a few weeks old when the drinking water became the same stinking slimy mess, and very scarce at that.

There were shipboard accidents, as there always are, and there was loneliness. Not the loneliness of days or weeks which, Heaven knows, is bad enough in the cargo steamers plodding over distant seas today, but a loneliness that had the leisure to feed on a man's soul in a complete vacuum of water and sky for months, years, at a time. Sailors being what they are, little of this has found its way into the written records, but one heart-torn entry in an early log from a ship called the *Rubicon* was decoded from its simple secret language to reveal this:

... My heart within me is ashes. I want to see my loving wife and press her to my bosom. But, O, my days are gone and past, no more to return forever. . . .

And later:

True undivided and sincere love united with its own object is one of the happy passions that possess the human heart. . . . Joanna, this day brings to my mind grateful reflections. This is the day that numbers thirty years of my dear's life. O, that I could lie in her arms tonight and recount the days that have passed away in youthful love and pleasure. . . .

And yet these men were lucky. Manual labor ashore began to lose dignity almost immediately with the coming of the slave trade, and the lower orders were held under a firm legal thumb with laws that were nothing less than brutal. Life ashore was based strictly on wealth and land. A man without land not only had no vote (except in Connecticut where personal property was accepted in its place), but in the New England colonies the very clothes he wore were regulated by statute. Only the wealthy wore what they pleased. Wages of a free farm laborer were small and irregular. He was customarily given board, lodging and a few shillings to spend now and then—because he was competing with white and Negro slaves. Twenty pounds "passage money" paid to a ship's captain would buy a good bond servant with half a dozen years to serve, and a "raw field hand," i.e., a newly landed Negro, could be had for half as much. There were no guilds or unions because they were forbidden by law, and even skilled craftsmen had their hours and wages determined entirely by an association of owners and masters in the same line of trade.

In sharp contrast to the lot of the landsman were such laws as the one passed in Massachusetts exempting fishermen during the season, and shipwrights and seamen at all times, from military duty—no small concession, considering the reception currently being tendered the colonists by their red-skinned neighbors in the backwoods. And the ordinary seaman's pay was good, about four pounds in hard cash a month. Better still, the crew often owned as much as a fifth of the cargo, or else they were allowed space in the ship in which to carry their own trade goods so as to share in the profits of the voyage.

Ashore, too, Jack and his mates were privileged characters. He was even protected from himself by law, as witness this Massachusetts provision:

No Master of Ships, having their vessels Riding within any of our Harbours in this jurisdiction, shall presume to Drink Healths, or suffer any Healths to be drunk within their Vessels by day or night. . . .

Also:

Whereas many Miscarriages are committed by Saylers, by their immoderate drinking and other vaine expences in Ordinaries, which oftentimes occasions prejudice and damage to the Masters and Owners of the vessels to which they belong, their men being oftentimes Arrested for Debts so made when their ships are ready to set saile: for Prevention whereof it is ordered . . . that no Innkeeper, Vitualler, or other Seller of Wine, Beer or Strong Liquors shall Arrest, Attach or recover by Law any Debts made by Sayler or Saylers aforesaid. . . .

With one hand the stern Puritans were passing laws against "immoderate great breeches" and other "wicked apparel" for the impoverished dandies ashore, and dealing out "eight stripes publikly administered" with a whip by way of discouraging fornication, while with the other they were wagging a tolerant finger at a deserting sailor or even one who refused obedience at sea. It is difficult to understand. Perhaps too few of them ever came back to make stronger measures worth while.

If this creates the impression that New Englanders were crowding the early shipping scenes in the colonies, it is not far wrong. The gentlemen planters in the South were not unaware of the lure of maritime profits and adventure, but in the lush region of Chesapeake Bay, and in Virginia and the Carolinas, they were comfortable ashore, while the folk up north were constantly occupied with dirty weather and a miserly soil, necessitating a great deal of sharp attention to the fundamental business of eking out a living. That living came more naturally from the sea. Southerners were to have their moment of glory charting the golden course of America's greatest days of sail when they built their Baltimore clippers; but in the beginning it was the New Englanders who were leading the colonists to sea, and their dominance cannot be laid entirely to soil and climate.

In a gloomy, self-righteous atmosphere of Puritan stay-at-homes, aided and abetted by a clergy and General Court who felt it their right, nay, their duty, to pass on such things as the cut of one's breeches, what would any independent young fellow do? Clear out by the most practical method at hand. The New England countryside was overrun with thin-lipped puritans and witch hunters, only the prosperous had any social standing, and it is more than likely that the lusty youth of the region did not so much follow the sea in those days as flee to it, embracing its savage hardships in quest of freedom, adventure and a possible fortune.

More than a wisecrack of the day was the grim saying, "There are no Sundays off soundings."

3

NEW LANDFALLS

IT WAS not long before the struggle at sea became also a struggle ashore. England had a civil war on her hands, and in the very years, the 1640s, when she would have liked best to put a stop once and for all to the shipbuilding nonsense across the sea she was helpless to do much about it.

At first the mother country's bad luck was also the colonies' bad luck. Cut off by the trouble across the sea from its former markets in England, the burgeoning American merchant marine began gathering barnacles on its idle hulls. America was feeling her first depression. Casting about for a new deal, the worried merchants and shipmasters of New England recalled that one Thomas Mayhew and the son of the governor of Massachusetts colony, John Winthrop, Jr., had sent a sloop to Bermuda a few years before, in 1636, loaded with corn and smoked pork. They had brought back a cargo of oranges, lemons and potatoes, and, what was more to the point, the voyage had netted a cash profit of over a hundred dollars, no mean return for a cash-starved trade. The actual cash was probably in doubloons, pistareens and the like, but it was good hard coin.

Eagerly the depression-ridden fleet set out for the new markets in Bermuda, Havana and other rich ports of the West Indies to reap while the illegal reaping was good. It meant an independent trade, free of duties and taxes, and, as it turned out, a prosperous one. Although the gentlemen at the Admiralty in London recognized it immediately for what it was—a dangerous precedent leading to a solid economic base on which the colonies could build their self-sufficiency—they were in no position to do much about it just then but fuss and fume and lay future plans for correcting this breach of good conduct.

No attempt is made here to fit these men and their troubles into separate watertight compartments of society, because in this case the fit would become a very awkward one. Everybody's troubles were everybody else's. For one thing, to use an apt term of the prize ring, most people in the colonial shipping world owned a piece of somebody else. More often than not, as many as a hundred people had a financial interest in one ship, including the sailors, who had a financial interest in the cargo, and more than one tavern keeper, who had a financial interest in a sailor. Then, too, most of the shipbuilders and owners had been to sea themselves at one time or another, so that any conflict beyond those of the barest physical nature had the quick and sympathetic attention of all hands ashore or afloat. Every matter of maritime trade, financial or legal, was the personal concern of all.

By 1650 the colonists' maritime trade had become three-pronged—coastwise, transatlantic and with the West Indies. As time went on the shoreside crowd, the builders and owners, were engendering a struggle all their own through the unfavorable attention their ships were drawing from a mother country whose feelings were rapidly growing less motherly. True, most of them were still engaged in coastwise trade, but some of the larger ones had already had the audacity to be crossing the Atlantic with alarming regularity.

In accord with the spirit of the times the British Parliament passed a series of statutes in 1663 providing, among other things, that nothing could be brought into the colonies that wasn't carried there in English ships, "whereof the master and three-fourths of the crew are English." That was not enough to stem the tide, however. A man named Edward Randolph, a British customs collector doubling as a sort of roving reporter for the home office, viewing the upstart colonists with the jaundiced eye that was becoming chronic in a good many English visitors of his day, was moved to write home in alarm in 1676 that the ships of Massachusetts "trafficked" with the West Indies and with most parts of Europe, carrying their own products and those of other colonies and distributing return cargoes among all the colonies and the West Indies, "so that there is little left for the merchants residing in England to import into any of the colonies."

His remarks could not have surprised the British authorities so much as pained them. If mere passing of laws could have choked off the trade it most certainly would have died a quick death. American ships were forbidden to haul American products anywhere else in the world but to England. Certainly there was no shilly-shallying in the language of the laws. One act of Parliament in 1672 had stated it bluntly: "To keep the colonies in firmer dependence upon the mother country, making them more beneficial to it."

With their sharp noses pointed to the trade winds the colonists were falling into the convenient habit of using the oppressive laws as an aid rather than a deterrent. The net result was to launch the shipbuilders and owners into working hand and glove with the men at sea on what rapidly became an honorable career of lawbreaking. Profit, as always, was the guiding force, and a kind of genteel piracy won enthusiastic support from gentlemen, properly backed financially, who set themselves up as privateers.

Any colonial merchant who felt he had been wronged by Spain or France—and what merchant did not, since the mother country was constantly at war with them?—would obtain letters of reprisal from the Crown authorizing him to make up what losses he could by plundering every Spanish or French ship that came along. It was a popular occupation, containing the happy ingredients of moral righteousness and profits mixed in suitable proportions, and the more damages collected the better.

A by-product of this wholehearted flouting of authority, and one whose value cannot be overestimated in the bloody years to come, was the impetus it gave to the Americans' skill in building ships. Lack of materials from England such as hemp rope and iron fittings forced never-ending labor toward simplification. Wood was used wherever possible, resulting in lighter, stronger frames, hence faster and more maneuverable vessels— two lifesaving necessities for the privateersmen. With a characteristic eye to economy the builders did not overlook the fact that simplification of rigging and hull not only saved rope but meant fewer hands needed to manage the vessel, and on the long voyages of those days with every hand in the pot, so to speak, this was no small item of expense.

In addition to privateering there were also fat profits to be had by evading the British revenue tariffs. Lord Bellamont, who was appointed the Crown's governor in New York in 1696, wrote plaintively of the town of Boston:

When ships come in, the masters swear to their manifests; that is, they swear to the number of parcels they bring, but the contents unknown; then the merchants being minded to run their goods, there's nothing to hinder them. Mr. Brenton, the Collector, is absent and has been these two years; his deputy is a merchant; the two waiters keep public houses, and besides this the coast is naturally cut out to favor unlawful trade. . . .

Lord Bellamont might have justifiably added that officials as well as the coast were so cut out. Bribery among officials of the Crown became almost an exact science, the scale of which could be computed by a ship's captain with as much accuracy as his dead reckoning, if not more. Forged papers in the skipper's ditty box were a part of his regular gear, and rare indeed was the Yankee shipmaster who could not prove to the inquisitive captain of a British cruiser that although his course appeared to be set for the forbidden shores of France, he was in truth headed virtuously for the docks of London.

Official dishonesty was accepted as a matter of course, like the weather. Without undue implications in singling out a particular case in point, it is interesting to note that even the plaintive Lord Bellamont, imbued no doubt with the spirit of the times, headed a syndicate of Englishmen capitalized at six thousand pounds to finance Captain Kidd. Poor old William Kidd, it is pretty well established now, was a plain, simple sea captain, a domesticated husband and father with a home of his own on what is now Wall Street, who was more a victim of English politics than he was a swashbuckling buccaneer. Indeed, up to the time of falling in with Lord Bellamont, Kidd enjoyed a local reputation (and a reward of 150 pounds) for loyal services to the King. He had every right to be looking forward to a deserved and comfortable retirement in the bosom of his family.

Unfortunately, in circumstances which were against him from the outset, Captain Kidd sailed away in the *Adventure Galley,* Madagascar-bound in the service of Bellamont and his syndicate of London backers, to engage in a series of misadventures which are too well known to bear repeating here. In justice to Kidd it need only be mentioned that he became a mild sort of pirate who never killed a prisoner or seized a prize unless on examination of the ship's papers it seemed warranted. He ended up, a broken old man approaching sixty, by being hanged at Execution Dock in London in 1701, disavowed by Lord Bellamont and everyone else involved in the case.

Meanwhile the British cabinet secretaries had been relieved of their frustrating job of supervising colonial shipping in 1696, and it was turned over to a board of conscientious gentlemen totally innocent of any real knowledge of the new breed of shipmasters and merchants with whom they were dealing. Administration of this body, called the Board of Trade and Plantations, was limited from the outset by lack of authority. The activity of its members consisted largely in shaking their heads over the interminable statutes passed by the legislatures of their faraway charges. The monotony was relieved only by pithy letters of complaint from colonial governors and by the angry protests of worried English merchants and shipmasters.

Finally the shipbuilders of the Thames district met in London in the winter of 1724-1725 and formally complained to the Lords of Trade:

In the eight years ending in 1720 we are informed that seven hundred sail of ships were built in New England, and that in the years since, as many if not more; and that the New England trade, by the tender of extraordinary inducements, has drawn over so many working shipwrights that there are not enough left to carry on the work.

Again Parliament shortened the apron strings. Laws became more explicit, the language tougher.

The results were about the same as those brought on by this country's national prohibition laws in a later generation. The laws were simply ignored. For the West Indies trade alone proved so logical, so sound for the ambitious Yankee traders that in spite of revival of trade with England it ranked in importance with the thriving coastwise and budding transatlantic commerce. It remained progressively so until the world became their oyster.

Linked inseparably with the venture south to the Indies was the colonists' brisk trade in rum and what they were in the habit of calling black ivory. For the Indies trade was a three-cornered affair hinging on rum, slaves and molasses. Together they comprised the foundation for more ships and hence more trouble than all the politicians ashore put together.

Like so many momentous occasions in history, the start of the slave trade had been an offhand sort of occurrence. A Dutch privateer found itself with twenty Negroes taken from a Spanish ship and, not knowing what to do with them, dropped anchor in the river at Jamestown in 1619, a year before Plymouth Rock had become anything more significant than just one more rock on the New England coast. The Negroes were offered cheap, and the Virginia settlers decided to trade tobacco for them. The swap was made and the Dutch sailed away, leaving behind them a cancerous growth that was to bring the parent body close to death before the disease was arrested.

Meanwhile the Virginians did not call them slaves; as late as 1660 Virginia court records were still referring to Negroes as indentured servants. There seemed to be a certain delicacy observed by common consent in the matter. But soon the House of Burgesses established slavery as the hereditary legal status of Negroes, defining them as a species of property. This is not to say that colonial slavery was confined to the South. The New Englanders had Indian slaves as early as 1637, and a more or less formal business developed, with traders nabbing Indians along the banks of the Kennebec River in Maine and selling them into slavery up and down the coast. It was the black ivory from Africa, however, that turned the trick in the West Indies trade and established Southern slavery on a solid and enduring footing.

The mechanics of this all-important trade worked like this: molasses was brought to New England and made into rum; the rum, highly prized among the Negroes on the west coast of Africa, brought its own price among the drinkers, a price that included any of their relatives or friends who might have the bad judgment to be lying about, and the resultant human cargoes were disposed of profitably in Boston, Newport and on south. Or most of the way south. Foreign ships for the most part maintained the supply in the deep South.

Not all the West Indies rum was drunk by Negroes. A flourishing local trade in fur was conducted with the Indians by the extremely profitable exchange of a few bottles of cheap rum or whisky for the entire season's catch of its drunken owner. Rum, it is generally agreed, had more to do with the destruction of the Indian tribes on the Eastern seaboard than all the wars in which they were engaged put together. The tribal chiefs, apparently recognizing this danger when one of the long series of Indian wars ended with the Treaty of Falmouth in 1726, begged without avail to have the sale of firewater to the young braves stopped.

Nothing loath to try their own poison, the colonists themselves were heroic drinkers. An anonymous coastal voyager returned from Philadelphia with this interesting entry in his diary: "Given cider and punch for lunch; rum and brandy before dinner; punch, Madeira, port, and sherry at dinner; punch and liquors with the ladies; and wine, spirit, and punch till bedtime; all in punch bowls big enough for a goose to swim in. . . . " Boston merchants happily estimated that nine hundred thousand gallons of rum were consumed annually in Massachusetts alone. This meant four gallons for every man, woman and child in that hardy colony, exclusive of the even vaster amounts of hard cider consumed, which, in view of the record, must have been used in place of water.

In some respects, at least, it must have been a full life and a merry one. The mother country had not yet had the necessary freedom to bring her precocious offspring to heel. But the day was rapidly approaching in England when problems closer to home were to be put temporarily aside in the interests of discipline across the sea.

A blood-red thread of courage running through this period of American venturing off soundings is the epic of the Nantucket whalers, fetching in their game from every watery corner of the earth. They led the colonists into the first years-long commercial voyages off shore, just as the West Indies trade lured them into an independent and solid commerce in the South. And just as American-built vessels had their local beginning in the shallops, pinkies, bugeyes and pinnaces that went scooning over the rivers and streams and coastal waters in search of new markets, so, too, did the swift, sturdy whaling ships parallel this growth in their ever-extending quest.

As the whale grew warier, the whalers, and particularly the Nantucketers, grew bolder and their voyages longer. Soon the sailors of Nantucket, who took and held the lead, were putting brick furnaces on their decks to use for reducing the blubber, and loading their small craft with miniature fleets of whale-boats and supplies for voyages planned to last two or three years. Oil for lighting was the incentive behind these epic whale hunts, since wax and tallow candles were too expensive for the majority of people. The voyages pretty well followed a pattern, reaching first to Greenland, then down over the rim of the South

Atlantic and on around to the Pacific, and finally to the Antarctic and the Arctic.

As time went on into the 1770s the oil of Yankee whalers was swamping the American market and was very near to cornering the British one. A tremendous advantage they had over their British competitors was their close-knit method of making it a community enterprise. The cooper made casks for the ship with his soundest and best seasoned wood for the very good reason that they might otherwise leak his own oil on the long voyage. The blacksmith forged the best iron he could find for the shanks of his harpoons, haunted, more than likely, by personal experience with other, lesser harpoons wrenching and twisting in the valuable carcass of a whale in which he had a one-hundredth interest. Profits of the labor were enjoyed by those directly engaged in it. The best testimony to its success was that high on the British Parliament's list of things to do something about was the colonists' world-wide fleet of whalers.

4

THE POWDER FLAG

As AMERICA'S ADVANCES on the sea grew swift and purposeful, what of the people—the distillers and carriage makers, the lawyers and money brokers, the mechanics in leather aprons, the paunchy gentlemen in ruffled shirt fronts and silk stockings—to most of whom the word shipping meant only a forest of masts knifing the sky over the housetops and taverns along the water fronts? What of them, as the struggle of ships and the men who sailed them took new form and swept in from the sea to fill the air with dangerous talk of "rights" and "freedom"?

To put it frankly, they were asleep. Waxing fat on Europe's wars, few took the trouble to notice that war abroad had fallen, for the moment, into disfavor. Every success of British arms had won new markets for the Americans. Every hour of war meant good prices for American products. But with the conclusion of the Seven Years' War in 1763 England was at peace. Now at last there was time for an irritable mother country to look about her and take stock of things, to dust off her badly mauled Navigation Acts and to jack up her committees to hear this and her boards to decide that.

True, the colonists were not in a position to do anything very drastic in the way of protecting themselves at this stage of the game. But typical of America's maritime career, and therefore worth noting early, have been the needs of a war-ridden Europe for food, ships and materials that have always given impetus to American shipbuilding and ship-using and which have, conversely, beguiled its citizens into the notion that the merchant fleet could always take care of itself. For many generations beyond the colonists' time American ships were to be considered strictly in the light of economics, with little regard for the naval aspects of a competent merchant service and none at all for a ship that did not show a profit. Only during periods of acute emergency were they considered an integral part of national defense; at such times dawned the realization that even in the absence of profits in slack periods the merchant marine should no more be allowed to expire than the postal service. The Island Empire knew this instinctively, as epitomized by its use of the term "merchant navy." For the United States a seventeen-billion-dollar lesson in building emergency ships for the Second World War was to be required to make the lesson stick.

With the Seven Years' War out of the way, and with the British national debt heavily increased, there was strong sentiment in England in favor of having the colonists share in paying the taxes. It was only logical, so went the reasoning, since England had helped defend the colonies against the French and Indians on this continent during the struggle. It hardly need be said this line of reasoning was not popular in the colonies. The Americans had no intention of helping to pay for the English war, not even the Indian part of it, especially as they felt they had done their share of fighting against the Indians and their French supporters and at their own expense.

The British decided that one way to increase revenues would be to put a stop to the Americans' open evasion of the Navigation Acts. That they were evading them was certainly true, as well they might be. Practically all manufactured goods from hatchets to hemp lines had to come from England, with the prices set in England and the cargoes carried in English bottoms. French, Spanish and other goods were legally obtainable, but first such cargoes had to go to England to pay duty at the customs and then be transshipped to America.

Writing of this situation in 1765, Daniel Dulany, a distinguished Maryland lawyer and politician, and a loyalist sympathizer at that, complained of the Crown's restrictions that with English profits, freight charges, commissions and taxes, British goods sent to America were being raised to six times their real value; that goods bought for sixpence in England could be exchanged for a bushel of wheat in North Carolina. It was a heads-I-win, tails-you-lose arrangement, since cargoes traveling in the opposite direction across the Atlantic were required to go first to England where English buyers resold them at their leisure.

It is hardly surprising, then, that among the first real troublemakers of all the British efforts to raise money was a new Molasses Act, for it was molasses brought in from the French West Indies from which New England's rum was made. There had been a similar act on the books as long before as 1733, but the duty of sixpence a gallon was such a prohibitive price for the rum distillers to pay that its only practical effect was to create the first of a caste that was to throw a very long shadow indeed— the bootlegger. To make the new act a more practical measure the duty was halved and a firm resolve taken to really collect it. To put teeth into the effort Parliament authorized the use of writs of assistance, a sort of search warrant covering an entire community that gave British customs officials the right to search any ship, warehouse or even private home for smuggled goods.

To the colonists it must have seemed that there were more acts than ships by this time, and they were in no mood to abide by any of them. Things had come to a pretty pass. American shipbuilding had reached a point where the Massachusetts colony, in a burst of civic pride that would challenge the lustiest chamber of commerce today, laid dubious claim to enough vessels to float every man, woman and child in its domain. It can be said with truth, however, that there were more sailors than farmers in New England. Lord Sheffield made some frightening calculations in 1769 that showed that even the Carolinians were moving languidly to sea. Along the entire American coast from the Carolinas northward, he pointed out, 389 ships totaling 20,000 tons had been built in that year. In 1771 he reported 24,000 tons, and in 1772 over 26,000 tons.

Nor was that the worst of it. American privateers were growing bolder, so bold that a dangerous state of mind now encouraged flouting the English laws as a kind of social grace. In years past there had been frequent cases of corrupt officials of the Crown doing the same thing, as exemplified by New York's governor, Lord Bellamont, and his equally shady successor, Colonel Benjamin Fletcher, who had been in the habit of wining and dining such notorious pirates of their era as Captain Tew.

But Governor Fletcher was admittedly a political pirate in his own right and was ultimately recalled to London to answer graft charges. Now, however, there was a new generation of more upright gentlemen whose profits brazenly gained through bootlegging and other illegal activities were overshadowed, at least in the public mind, by their courageous defiance of the ever-increasing strictures on their commerce. In fact nine tenths of the colonial merchants and skippers had become smugglers as the break with England neared. Such men as John Hancock, a prince of contraband traders, on the eve of Paul Revere's ride had for counsel before the Admiralty Court in Boston none other than John Adams answering for him a half-million-dollar suit in penalties as a smuggler.

When the harried Board of Trade and Plantations finally decided to act, its attempt to enforce the Navigation Acts was the spark in the touchhole that set the guns to booming. One quarter of all the signers of the Declaration of Independence were bred to commerce, to the command of ships and to contraband trade. Men like Hancock, Trumbull and their friends were merchants first, statesmen second. Their every evasion of the English statutes they considered a blow for liberty. Thus the count in their indictment drawn up against the King of England, "of cutting off our trade in all parts of the world."

And so we find the rebellious sailors hoisting the powder flag, cutting holes in their bulwarks for guns and spreading their sails for conflict. The new Continental Congress, convulsed in a series of financial squabbles that would do credit to a Senate finance committee today, dredged up a plan backed with hard-wrung funds for establishing a navy of some thirty converted merchant vessels. These were duly and hastily commissioned, which was well, because as the echoing shots for liberty crackled along the road from Concord, the Americans stood without one fighting ship.

5

MERCHANT FIGHTERS

Pipes and drums echoed through the narrow street down which a band of boisterous men was marching. Rigged in shoregoing waistcoats of scarlet, blue or green, some with bandoleers and muskets slung over their shoulders and each with a cockade, the mark of the military, mounted on his hat, they swung along behind their grinning leader roaring a song:

> All you that have bad masters,
> And cannot get your due,
> Come, come, my brave boys
> And join our ship's crew!

Men, boys and a few teary-eyed women scurried along the fringe of the parade. At a corner the crowd thickened, the leader waved down the music and the column shuffled to a halt. He called for quiet. In jovial, comradely tones he told a comical story and the crowd was with him. Gravely, then, he spoke of the Redcoats and of the American blood spilled at Concord. He had a keen, twinkling eye for any husky youngster in his audience as he spoke persuasively of a life at sea, with heavy accent on prize money and glory. He named a rendezvous for "gentlemen adventurers." The music started again, the crowd cheered.

With any luck at all the recruiting officer would have his crew by nightfall. But, luck or not, he'd have them. Mine host at the rendezvous, which more than likely was the Mariner's Nook or the Sign of the Gold Anchor or whatever happened to be the most popular water-front tavern at the moment, would see to that. The punch and grog were free, paid for by the ship's owners, the company was good, and drunk or sober Master Jack would be carried, dragged or driven to his ship and glory before the night was out.

Not many would need to be driven. Three days before the battle on Breed's Hill, or Bunker Hill as it was later to be called, Colonel Washington, about to be upped to General and Commander in Chief by the Second Continental Congress sitting at Philadelphia, had already lent his weight to the call for army volunteers. Rumor had it that army pay was not so good—about six dollars and sixty-five cents a month when there was any pay at all—and discipline was harsh.

A privateersman could do better than that. When he "signed on" his articles of agreement provided that "If anyone shall first discover a saile which shall prove to be a Prize, he will be entitled to Five Hundred Dollars. . . . If he loose a leg or an arm he shall be entitled to Four Thousand Dollars . . . an eye, Two Thousand Dollars. . . ."

As to discipline, the treatment of these "gentlemen seamen" could almost be termed loving. For abandonment of post, for instance, or for disobeying commands of the captain or officers, and if adjudged guilty by three officers, the captain being one, the culprit was then required to forfeit any prize taken. Competition among ships for crews was keen, and the "gentlemen seamen," who in large measure were no seamen at all but included doctors, lawyers, merchants and even ministers of the cloth, went swarming down to the harbors to join their ships. Decks were cleared for mounting batteries of Long Toms and

Long Nines, hammocks were slung for doubled and tripled crews, chests of muskets, cutlasses, boarding pikes and shot were stowed aboard, and the sound of drilling men waiting for a chance to slip to sea echoed on the wharves day and night.

The chance did not come easily. In the hands of the enemy was the enormous advantage of sea power. Boston was occupied; so each in their turn were Newport, New York, Philadelphia, Charleston, Savannah. Pressed for haven, the privateers made the sheltering waters of Salem their headquarters, along with neighboring ports like Marblehead and Beverly. From the start the hastily organized American navy was almost helpless. When a year had passed and Thomas Jefferson sat down to apply his widely heralded erudition in writing "without book or paper" the Declaration of Independence, the ships of the navy, in spite of heroes like John Paul Jones, were well on their way to being swept from the Atlantic by superior British squadrons.

Meanwhile, the merchant ships of Salem and her neighbors crept to sea and descended on the far-flung British fleet. Accustomed to being armed to the teeth with cutlass and cannon as well as forged papers as a matter of course, and through force of circumstances having learned to construct swift and maneuverable ships, they outwitted, outfought and outran British frigates convoying the rich and ponderous merchantmen. Ships from Delaware, Baltimore and Charleston swelled the fighting merchant navy to nearly a thousand vessels as the exodus to sea gathered momentum. From Salem alone sailed 158 armed craft and four thousand men. Their ships ranged in size from those as large as the *Deane,* with her thirty cannon and crew of two hundred, down to some as small as the *Wasp,* with no guns at all, a crew of nine armed only with muskets, pistols and cutlasses—and no doubt with more changes of flags than shirts. But, large or small, they preyed on English ships wherever they found them. They raided in the English Channel and the North Sea. They loitered impudently off Liverpool and Plymouth.

Britain's commerce was confused, her merchants and ship-owners were exasperated. Insurance rates in London ballooned out of sight, with underwriters charging a premium of twenty-five per cent for insuring a merchant vessel. By way of Spain came a British report in 1777 bitterly complaining of the situation:

Everything continues exceedingly dear and we are happy if we can get anything for money by reason of the quantity of vessels taken by the Americans. A fleet of vessels came from Ireland a few days ago. Some sixty vessels that departed from Ireland, not above twenty-eight arrived in this and neighboring islands, the others, it is thought, being all taken by American privateers. If this American war continues much longer we shall all die of hunger. . . .

The financial pinch had British merchants pressing for peace before the war had fairly begun.

But there was trouble ashore. With the ports in their hands and with their overwhelming fleet the British were in a position to land large bodies of troops anywhere they chose on the American coast. They could shift whole armies from port to port with a neatness and dispatch that could never be matched by the foot-slogging patriots of Washington's army. They could, but they did not.

Why they failed to do so is one of the mysteries of the early fumbling by the British that had the Americans puzzled from the beginning. It was matched in its folly only by the inexplicable earlier withdrawal of their troops from Boston to Halifax in a large fleet of ships—enough troops to have completely wiped out the rallying squirrel hunters and farmers of Concord. It led Alexander Hamilton to remark after the war was over that

"All the British need have done was to blockade our ports with twenty-five frigates and ten ships of the line. But, thank God, they did nothing of the sort."

Even so, the Continental Army was having its troubles. There was money trouble, as always, but there was also man trouble. Men, young and old, were shouldering their sea chests and marching down to the sea in such numbers that Henry Knox, the plump, pleasant-faced bookseller of Boston who was later to become Washington's Secretary of War, was desperately pressed for troops to man his artillery. Total war was a refinement of civilization yet to come, and the majority of men in those days were more than willing to exercise their right to stay quietly at home for the duration and argue politics in the village tavern. Rough estimates fix three million as the number of people living in the colonies, including half a million Negroes, most of whom had no choice in what they did. Only half the total, it is further estimated, were rebels. That should have left, with a generous allowance for the physically unfit, at least a quarter of a million men able and politically minded to bear arms.

But Congress pessimistically authorized an army of only twenty thousand, and even this modest quota was never filled. It is true that irregular troops sporadically increased the total of the rebel forces when the spirit and the weather moved them, but never at any time did their number equal the number of men who had cast their lot with the sea.

Nor is this very surprising. Hull down on the horizon were adventure and gold for the taking. In the mud of Trenton and Valley Forge were hunger, ever-tightening discipline and monthly pay that had sunk in buying power to about sixteen cents. Lack of equipment was appalling, and there was no dodging the Redcoats as British frigates were being dodged and outrun at sea. American soldiers were jeeringly called Homespuns, a name that stuck. It was hardly calculated to have recruiting appeal for the young, although there was a romantic side to the creation of the Homespuns. In the first bitter winter of the war a call went out for thirteen thousand warm coats, and immediately a great army of loyal women went to work supplying them. Inside each coat was sewed a label with the name of the town from which it came and the name of its maker. Many a romance blossomed from this source, and the "coat roll" still to be found in some New England towns became not only a roll of honor but also a convenient sort of address book for a romantically minded soldiery.

By and large, however, this was thin gruel for a soldier's life. There is no doubt that the privateers were robbing the army.

At sea there were careers to be shared with ships like the *Grand Turk,* a Hanover-built vessel designed and owned by the most famous shipbuilding family of Salem, the Derby family. Her record illustrates on a grand scale the privateersman's harvest. This greatest of all Continental vessels, as they were called in more dignified moments, carried more canvas than any ship yet launched anywhere. In less than two years of prowling the North Atlantic and the English coast she safely delivered some sixteen British ships to the American cause, and the financial residue of her prizes received by over three hundred members of her various crews was ample to set them up for life, assuming that any sailor would be so minded to hang on to his money.

This does not mean that the struggle at sea was without its hardships. Gangrene killed more men than grapeshot or cutlass or the punishing sea itself. To the traditional horrors of the fo'c'sle there were now added the blood and stench of the dying, the very excellent chance of falling victim to the ship's doctor who, significantly, was always called a surgeon, or, worse than these, to end up in an English prison waiting for a trial that never came. So scarce were powder and guns that many of the smaller vessels sailed totally unarmed, expecting to seize them from the British. What is more, they did. Certainly the accomplishments and the gallantry of the privateersmen are not to be discounted because their weather eye was cocked for a likely prize.

From a more patriotic standpoint, and one that cheered a Congress frantic for money, was the happy circumstance that these sea fighters frequently financed themselves. Furthermore they were reckless, loyal and obviously imbued with a will to independence, or they might easily have chosen to go over to the Crown with certain assurance of a warm welcome and of basking in its protection and later rewards. Such a course was not beyond the range of possibility, as witness Benjamin Franklin's son, William, who became president of the Board of Loyalists, much to his father's humiliation, and who at the end of the war went to live in England on a British government pension, never to return to his native land.

Nor was the looting of English merchantmen the only service performed by the privateers. It is difficult to imagine how the affairs of state of the struggling young nation could have been carried on at all without these ships to carry diplomatic officials to France, dispatches and gold to Europe, and to bring back sorely needed ammunition and supplies.

Theirs is a record of telling blows struck in the face of overwhelming odds. Cursed as they undoubtedly were by the recruiting sergeants of the Continental Army, and swept at last from the sea by British frigates superior in size and number, the privateersmen of '76 must have occupied at least a small corner in the heart of the commander in chief surveying the smoking battlefield of Yorktown when he remarked to his officers, "The work is done, and well done."

PART 2

America Gets Her Sea Legs

6

PEACE AND POVERTY

WAR'S END found the nation stripped of its hard-wrung wealth, looking about for the tools of peace. There were not many. The battle at sea had cost the New England states alone nearly a thousand ships—virtually all of them. Their fishing fleet, an indispensable source of food as well as income, had been destroyed. Among the whalers of Nantucket and elsewhere along the coast, English ships had accomplished the task set them with thoroughness. Of a whaling fleet of several hundred stout vessels there remained less than a hundred veterans.

A couple of dozen earnest gentlemen, gathered together in a hired hall as the Congress of the United States, were attempting to govern thirteen disunited states with one hand while begging for funds with the other. But there were no funds to be had. Nor did they have the authority to raise any if there were, not even for the hire of the hall. A day came when there was not one dollar on the treasury books.

Across the ocean the mother country, with all the shrewishness of a rejected relative, bore down vindictively with more Acts of Parliament. English merchants were forbidden, regardless of price, to purchase the highly prized American-built ships. Worse, the Barbary pirates, long a thorn in the side of all countries with shipping in the Mediterranean, were encouraged by

Europe to sabotage what little commerce the upstart nation retained.

Peace had come and times were hard.

Things were worst in the northern maritime states. The depression in Rhode Island brought industry there to a standstill. Ironically, there was money everywhere. The trouble was that there were too many kinds, some of it in foreign gold and silver coinage, much of it in land warrants and shaky government certificates of indebtedness, and all of it of fluctuating value. Speculators and quick-change artists reveled in a wild money market of their own creation. Only the foreign-exchange brokers, the lawyers (thriving as always in disaster) and the mortgage holders seemed to understand what was going on. Even George Washington wrote anxiously from the South that he had put off the tax collector three times, and now he feared he would have to let the sheriff seize some of his land to satisfy taxes.

From the back country disquieting reports came drifting in that the settlers, many of them army veterans, were making strange proposals for relief, backed with threats of rebellion. In a bewildering depression of plenty, these people were offering their produce and livestock in lieu of the shaky currency which they did not possess. Indignantly creditors and lawmakers alike turned them down. The settlers grew desperate. Word flashed over the countryside that an ex-soldier of the Revolution, Captain Daniel Shays, was leading an armed band of farmers from western Massachusetts in a series of raids on the courts to stop the foreclosures on their land.

Indignation grew to alarm; alarm led to strong measures. "God forbid," wrote Thomas Jefferson of this event, "that we should have twenty years without a rebellion." But for the most part the Founding Fathers didn't look at it that way, and Shays' Rebellion was broken up by the militia in the winter of 1787.

If the rebellion accomplished nothing else, however, it impressed on Congress the temper of the times. It gave impetus to the lagging movement for a better organized confederation, and this in turn gave hope to the shipowners and sailors, long suffering under a government impotent at home and abroad, that their ships and persons would cease to be fair game for everybody.

Unhappily Congress was slow to jell, principally for lack of authority. What authority it did have it failed to use to encourage or even protect the new merchant fleet that was slowly and painfully being pieced together out of the ruins of the old. It seemed that the brave showing of the privateers was to be their own undoing, as if by their deeds Congress and the people at large had been lulled into the comfortable belief that the peacetime fate of the merchant marine was no concern of theirs. The war was over; let American ships seek their own fair winds. In any future war—and few people really believed there would be one, at least not for a long time—let the merchant fleet rally round as it had in the past.

A momentous thing happened in the decade following the Revolution which, bolstered by the signing of the Constitution a few years later with its resultant stronger government, enabled the young nation to raise itself by its bootstraps. This was the opening of the China trade in 1784.

Up to that time and a few years beyond it, as has already been seen, things had been going from bad to worse. Sailors returning from the war were on the beach by the hundreds (the country was too small to speak of anything by the thousands yet). Warehouses were full. What ships there were lay rotting at their docks. All hands were eager to put to sea again—and those that were able did—but the only markets lying over the known horizon were forbidden British markets. Britannia was ruling the waves with a heavier hand than ever, biding the time when her recalcitrant and disorganized ex-colonies of adventurers should come to their senses.

In the seaport towns there had been a lot of talk about possible trade with China, but China was a long way off, its people hated foreigners, and anyhow the British had got there first. Nobody felt like doing much about it until sheer hunger drove them to it. It was one of those slender moments during which the fate of a great many people would depend on the success of a few.

A certain Major Samuel Shaw of Boston, a young man who had served as aide-de-camp to General Henry Knox and had lost his fortune in the war, had made an earlier attempt to reach China in 1783. He had sailed from Boston in a tiny fifty-five-ton sloop, the *Harriet,* with a cargo of ginseng root, hoping to trade it for silk and tea. Ginseng grew wild in the backwoods and was known to be highly esteemed by the Chinese for its medicinal qualities. At the Cape of Good Hope, however, he was offered twice as much tea for his root by some English East India men who were doubtless anxious to head him off from their private preserve in China. Shaw accepted the bargain and returned home.

But in February of the following year, backed by a group of merchants willing to do anything to relieve the pressure of stagnant trade at home, he sailed from New York with another cargo composed mainly of ginseng in a 360-ton vessel optimistically named the *Empress of China.* For this voyage the twenty-nine-year-old Major Shaw was commissioned as supercargo. Sending a supercargo, which is a sort of seagoing business manager, was a straw in the wind showing the future direction of American shipowning. Seamen were cheap, and gone was the crew's share in the cargo. Ships and cargoes were

CLIPPER SHIP *WESTWARD HO*

Built by Donald McKay in 1852. She burned at Callao in 1864. From a painting by Charles Rosner.

CLIPPER SHIP *FLYING CLOUD*

Built in 1851, she was probably most famed of the McKay-built clippers
She was finally scrapped in 1875. From a painting by Warren Sheppard.

CLIPPER SHIP *EMPRESS OF THE SEAS*

Another famous McKay ship. She made two trips to California during th
gold rush and sailed in the Australian trade until she burned in 1861.

owned ashore now. Most captains were hired only to command them, crews were hired to work them and a supercargo went along to make sure the ship returned a profit for the stockholders at home. The dividing lines were not so sharp as they would later become, but they were growing visible. Not taking any undue chances, the *Empress of China*'s owners decided to try out Paul Revere's new invention for copper-bottoming a ship's hull, and the *Empress* was so sheathed, the first in America, in order to prevent fouling during the long voyage around the Cape and through the Indian Ocean.

Major Shaw's job was a ticklish one. Even Congress seemed to realize this. He was armed with a sea letter signed by the President and the Secretary of Congress, which is an eye-catching precursor of the Good Neighbor policy. It began: "Most serene, most puissant, high, illustrious, noble, honorable, venerable, wise and prudent emperors, kings, republics, princes, dukes, earls, barons, lords, burgomasters, counsellors . . . who shall see these patents or hear them read . . . "

Six months out of New York, on August 23, 1784, the clank of the *Empress of China*'s let-go cable echoed over the water at Whampoa in the Canton River, and Major Shaw swung down the pilot ladder to try his luck ashore. His welcome, to abuse the meaning of the word, was decidedly cool. Without benefit of experience or aid from any source he quietly set about trading his cargo for the fabled silk and tea of the Orient. Through an almost unbelievable maze of obstacles presented by the organized channels of British trade, and over, around and through the pitfalls of Chinese suspicion, traditional isolationism and graft which was a concomitant of all their dealings with the foreign devils, the persistent major threaded his way, profitably expounding the virtues of his medicinal root.

His success was remarkable. When at last he sailed into New York harbor fifteen months later he was able to show his anxiously waiting backers a profit of $30,000 on their total outlay for the venture. This modest profit of twenty-five per cent— modest if the terrific gamble is considered, to say nothing of the months of waiting to learn whether your life's savings have been fattened or lost forever—created a sensation along the water fronts, for it showed in a practical way that a profit in trade with China was possible.

By this single successful voyage news of the China trade filled the sails of every idle vessel. As more and more Yankee ships swung into the Canton River eagerly seeking outlets for the glutted markets at home, the names of their customers, the Hong merchants, became household words as well known as na- tionally advertised brands of soap and cigarettes are today. Shaw himself returned to Canton as United States Consul, and his record of fair dealing and friendliness with the Chinese eventually gave the Yankee traders a decidedly favored position with the kingly merchants of the River of Flowers.

Kingly is the word for them. Taking their name from the rich, spice-laden warehouses called hongs, they enjoyed a mo- nopoly of trading with foreigners for which they paid the gov- ernment at Peking cash sums amounting to nearly $300,000 each, as licensing fees. In addition they were bonded for the good behavior of their foreign customers. The most famous of them all, Kwan Houqua, was a great friend of Major Shaw. This tall, slender, ascetic-looking Chinese with large liquid eyes, drooping mustaches and goatee, and swathed in rich brocaded silks, kept no books on his vast accounts with his American customers, and he matched Shaw's reputation for generosity as well as honesty in his dealings. Houqua became one of the richest men in the world, with a fortune estimated at well over thirty million dollars. Needless to say, his friendship was of immeasurable value in helping to foster and develop this vital new trade with the raw young nation in the western world.

Lifesaver that it was, however, the China trade was slow to get firmly established. For one thing the British, anxious to head it off, were offering every American ship that touched on the African coast and elsewhere en route to Canton such tempting profits to leave their American cargoes with them that many shortsighted, or perhaps overeager, shipmasters and supercargoes were selling out and turning their ships around for home. There was the *Grand Turk*, for instance, the same privateersman of Revolutionary War days still earning profits for her shareholders, which might have beaten the *Empress of China* into the Canton River on her first voyage had not her skipper, Captain Jonathan Ingersoll, accepted the bird in hand proffered by the worried English merchants he found at the Cape. Even so, Captain Ingersoll was not so easily bought off. With information culled from English skippers at the Cape concerning the Canton trade, he promptly made a second voyage and put it to good use.

And then, just when it looked like fair sailing, the trade showed alarming signs of withering away. As other ships arrived home in the months following the triumphant return of the *Empress of China* in the spring of 1785, they brought reports of an oversold market. For although the American demand for the tea and silk brought from Canton was lusty enough, it developed that the demand of the effete mandarins for the cargoes from America was not equally enthusiastic. Their finicky tastes did not include an insatiable desire for ginseng root, corn, salt fish, barrel staves and shingles. American ships began to clutter the Canton Roads off Whampoa, unable to dispose of their cargoes and unwilling to admit defeat and return home. In Salem and Boston and all along the coast down to New York, clerks in snuff-brown coats sat on their high stools doing most of their calculating in red ink, while portly gentlemen in the front offices were stepping out onto the wharves to rub their chins thoughtfully and peer out to sea with increasing frequency.

That the China trade was ultimately saved and continued to flourish for years to come has obscured the all-important fact that hardly had it become established when it threatened to collapse, until two Boston ships sailed in the opposite direction from all the others, around the Horn to the rescue.

It was recalled by some Bostonians that John Ledyard, a Connecticut man who had sailed with Captain Cook on his third voyage, had published a journal in Hartford in 1783 which had been read with great interest. In it he had suggested that fur could be obtained from the northwest coast of America and traded with profit to the Chinese, explaining how the Indians in the Nootka Sound region willingly bartered sea-otter pelts worth anywhere up to a hundred dollars apiece for beads, knives and cheap trinkets. Ledyard had, in fact, tried to fit out an expedition to the Pacific Northwest himself but, failing, had gone off to Europe in 1785 to try his luck there, where Thomas Jefferson, Lafayette and John Paul Jones had given him their sympathetic ears but no money. In London he had better luck. Finally he set off in 1786 to try the overland route across Europe and Russia, but it was a short-lived venture that ended with his expulsion by the Russians.

Meanwhile the Bostonians formed a stock company with such substantial merchant adventurers as Joseph Barrell, Charles Bullfinch and the ubiquitous John Derby among them. They purchased an eighty-three-foot ship with two decks and mounting ten guns, prophetically named her the *Columbia* and, on September 30, 1787, dispatched her from Boston in company with a little ninety-ton sloop, the *Lady Washington,* to investigate Ledyard's claims. With the fervent good wishes of their shareholders and with $50,000 of their money invested, these two vessels, which together could just carry the cargo of an ordinary coal barge today, rounded Cape Horn and beat their way up the long western reaches of two continents to the promised land on Nootka Sound, some two hundred miles north of what is now Victoria, British Columbia.

To everyone's surprise they found two British ships there and a third one building, all under the command of Captain John Meares. Captain Meares had traded a pair of pistols with an Indian chief named Maquinna for a lease of the country thereabouts, but to the vast relief of the Americans his interest was chiefly of an exploratory nature; his particular delight seemed to be the naming of islands, straits and sounds right and left. He invited the two American skippers, Captain Gray and Captain Kendrick, to attend the ceremony of the launching of his new vessel, and since the event was only three days off, they swallowed their tongues and tarried.

This was to be the first ship-launching in Northwest America, the beginning of an economy linked with the other extremity of the continent generations before the overland pioneers settled the West. A picture of the scene on that warm Indian-summer day in 1788 is easily imagined by a look at the entry in Captain Meares's journal for the day of the launching:

At noon an event to which we had so long looked with anxious expectation, and had been the fruit of so much care and labor, was ripe for accomplishment. The vessel was then ready to quit the stocks, and, to give all due honor to such an important scene, we adopted, as far as was in our power, the ceremony of other dockyards. As soon as the tide was at its proper height, the English ensign was displayed on the shore and on board the new vessel, which at the proper moment was named the *Northwest America,* as being the first bottom ever built and launched in this part of the globe. It was a moment of much expectation; the circumstances of our situation made us look to it with more than common hope. Maquinna, Callicum, and a large body of

their people who had received information of the launch, were
come to behold it. The Chinese carpenters did not very well
conceive the last operation of a business in which they themselves had been so much and so materially concerned, nor shall
we forget to mention the chief of the Sandwich Islands, whose
every power was absorbed in the business that approached, and
who had determined to be on board the vessel when she glided
into the water. The presence of the Americans [*Columbia* and
Lady Washington] ought also to be considered when we are
describing the attendant ceremony of this important crisis,
which, from the labor that produced it, the scene that sur-
rounded it, the spectators that beheld it, and the commercial
advantages as well as civilizing ideas connected with it, will
attach some little consequence to its proceeding in the mind of
the philosopher as well as in the view of the politician, but our
suspense was not of long duration. On the firing of a gun, the
vessel started from the ways like a shot; indeed she went off with
so much velocity that she had nearly made her way out of the
harbor; for the fact was that, not being very much accustomed
to this business, we had forgotten to place an anchor and cable
aboard to bring her up, which is the usual practise on these occasions. The boats, however, soon towed her to her intended
station, and in a short time the *Northwest America* was anchored. . . .

When the Englishmen were gone the Americans promptly
set about collecting the cargo for which they had come. Their
fondest hopes were realized. In one place along the sound, for
instance, they obtained $8,000 worth of sea-otter pelts for about
$100 worth of cheap chisels. When the *Columbia*'s holds were
filled with the glossy fur, most of it of the precious jet-black
variety, Captain Gray left the *Lady Washington* behind to continue the trade and sailed across the Pacific via the Sandwich
Islands to Canton, where he exchanged his cargo with the eager
Chinese at the rate of some $750 a pelt. Loaded with Cantonese
tea, he then sailed on westward around the world to Boston,

completing a voyage of 41,899 miles by the ship's log, and by the calendar one that had lasted within a month of three years. His welcome home must have been an enthusiastic one. Imagine waiting three years without word of any kind to find out what had happened to your share of $50,000—which was more like half a million in those days.

The *Columbia* had weathered the Horn and circled the globe, the first American vessel to do either of these things. But the important thing to the worried merchants of Boston was that their ship had shown the way to a continuing trade with the shrewd merchants of Canton in a language everybody could understand, the language of dollars. And once again the dollars rolled in from the China trade. Records show examples of outfits costing as little as $9,000 trading a fur cargo valued at $60,000, and a $50,000 outfit yielding a gross return of $284,000.

Prospering ships meant prospering sailors. On her first voyage in the fur trade, while the depression was still on, the *Columbia*'s ordinary seamen were paid five dollars a month, able-bodied seamen seven dollars and a half. After that first successful voyage, as the new trade sent more and more ships to sea, firms like J. & T. Lamb of Massachusetts were paying boys eight and ten dollars a month, ordinary seamen fourteen to seventeen dollars, able seamen eighteen, and junior officers twenty-four dollars. By 1812 Senator Lloyd of Massachusetts was able to report that the average pay of American seamen was twenty-two dollars and a half a month. Wages in comparable trades ashore also rose at the turn of the century to as high as a dollar a day, out of which the worker, unlike the seaman of course, housed and fed himself.

As for the *Columbia,* a terse entry in another sort of record tells a story all its own: "The ship *Columbia,* Captain Gray, arrived Boston Aug. 10, 1790. Cleared port on a second voyage to the Pacific Northwest Sept. 28, 1790. . . . " Three years of icy gales and tropic blasts, of putrid food and undrinkable water, of illness, wrenching loneliness and all the refined tortures of a life at sea—and Captain Gray turns his ship around to sail away for Cape Stiff again and the wilderness of the Pacific, just seven weeks after arriving home. Here was a breed of men hard to beat.

That on his second voyage Captain Gray discovered the "Great River of the West," now known as the Columbia River, which had been sought by explorers probing the coast from Mexico to Alaska for years, and that he thereby claimed the vast region that now includes Oregon, Washington and Idaho for the United States, is almost anticlimactic in the bright light of this Yankee skipper's courage and determination in following a tradition that has no end in the ageless struggle with the sea.

7

PEPPER AND SPICE AND
FRIENDS IN CONGRESS

TRUE TO the old saying that it never rains but it pours, with the China trade thriving there came sailing home to Salem in 1796 the schooner *Rajah,* Captain Jonathan Carnes commanding, chockablock with pepper.

On the wharf the *Rajah's* elated skipper was closemouthed, but his shrewd eyes must have twinkled over his secret. For up to this time the pepper and spices of the Orient had been controlled by an ages-long series of monopolies, first by the slow and devious caravans that had hauled the stuff overland from its unknown sources in the mysterious East to the markets of the Levant and Europe, later by the Portuguese, then the Dutch and finally by the English, who brought it from the coasts of Brazil and from the East around by the Cape of Good Hope. From Europe it had to cross the Atlantic to reach the tables of those Americans who could afford to pay for such luxuries. And a luxury it must have been, selling as it did as late as 1699 at eight shillings a pound and at the time of the *Rajah's* voyage at thirty-seven cents a pound—when thirty-seven cents was more like three dollars today.

Now Captain Carnes had changed all this. The excitement of the crowd on the wharf, and the mounting envy of rival merchants mentally totting up the profits of the *Rajah's* voyage, is

73

easily imagined as her cargo was tumbled from the holds. At a cost of not more than $18,000 for the voyage, including the schooner's magic cargo, and with the pepper selling in a wild market for about $125,000, he returned to the vessel's owners a profit of seven hundred per cent!

In darkest secrecy the captain slipped away again on a second voyage. Others followed, but he managed to shake them off before setting a true course for his secret sources on the northwest coast of Sumatra. Their names were as exotic as the cargo he sought—Benkulen, Padang, Analaboo, Tally-Pow, Labuan-Haji. On this voyage, too, and for nearly five years to come, Captain Carnes managed to keep his secret, learned during an earlier voyage on a tip from a native.

There was a claim of prior discovery, as usual, this one made by William Vans of Salem, that he and Jonathan Freeman were actually the first to open the pepper trade to America in the brigantine *Cadet* in 1788, eight years before Captain Carnes. Regardless of who was first to discover the source, in 1791 less than five hundred pounds of pepper were exported from the United States, while the customhouse records of Salem alone show that in 1805 that port exported to European markets over seven and a half million pounds which Salem ships had brought home first and then reshipped across the Atlantic.

Inevitably, Captain Carnes's long-nosed rivals tracked him down at last, and the "Spice Islands" were thrown open to Yankee trade, a trade destined to persist for forty years and to come very close to cornering the world market just as the Nantucket whalers had done before the war. Salem ships almost exclusively boomed the trade until stiff competition and thinning profits once again sent them questing other cargoes in far, lonely stretches of other seas.

By now Americans seemed to be fools for luck. Almost anything to which they turned a hand had the Midas touch. In

1805 a twenty-one-year-old Bostonian named Frederic Tudor took a notion to capitalize on the short summers and long winters of his native state by shipping ice to the tropics. It was an occasion of vast amusement to the hardheaded New Englanders when he had his first cargo of 130 tons hauled to Charlestown and loaded aboard a brig for Martinique. The sailors were sure the ice would melt and swamp the brig, and he had great trouble securing a crew. As it turned out, the scoffers were all dead right. The cargo melted in Martinique before he could sell it, leading him to record in his diary: "I found myself without money and without friends, and with only a cargo of ice in the torrid zone to depend on for the supply of both."

But Tudor refused to give up. On subsequent voyages he learned the importance of cutting the ice properly on the ponds, of stowing it in blocks between thick blankets of white-pine sawdust and building icehouses in foreign ports to receive it. It was a long hard struggle involving frustrating debts and even jail, but in the end he was able to exclaim happily in what he labeled his "Ice House Diary": "Thus is the winter of my discontent made glorious summer. . . . Drink, Spaniard, and be cool, that I who have suffered so much in the cause may be able to go home and keep myself warm!"

Warm and snug he was kept, too, for Frederic Tudor's ice trade made him rich and established the fortune of more than one Boston family that followed his lead in sending ice as far south as Rio and halfway around the world to Calcutta. By 1857 the Boston Board of Trade was able to report that in the previous year 363 cargoes totaling 146,000 tons of ice were shipped from that port to fifty-three places in the United States, the West Indies, the East Indies, China, the Philippines and Australia. For a generation after the Civil War, until cheap artificial ice was invented, this export trade increased and prospered. Not Boston alone, but every New England village with a pond near tidewater was able to turn this Yankee liability into an asset through the persistence and genius of Frederic Tudor.

And then there is the case, in Tudor's time at the turn of the century, of a crackpot in Newburyport who was called "the luckiest man in America." Everything he attempted seemed to bring him in money. He assumed the title of Lord—Lord Timothy Dexter—and by way of self-aggrandizement he maintained a personal poet laureate, had statues erected to himself, gravely conducted his own funeral and otherwise enjoyed life according to his lights. But if he was a fool, he made it pay. On one occasion he allowed a group of sly merchants to fill up one of his ships sailing for the West Indies with warming pans— a ruinous cargo, surely. But on arrival the pans were eagerly snatched up by the natives, who found their long handles and shallow draft excellent for skimming boiling molasses vats in the manufacture of rum.

Times were booming. New England ice, furs from the Pacific, even warming pans for the tropics had their markets. Warehouses were stuffed with tea, silk and spices from the Orient, wines from France and Portugal, iron chain and cotton duck from Russia, general merchandise from England, sugar and molasses from the West Indies, hides and wool from Chile, Brazil and California, coffee from Arabia, fruits from the Mediterranean. Every sailor worth his salt had a berth. The hold of every ship was filled. A prosperous coastal trade was bringing the country's seaports closer together, helping to unify the nation. It was nothing for Boston to have a hundred vessels clearing port in a single day—ships, brigs, schooners and lesser craft—with four times that number busily loading, unloading or being fitted out at her eighty wharves and quays. Pressing close on her heels in the race for trade were Salem, Baltimore, Philadelphia and New York.

Of course everything is relative. In those days nobody was so busy that he had no time to pause for a swallow of ale or a tipple of port at the Sign of the Jolly Tar at almost any time of day; nor were cargoes so overwhelming that a shipmaster didn't know their contents and value right down to the last hogshead of cheap "tradin' likker." For the sake of perspective, consider that if the eye-popping spectacle of a present-day Liberty ship had presented itself in Boston harbor, such a ship would have required no more than six voyages to transport the cargoes of every vessel in the harbor. Furthermore, supposing the cargoes were bound for Canton, the Liberty's six voyages would take no longer than the time consumed by Major Shaw in making one such voyage in the *Empress of China*. A couple of trips more by the modern freighter would have relieved Baltimore ships of all their freight, and Baltimore ranked third as a commercial port. What a monster of the deep like the 53,000-ton *S.S. United States* could have done by way of transport along those tranquil water fronts may be left to the imagination.

Even so, a hundred seagoing vessels clearing port every day is a lot of business regardless of size. Not so many less than that were sailing from other bustling, rapidly growing ports like Philadelphia, which, despite lying a hundred miles or so from open water and the menace of tide rips off the mouth of Delaware Bay, could boast that it had doubled its population in ten years, from some forty thousand to 81,009 people, as shown by the census of 1800. The billowing sails and tall spars of a merchant fleet shaking off the shackles of war-waste and depression had again clawhauled its way into an era of prosperity.

Nothing succeeds like success. Congress, with money in its coffers at last and with considerably more authority, sat up and took notice of the winning struggle at sea. In an expansive mood it decided to give actual support to shipping with an act providing a ten-per-cent discount on import duties on cargoes carried in American ships. Further, with an eye to monopolizing the China trade, it provided that duties on tea should be especially low for American vessels, thus making it unprofitable for foreign ships to handle it.

During these halcyon days of Congressional favor beginning in the 1790s and extending beyond the turn of the century, no less than fifty laws helpful to shipping found their way onto the books. They ranged from measures encouraging shipbuilding to provisions for the protection of coastwise trade. American-owned-and-built ships, for example, could enter American ports upon payment of six cents a ton, while foreign-built-and-owned vessels were required to pay as high as sixty cents. Furthermore, American vessels in the coastal trade paid their tonnage fees once a year, while foreign ships paid for each port entered.

All this for a breed of seafarers long used to thriving on disaster. The goose hung high indeed—perhaps too high. Envy from abroad was to be expected and could be coped with; war, weather and politics were old tribulations and could also be coped with; but had they known and understood that the most implacable enemy of their spreading sails and fleet wooden hulls was quietly a-borning on their own shores it is possible they would not have faced the future with such equanimity. Possible but not probable. A profession that was content to let the chronometer lie idle for fifty years after its perfection could hardly be expected to stir with much resolve against anything as preposterous as the scheme of a former victualer and handy man of the Continental Army, one John Fitch, whose fantastic claim was that vessels propelled by steam would soon be crossing the Atlantic Ocean.

To substantiate his claim Fitch had sent such a vessel of his own creation chuffing up the Delaware River in 1787 in the presence of a crowd that included most of the members of the Constitutional Convention then sitting in Philadelphia; but perhaps because that year was such an eventful one, those most concerned had no time to take stock of such nonsense. It does seem as if he had miscalculated the psychological moment for attracting public support for his outlandish contraption, what with Captain Shays' rebellious farmers being run to earth by the Boston militia, Captain Gray setting forth on his momentous voyage to the Pacific Northwest with the *Columbia* and *Lady Washington* to revitalize the China trade, and the famous *Grand Turk* returning to Salem from her voyage around the Horn with a fabulous cargo of silk. Certainly it was a poor year in which to try to beguile honest folk with harebrained schemes for abandoning the centuries-old tested methods of wresting their livelihood from the sea.

Even poor John Fitch himself, who from his copious journal and letter writing appears to have been as handy with his quill as he was with his steam-fitter's tools, must have sensed the hopelessness of his position when he wrote to a friend in that noteworthy year: "This, sir, whether I bring it to perfection or not, will be the mode of crossing the Atlantick . . . for packets and armed vessels."

8

SLOW BELL

IF EVER THERE was an event in the story of America's ships and sailors which fails to fit snugly into its own watertight compartment, it is the coming of steam. To attempt to determine who was the first steam navigator on either side of the Atlantic is as pointless as trying to name the first sailor. What matter who was first unless his act was of some consequence in directing or giving impetus to the future? Most likely the first sailor was a hairy, slant-skulled fellow who fell out of his tree into the water and, finding himself miraculously kept afloat by clinging to a branch, paddled his way to shore.

Similarly inconsequential though more specific is a machine described by Hero of Alexandria which was set moving with steam by some unsung genius about 130 B.C. More specifically still, a Spaniard, Don Blasco de Garay, was trying to convince his king, and more especially the royal treasurer, of the virtues of the steam-spouting *S.S. Steinitz* in Barcelona harbor as early as 1543. In the time-honored way of treasurers, this one overrode the favorable report of a royal commission and opposed the steamboat. The idea was therefore dropped by the king and Don Blasco alike, in spite of the fact that the *Steinitz* had steamed at a speed of "some two leagues in three hours," which was considerably faster than the fleetest galleys of the day. It is a temptation to say that the attitude of the king's treasurer was significant of events to come, but opposition to a new idea, be it steamboats or cuffless trousers, is too familiar a human burden to be identified by profession. Besides, a steamboat had not yet been built, apparently, that was good enough really to scare anybody.

Down through the years Frenchmen, Scotsmen and Englishmen were all groping for a practical means of using a cylinder and piston driven by steam to propel their crafts through the water. Not until the hurly-burly of trade with China and the Spice Islands was in full swing, however, did John Fitch come forward to point the way. His voyages by steam navigation were so successful and the ultimate conquest of steam over sail so compelling, particularly for the wood-wind sailors of this country, that its American beginnings crowd into the story of our struggle with the sea.

John Fitch may justly be called the father of American steam navigation. True, his claim was disputed by a millwright from Berkeley County, Virginia, named James Rumsey, whose steamboat was good enough to win him exclusive rights on the rivers of Virginia, Maryland and New York in 1787, a year or so after Fitch had built his first boat, but Rumsey does not seem to have done much with his invention. This may have been because Rumsey's craft was powered by jet propulsion, a method advocated by Benjamin Franklin, which proved unsatisfactory for large vessels because of the excessive friction of water charging through the pipes from bow to stern. It was Fitch who carried on the struggle alone, against ignorance, prejudice and lack of funds, until he brought steam navigation to a practical point of development sixteen years before the successful ex-portrait painter, Robert Fulton, came splashing noisily onto the scene.

John Fitch was a Connecticut farmer's son who went to sea

at seventeen. He gave it up to try his hand as a clockmaker, brass founder and silversmith before turning to the more lucrative business of purveying supplies to Washington's Continental Army. After the Revolution, with a substantial stake, he bought some land in Virginia and was appointed a deputy surveyor for Kentucky. He got the idea of steam navigation while roaming over the great rivers of the region making maps. But to try out his ideas cost money, and it is almost superfluous to say that none of the state legislatures to which he applied would grant him the assistance required for such an expensive hobby. However, after building an experimental boat, he did ultimately succeed in organizing and partly financing a private company through his efforts in making a map of what was later to be known as the Northwest Territory and printing it on a cider press. The sale of his maps brought him about eight hundred dollars, and in 1786, with half of the company's shares retained for himself, he managed to get a second steamboat constructed.

His first boat had been little more advanced than Rumsey's, nor was his second one, propelled as it was by a series of upright oars, six on a side, worked by cranks coupled to a steam engine. But to the wonder of all who beheld it the latter craft traveled up the Delaware at better than three miles an hour on the eventful summer day of its trial run in 1787. With this success Fitch redoubled his earlier discouraging efforts to secure additional funds and aid from various states and the Central Government, as it was then called, to develop his steamboat.

By this time he had worked himself into a frenzy over his plans. No other thought possessed him. Years before, after a wretched marriage, he had left his wife. He later wrote: "I know nothing so perplexing and vexatious to a man of feelings as a turbulent Wife and Steamboat building. I experienced the former, and quit in season, and had I been in my right sences,

I should undoubtedly have treated the latter in the same manner." He did finally succeed in persuading several state legislatures, including that of Virginia, to grant him certain exclusive rights to steam navigation on their inland waters. Thus encouraged, Fitch and his associates built a third steamboat, this time with its twelve-inch cylinder driving broad upright paddles at the stern.

This was his most successful venture. After many trials and mechanical changes a cabin for passengers was built on the foredeck, and there appeared the following announcement in the *Pennsylvania Packet* on June 14, 1790:

THE STEAMBOAT

is now ready to take passengers, and is intended to set off from Arch Street Ferry in Philadelphia every Monday, Wednesday, and Friday, for Burlington, Bristol, Bordentown, & Trenton, to return on Tuesdays, Thursdays and Saturdays. Price for passengers 2/6 to Burlington and Bristol, 3/9 to Bordentown, 5s. to Trenton.

During the summer and fall of 1790 the boat ran regularly at a speed of seven or eight miles an hour between Philadelphia and various river towns. Then came disaster. In order to comply with Virginia's requirement that at least two steam vessels be in operation on the waters of that state by November 9, 1790, another boat, fittingly named *Perseverence,* was under construction. When nearly completed it was torn from its moorings in a violent storm and tossed up on an island beach where it could not be refloated in time to fulfill the conditions under which Virginia's privileges had been granted. At this, Fitch's faint-hearted company dissolved. A Philadelphia merchant who was later to run sailing ships to Europe, Thomas P. Cope, wrote of this: "Fitch became bankrupt and broken-hearted.

Often have I seen him stalking about like a troubled spectre, with downcast eye and lowering countenance, his coarse soiled linen peeping through at the elbows of a tattered garment. . . . "

Snubbed at every turn in his quest of financial aid—even by the usually imaginative Benjamin Franklin—until his persistence earned him the name of madman, Fitch sailed in desperation to Europe. His mission failed both in France and England. It is perhaps significant that while he was in London his drawings and papers were loaned by the American consul in France to the engaging Robert Fulton, who kept them for several months. Fitch, then fifty-one years old, worked his passage home as an ordinary seaman. In New York, in 1796, he was puttering about the Collect Pond, where the Tombs Prison now stands, fitting a borrowed yawl with a steam engine and, remarkable as it seems, a screw propeller. The screw propeller is generally credited to Colonel John Stevens and other later experimenters, but there is no doubt that Fitch used it first.

Nevertheless, it appears that by this time only the owner of the borrowed yawl was interested in Fitch's work, for obvious reasons perhaps. When even this patron took back his yawl, leaving him high and dry, Fitch gave up the ghost. He wrote in his journal: "The day will come when some more powerful man will get fame and riches from *my* invention, but nobody will believe that poor John Fitch can do anything worthy of attention. . . ." Alone and ignored, poor John Fitch returned to the scenes of his younger days in the Kentucky wilderness and there poisoned himself. Too late by several years, a committee of the New York legislature finally recorded that "The steamboats built by Livingston and Fulton were, in substance, the invention patented to John Fitch in 1791." Fitch's observations on this belated recognition might make interesting reading, had the frustrated genius been able to pass down one last entry from a heavenly journal.

Fitch's hard-won steamboat patents no more established successful steam navigation in America than did successful steam tugs like Symington's famous *Charlotte Dundas* do so abroad ten years later. Few men understood the principle of the steam engine, and fewer still knew how to build a steamboat; hardly anyone wanted to.

Then, too, shipping men claimed that the engine, boilers and fuel took up too much space, leaving no room for the profitable carrying of cargo. Nor could the cost of operation compare with the use of the wind. In addition to all these loudly voiced objections was the customary indifference of the country at large to any kind of change; and thickly overlying the whole like a choking marine growth was the frightened opposition of shipowners. In their struggle against the encroachment of steam—when at last it became a struggle—the shipowners first reverted to the traditional tactic of ridicule. This failing, they were to fight it down the years to their last ragged sail.

So, despite the infant steam, the high tide of America's career in the art of the sea was to be reached in sail. It was a career destined to span in its greatness only eighty years, beginning with the launching of the China trade, and to end in disaster as so many careers have ended, because of the blinding light of its own success.

Meanwhile, proof of the unity and strength of the young nation had yet to be demonstrated to a skeptical world by force of arms. It was to be a demonstration which would bring with it a second paralysis of trade within a generation, because the United States still failed to understand the inseparableness of her navy and merchant marine.

9

WAR FEVER

AMERICAN INVENTIONS have a way of geting us into trouble with alarming frequency. At one stage in our history American steamboats and screw propellers gave England a naval fleet that automatically turned what there was of our own into obsolete junk. At another, American-devised extreme clipper ships led us down the primrose path of sail when steam was conquering the world. To this day Pearl Harbor bears the scars of the United States-invented dive bomber, as imitated and refined by the Japanese.

Likewise, there is a strong case for the argument that a twenty-eight-year-old Yale graduate, while job hunting in Georgia, hit upon an invention which led this country into a series of armed conflicts that finally brought down on our heads the War of 1812. Before his invention this country needed so many more things than it had to sell that we were a struggling nation of importers, much sought after as customers. In the twenty years following his invention, with cotton having become our most valuable export, the United States became the greatest, most successful and most envied neutral commerce carrier in a world at war. Naturally we were ripe for trouble.

Eli Whitney was staying at Mulberry Grove, the plantation home of Nathanael Greene's widow on the Savannah River, in 1793, waiting for a teacher's berth to turn up, when he heard the planters discussing with despair the labor of separating cotton from its seed by pulling it off by hand. It struck him as simple and logical that the fiber could be combed away from the seed with a set of revolving wire brushes, and, to prevent the seed from going through, another roller could be set close by the comb roller. It was one of those simple ideas that makes everybody wonder why he didn't think of it himself. In fact claims have been made for the Widow Greene herself that she did first suggest the idea.

In any case the building in which the cotton gin was placed was broken into and the machine carried off. In the absence of workable patent laws the gin quickly became public property. Slavery became fabulously profitable. Planters moved small armies of slaves westward into the lush fields of Alabama and Mississippi to raise and reap the harvest. A year or so before Whitney's cotton gin—by which name it came to be identified, regardless of the claims for his hostess—only thirty-eight bales, by modern measurement, had been sent abroad. In the years immediately following the invention cotton became the country's biggest and most profitable export. Shipping increased by leaps and bounds.

Stimulated as usual by war abroad—it was Napoleon this time—a mounting prosperity was at hand for the Yankee traders. Sea captains were retiring as young as thirty with funds enough to set up as merchants and to indulge themselves in the long-denied shoreside pleasures of politics, horses and suing at law. Such was the demand for American-built ships that every sixth vessel launched was "sold foreign."

It was a situation that irritated the British. Aggravating their jealousy of our incredibly large profits was the fact that we were carrying cargoes to France, with whom they were at war. And France didn't like it because we were carrying goods to England. In fact the only foreigners who did like it were the Barbary pirates, and their approval was decidedly negative since their sole interest in American prosperity was in the fat bribes we were paying them to leave our ships alone.

In the beginning the most pressing troubles were with the French. The liberal ideas of the newly founded French Republic had frightened the aristocracy of Europe who were afraid foolish notions of *liberté, égalité* and *fraternité* might spread among common people everywhere. England and her various allies had promptly set about to destroy the republic by waging an undeclared war which they said was "to avenge the death of the French king." The British began by nabbing all neutral ships on the high seas with cargoes for France and holding them in English ports. France struck back, claiming that England was trying to starve her into submission. Soon the American minister to Paris was complaining about French privateers capturing American vessels and treating them as prizes on various legal technicalities, often using captured American sailors in exchange for French sailors captured by the British.

Of course everybody in this country wanted to keep out of the European war. But in spite of a sort of neutrality—President Washington had issued a neutrality proclamation in 1793 without actually using the word "neutrality"—both belligerents seized American ships, cargoes and seamen. It began to look as if the United States would have to get off the high seas. Generally speaking, the British were taking our sailors and the French were taking our ships. Perhaps because of the difficulty of determining the cash value of a sailor, however, American resentment was greater against the French, who despoiled us in some seven years of several hundred ships and their cargoes valued at over twenty million dollars.

Congress, lulled by flimsy treaties with the Barbary pirates—the Sultan of Morocco, the Dey of Algiers, the Bashaw of Tripoli and the Bey of Tunis—had called a halt to the expensive building of six frigates a few years earlier, and these lay on their stocks unfinished. But in desperation, with American merchant ships being driven from the high seas, work was begun again in 1797 in feverish earnest. Thus was born, if the helter-skelter arrangements of the Revolutionary War are excepted, the full-dress United States Navy, with the launching of the frigates *Constitution, United States* and *Constellation.*

Along the water fronts the air was alive with talk of war. Treaties with the French Republic were set aside. The call went out for ten thousand volunteers to serve in the armed forces for an enlistment of three years. George Washington, who had been succeeded in the presidency by John Adams the year before, in 1797, was recalled from Mount Vernon to take command of the army. In the theaters people were singing "Hail Columbia, Happy Land." Everywhere were shouts of "Adams and Liberty!" and "Our infant Navy!"

At last the order came through:

Instructions to the Commanders of armed vessels belonging to the United States:

You are hereby authorized, instructed, and directed to subdue, seize, and take any armed vessels of the French Republic.
JOHN ADAMS
PRESIDENT OF THE UNITED STATES

This time there was no lack of crews for official naval vessels. President Adams, shrewdly drawing on his experience in the last war, made it a point to learn the prevailing scale of wages ashore and afloat and then cannily raised the bid. Skilled mechanics ashore were being paid fourteen dollars a month, and merchant seamen eight to ten dollars. Enlisted United States sailors were therefore offered fifteen to seventeen dollars a month and tempted with a ration list half again as large as that of the British Navy. Furthermore, American merchant ships, by which was meant the lusty privateers, were forbidden by regulation to take prizes. Since they were allowed to carry guns for their own defense, however, and in view of their past record, it is doubtful if these regulations would have been worth the paper they were writtten on had the struggle developed into a full-dress war of any duration.

This it did not do, thanks to the small, badly organized but tough-fighting newborn United States Navy. Manned mostly by former merchant officers and seamen, and with eight of the so-called naval vessels merely converted merchantmen, the ships of the fleet fought a series of individual bloody engagements that had the French on the run from the start. One of the bloodiest was fought by the *Constellation,* which fell upon the French ship *L'Insurgente* while prowling the Leeward Islands off St. Kitts in the West Indies. *L'Insurgente* was the fastest ship in the French Navy, if not the world, but when Captain Truxton and his men were through with her she lay a helpless wreck with seventy casualties. The victory had cost the Americans three men. Less than a year later the *Constellation* fought the most daring battle of all when she attacked and cut to pieces the French ship *Vengeance,* a war vessel that outgunned the Americans five to three in weight of broadside. Finally, with the triumph of the *Boston* over the *Berceau,* the French were willing to sign a treaty of peace in 1801. Besides the two battleships it had cost the French to learn that the Americans would, in the end, fight, it had cost them over eighty merchant vessels and considerable national pride.

Since this undeclared war was fought largely for commerce,

a trial balance cast up by Fletcher Pratt in his history of the navy makes interesting reading:

National revenue from customs on imports, 1798-1801 (protected by navy)	$30,000,000
National revenue from customs during four years preceding (unprotected)	23,000,000
Gain	$7,000,000
Minus cost of navy	6,000,000
Credit balance	$1,000,000
Plus value of French ships taken	700,000
Total credit balance	$1,700,000

A pretty fair investment any way you look at it. But with the war, or rather the quasi war, ended, what did Congress decide to do with a fleet specifically built *"to defend the merchant marine,"* in accordance with Washington's fifth annual address to that body? It promptly decided that the navy could shift for itself. Under the provisions of the Peace Establishment Act of March 3, 1801, the ships were sold as they came home, and those unsold were decommissioned and roofed over on the mud. Rations and pay were reduced and blanket dismissals were given out, leaving only nine captains, thirty-six lieutenants and 150 midshipmen in service. This accomplished, the lawmakers turned to more pressing matters, which included earmarking funds for the annual tribute to the Barbary pirates.

"If there were no Algiers," remarked a British lord to Benjamin Franklin, "it would be worth England's while to build one." For a hundred years and more the Barbary pirates had certainly been a peculiarly paying proposition for England.

These African corsairs, comprising Moroccans, Tunisians, Algerians and Tripolitans, by looting the ships of weak or peaceful nations, served the very useful purpose, from the British point of view, of keeping steady the balance of trade. England paid them tribute, too, but that was part of the bargain. The British were quite frank about it, as Lord Sheffield's observation in a publication of 1784 had made brutally clear. "It is not probable," he declared, "that the American States will have a very free trade in the Mediterranean; it will not be in the interest of any of the great maritime powers to protect them from the Barbary states. They cannot protect themselves from the latter; they cannot pretend to a Navy."

Maybe so. But one thing at a time. For in spite of subduing the French, things were happening fast at the turn of the century. Across the sea Europe was crumbling under the armies of a dictator. In America trade in general and shipping in particular were booming. Despite continuing depredations by the French, treaties or no treaties, and despite the irritating if not actually damaging impressment of American seamen by the British, the merchant fleet had doubled in size in ten years. As in all periods of restlessness and development the pieces in the jigsaw puzzle of events in the first decade of the 1800s were numerous and seemingly unrelated. They shape a story according to the point of view taken.

From a sailor's standpoint, everybody was getting rich except the men who sailed the ships. Shore wages had again risen to as much as a dollar a day, while sailors in New York were still being paid ten dollars a month. Up the coast, wages for a sailor shipping out of Massachusetts ports were a little higher, but then so were shore wages. The seamen were taking the lumps, risking life and liberty at the hands of the British, French and African pirates, to say nothing of ordinary sea risks, while landsmen were stowing away the profits in their long socks under the mattress. Windy tales were told over glasses along the water front of vanished ships, floggings on British men-of-war and starvation or worse in African dungeons. Nobody had heard the word propaganda in those days, but the yarns had enough basis in fact to make very good spinning. There was a rising feeling in favor of a fight. Just who was to be fought didn't matter—everybody had his own ideas about that—but fighting meant action, release and possible gain.

One solid, incontrovertible fact was the grinding wage of ten dollars a month. Every sailor could agree on the villainy of that. The trouble was that there was nobody to speak for the seamen as a body, even if anyone had been willing to listen; and since most people were too busy making money from the harvest of the sea, listeners were very, very scarce. In colonial times there had been maritime organizations, but their memberships usually consisted of politicians with axes to grind. In Massachusetts the frank purpose of the Caulker's Club, for instance, was "to lay plans for introducing certain persons into places of trust and power." Down in Philadelphia a shipmasters' society had been founded in 1765 called "The Society for the Relief of Poor and Distressed Masters of Ships, Their Widows and Orphans." The Society, which continued to meet regularly as late as 1922, held its monthly meetings in a room off Carpenter's Court, which today is a passageway leading up to Old Carpenter's Hall from Chestnut Street.

From the beginning the pilots were unruly. They were known to strike when their rates were reduced or when a rule which displeased them was passed. In those early days when the whole length of the Delaware was considered to be within the port of Philadelphia they could thus tie up the river for commerce. Later, in New York City, the shipwrights had incorporated themselves into a loose organization, but it didn't amount to much—and, anyway, shipwrights are not sailors. The sailors were out of luck, and in November 1803, in New York, they decided to strike.

Who the leaders of this first notable American strike were is not clear. One thing was definite, though: it was no backhanded affair to "lay plans for introducing certain persons into places of trust and power." Known simply as "The Sailors' Strike," it stemmed straight from the fo'c'sles, or perhaps in the interest of accuracy it should be said, straight from the water-front ale-houses, where most sailor business was transacted. Demanding a raise to fourteen dollars a month, they refused to sail the ships unless something was done about it. Nothing was done about it, though, and when their demands were turned down they formed in a body, marched yelling and singing through the streets, gathering forces as they went, and ended up in a bloody free-for-all with the constables, who threw the leaders in jail. Wages remained at ten dollars.

In the vaulting times with the breath of war abroad fanning every conflicting point of view, the feeling of one and all, man, woman and child, was the same concerning the Barbary pirates. Ambassador Charles Cotesworth Pinckney took the words out of everybody's mouth with his popularly misquoted protest, "Millions for defense, but not one cent for tribute!" (What he actually said was ". . . not a *damned penny* for tribute!") This was quite a mouthful, in view of the fact that the Dey of Algiers alone had seven kings and two republics paying tribute to him. And one of the republics, the United States, had contributed over a million dollars as its share. To add insult to injury, one of our recently victorious naval vessels, the *George Washington,* Captain Bainbridge commanding, sailed into the Mediterranean to pay the annual tribute to the Dey and was required to continue her voyage to Constantinople with a cargo of livestock and slaves for the Sultan there. Worse, she was forced to pull down the national ensign and fly the Algerian flag!

Everyone seemed agreed that the Dey of Algiers was about the most offensive of these international racketeers in every sense of the word. The American consul there, William Eaton, who was soon to prove a man of action rather than words, described him as "a huge, shaggy beast, sitting on his rump on a low bench, with his hind legs gathered up like a tailor or a bear, who extended his fore paw as if to receive something to eat. . . . He grinned several times, but made little noise."

Something had to be done about this gentleman and his co-horts. In desperation—and being free of the French for the moment—several naval expeditions were sent into the Mediterranean to settle the score by force. However, the understanding that naval warfare seldom accomplishes subjugation of an enemy without co-ordinated land operations was not a part of the navy's mental equipment, and among other frustrations the *Philadelphia* was captured at Tripoli and her crew imprisoned. There was supposed to be a blockade against Tripoli, but just who was actually blockaded was never quite clear. Certainly with the prospect of the captured *Philadelphia* being turned against them as a powerful raider, a blockade was not getting the American Mediterranean squadron anywhere.

In the end it took an ex-sergeant of the American Revolutionary Army and a handful of U. S. Marines to get "the situation well in hand."

William Eaton, the ex-sergeant, had come up the hard way. From the army he went to Dartmouth College, where he worked his way through, then spent seven more years on active military duty doing Indian fighting as an army captain. Eventually he got himself appointed United States Consul at Tunis. But he soon sickened of the job. He was shocked and disgusted at what he considered the wishy-washy attempts of the American government to appease the Barbary Powers with "presents," which he was often required to present in person. The only thing that kept him from resigning was the breaking out of hostilities with Tripoli. This cheered Eaton's fighting spirit and he decided to stay around and lend a hand.

From the look of things to Eaton, the Bashaw of Tripoli's Achilles' heel was his brother Hamet. This Hamet was a weak-livered sort of fellow who was afraid to take over the throne which his younger brother had usurped by the simple expedient of murdering all his brothers but Hamet, who had escaped to Tunis. Eaton made it a point to befriend Hamet and fire him with ambition to regain his rights. The subsequent wining and dining and outright bribing, as well as the organizing and arming of Hamet's followers, put Eaton in debt for some $23,000. Perhaps recalling the ringing cry of the home folks, "Millions for defense, but not one cent for tribute!" he returned to Washington for the double purpose of settling accounts and getting official approval of his plans for his fifth-column work against Tripoli.

Loose talk about millions was one thing, however, and actually ponying up $23,000 quite another as far as Congress was concerned. Eaton's one-man effort seemed about to be buried under a hopeless pile of red tape and interdepartmental correspondence between the State Department, the Navy Department and Congress. Then, like a lightning shock clearing the air, news of Decatur's heroic night attack and burning of the pirate-held *Philadelphia* in Tripoli harbor reached Washington. Eaton's star was on the rise. While the *Philadelphia* had been in the hands of the Tripolitans her speed and gun power had been a constant threat to the hovering American squadron, keeping it paralyzed and out of action. Now, by Decatur's daring raid in the harbor and destruction of the vessel, the navy was free at last to take the initiative. Supplies, cash, everything was granted, and Eaton himself was appointed Navy Agent to the Barbary States, by way of giving him official status. Eaton

JOHN FITCH'S SECOND STEAMER

The artist concentrated on the mechanically operated oars and forgot the smokestack.

JOHN FITCH'S THIRD STEAMER

This little vessel, well ahead of Fulton's, looked and worked like the real thing.

A BLACK BALL LINE PACKET

Sailing days were the first of each month, and the Atlantic Ferry was under way.

THE BLACK BALL LINE STEAM PACKET *UNITED STATES*

Built in 1847, she was sold after two years' service to the Prussian government

promptly set sail, but before he could get back to Hamet and his makeshift army, another report reached Washington—bad news this time. Impatient of waiting for Eaton, Hamet had taken things into his own hands, suffered a defeat at the hands of his brother's forces and was now holed up in Alexandria. American aid was thereupon withdrawn, official heads nodded knowingly and Eaton was left to carry out his rather vague mission on his own.

He reached Cairo in the winter of 1804. Knowing the importance of making a favorable impression in that region, he took on the airs and title of a general, rigging himself out in feathers, sash and other glittering military appurtenances. His actual command consisted of nine Americans, six of whom were United States Marines. This doughty band set out in search of Hamet. They found him eventually, being held for ransom out on the desert. After paying off his kidnapers, they reorganized the "army," assured Hamet of support from the United States fleet with which they were to rendezvous at Derna and sallied forth on a five-hundred-mile march across the blazing crucible that is the Barca Desert.

The tale of Eaton's march is a saga in itself. After strikes by the camel drivers, desertions by the Arabs, quarrels with the fainthearted Hamet and an outright mutiny, Eaton's tattered and shriveled forces straggled onto the heights above the walled city of Derna fifty days later and found to their joy that the American fleet, having sighted their campfires along the coast, was waiting for them. Thus the forces for a land-and-sea action were joined.

While the United States ships *Argus, Hornet* and *Nautilus* bombarded the city's fortifications from the sea, General Eaton put himself at the head of his thirty-eight loyal Greek cannoneers and six U. S. Marines and, sending Hamet's unreliable horsemen off on a diversionary feint, charged the enemy's loopholed wall from the land side. By four o'clock that afternoon, as Eaton lay wounded, the American flag was hoisted for the first time over a fortification in the Old World. The fall of Derna, Tripoli's second city, resulted in a treaty of peace with the shocked Bashaw and the release of the American seamen held in his dungeons. Still more important, William Eaton, with his Greeks and marines backed by United States Navy guns, had demonstrated to the Barbary pirates and the world at large that the American republic was no longer an ex-colony unable to defend itself.

The Yankee powder flag was at the mizzen again. Let France and England beware.

10

STEAM, HALF AHEAD

MOST PEOPLE in the seaport towns had their uneasy gaze fixed seaward in these troubled years, what with the nation laying about her with gunfire, treaties and threats. Still, as suggested earlier, one of the very causes of all the international squabbling was the thriving state of commercial affairs at home, a result of Whitney's cotton gin and the consequent increase in cotton production.

An important personality in the jigsaw picture of this period was a young Irish-American, Robert Fulton, who had been haunting the official chambers of Napoleon's government in Paris with a scheme for invading England with the aid of a "submarine boat" that fired torpedoes. But the young man was thought to have too many other bees in his bonnet, one of the most outlandish of which was to build a steamboat and none of which had yet been successfully demonstrated—at least so far as his French listeners were concerned. So Napoleon postponed his invasion of England till a more practical means than a submarine could be devised.

Fortunately for Fulton, his plans for a steamboat were symptomatic of the bustling times at home, for it was on the East River in New York, in 1807, that he chose to launch his boat.

A favorite picture conjured up by mention of the discovery of steam propulsion is that of Fulton's gallant craft, the *Clermont,* making history with every turn of her creaking paddle wheels on the waters of the Hudson. Or of Watt eying in picturesque wonder the hissing teakettle. Of course, as witness John Fitch, Fulton did not "invent the steamboat," any more than did Watt "invent the steam engine." As a matter of fact neither of them invented anything. Watt's very solid contributions to the science of steam were mechanical improvements coinciding with the rise of industrialization in New England, which in turn was made possible by the use of spinning machinery based on the already familiar use of steam. As for steamboats, they had been churning up a lot of water since Fitch's efforts down to the time when Robert Fulton, backed by his charm, his persistence and his political influence, made them a paying proposition.

At least sixteen steamboats had been built in America before the launching of the *Clermont.* Still others had been built abroad. One of them, built in Germany by Denis Papin, a Frenchman, just a hundred years before Fulton's so enraged the astonished boatmen on the River Fulda as it approached the town of Münden that they attacked its builder and destroyed his boat. Papin apparently considered himself lucky to escape with his life, and he left the tricky business of steamboating to others.

If Fulton was given to reflection on the misfortunes of his predecessors, a trait which, if it existed, has escaped the notice of historians, it is quite likely he dismissed their failures with some such solemn bromide as "results are what count." Fulton himself was certainly a "results" man. In contrast to the plodding, scientific approach of poor John Fitch, Fulton had all the qualities necessary for ramming a newfangled contraption down the throats of an unwilling public with its mind on more pressing matters. He was handsome, a good talker and a promoter *par excellence.* He had imagination and he had also undoubted ability. He even had the kindly eye and open pocketbook of the powerful Robert R. Livingston, successful lawyer and politician and New York's first chancellor, as well as the inspiration of a devoted sweetheart who had the good fortune to be a niece of Chancellor Livingston. What more could any man want?

Livingston was no newcomer to steamboating. He had experimented with a boat of his own back in 1798 after taking over the exclusive privileges granted by the New York legislature to John Fitch eleven years earlier. But Livingston's steamboat could make only three miles an hour, one mile short of the requirement of the grant, and he had abandoned the project when the grant's time limit ran out. Fulton met him in Paris in 1803 while Livingston was United States Minister there, and together they experimented with two steamboats on the Seine. But the first one sank when its engine dropped through the bottom, and the second one moved too slowly to be of any value.

Back home again Fulton set to work on the *Clermont,* named after the Livingston family estate on the Hudson. With great difficulty he managed to have the machinery which was built by Boulton & Watt, a British firm, brought over to New York despite British government restrictions, and with the help of Charles Brown, a New York shipbuilder, he constructed the hull. If Fulton created nothing new in steam propulsion, his success was nonetheless deserved if only because of his skillful employment of the best features of the other steamboats that had already wheezed their way into history. His *Clermont* was a thoroughly practical vessel, built to make money rather than to prove any new theories. He distributed his weights so that the wooden hull would float on an even keel, no mean feat in those days, what with her ponderous boiler, twenty feet long, set in masonry and her condenser in a large cold-water cistern.

The *Clermont* foreshadowed the slab-sided freighters of today. Fulton wrote in his instructions to the builders: *"Clermont . . . should be built almost wall-sided, if sixteen feet at bottom she need not be more than eighteen on deck. Straight sides will be strong, since it fits the mill work and prevents motion in the waves."* No ship designer up to that time had considered the shape of his craft with an eye to preventing motion at sea. Or if he had, none had brought it to public attention.

One innovation he did fail to incorporate in his craft, however—the screw propeller. There must have been some defects in the screws of the time, for they were not put into general use for nearly forty years afterward in spite of improvements made by Colonel John Stevens on Fitch's invention. The colonel had had a steamboat driven by a four-bladed screw propeller plying the waters around New York harbor in the summer of 1802. By 1804 he was operating a small twin-screw boat as a ferry between Hoboken and New York—three years before the *Clermont* was built—but no one except his son seemed much interested in following up the screw-propeller idea at the time.

When at last the *Clermont* was ready to sail, after all the struggles of inventors of the past, after numerous proved and successful steamboats and after Fulton's own practical efforts now brought to fruition—after all that, a skeptical crowd gathered on the pierhead where the vessel was docked, getting up steam. They had come to jeer. "The morning I left New York," Fulton wrote to a friend, "there were not thirty persons who believed that the boat would ever move one mile an hour or be of the least utility; and while we were passing off the wharf, which was crowded with spectators, I heard a number of sarcastic remarks . . . . " Typical was the cautious announcement of the *American Citizen* in its August 7, 1807, issue:

Mr. Fulton's ingenious Steamboat invented with a View to the Navigation of the Mississippi from New Orleans upwards, sails today from the North River, near the State Prison, to Albany. The Velocity of the Steamboat is calculated at four miles an hour; it is said that it will make a progress of two against the Current of the Mississippi, and if so it will certainly be a very valuable acquisition to the Commerce of the Western States.

"If so," it certainly would!

At last the order was given to cast off. A long blast was blown on a big tin horn as a warning to near-by boats, and then, as reported by the New York *Evening Post,* "there was a strange creaking, whirring, churning sound, a hiss of the escaping steam; the awkward-looking wheels, towering full seven feet above the deck on either side begun to turn, and we were really started on the first steamboat voyage on the Hudson." So with a passenger list of some fifty people, we find the handsome ex-portrait painter and Jack-of-all-trades triumphantly breasting the Hudson at five miles an hour in his new vessel to the astonishment of all who beheld it.

It must have been a sight to give one pause, at that, what with its thirty-foot-high stack roaring flames and sparks from the dry white-pine fuel, its machinery exposed to view and groaning in its labors while a man with a pot of molten lead scurried about to stop leaks of escaping steam, and its adventurous passengers crowded onto the two small decks at bow and stern. "Bottomside" was the first of a new and indomitable breed, the chief engineer, and, prophetically, he was a Scotsman. Among the passengers was Harriett Livingston. It is not difficult to imagine the look in her eyes when Fulton, in the best Hollywood style, seized the occasion of this voyage that meant so much to them both to announce their forthcoming marriage.

They made the 160-mile run up to Albany in thirty-two hours, against a headwind that prevented the use of the sails she carried as insurance, and returned to New York in thirty hours. Not everyone was happy about the *Clermont's* success. Foreseeing trouble ahead, the river boatmen damaged her time and again, sometimes by ramming her on the river or by destroying her paddle wheels while she was tied up at the dock. To protect the wheels Fulton was obliged to enclose them with heavy timbers. But in the impending battle of steam this was only a skirmish. Fulton himself, ironically, had a hand in delaying steam's progress. In his efforts to hang onto his legal monopoly in New York waters he engaged in a series of lawsuits, one of which resulted in his acquiring two steamboats from a Captain Bunker, called the *Hope* and the *Perseverance,* which were copies of his *Clermont.* As soon as they were turned over to him by the court he broke them up, which is one way of getting rid of dangerous rivals.

Even so, Fulton's exclusive steam-navigation rights had the effect of stimulating a healthy competition in broader fields, for when Colonel Stevens and his son Robert of propeller fame were eventually forced out of Fulton's preserve, they decided to take their side-wheeler, *Phoenix,* which had been running on the Hudson, around to Philadelphia. It meant an outside passage for the first time, and thus Fulton may be said, in a negative sort of way, to have sent steam nosing its way to sea.

To sea and conquest. A conquest to be challenged only by the white wings of the clippers casting their swift shadows over the world's oceans in a last fateful struggle to survive.

11

"Lest Britain Should Take a Few Men by Mistake . . ."

DOWN IN Washington a gentleman-farmer President, if he thought about a steamboat at all, probably thought of it as a smoky, smelly nuisance. He had enough worries fretting over the trouble into which Yankee sailboats were leading the nation. More and more the trouble was narrowing down to squabbles with the English. England felt that she had a special grievance against the Americans, for, while she was fighting for her life against Napoleon, her sailors, the backbone of British resistance, were deserting her men-of-war by the thousands to escape the brutality and horrible food in the British Navy.

Ten dollars a month, low as it was, looked good to a British sailor who more often than not never got paid at all and then only when his ship was safely anchored well out in the harbor of its home port so he could not draw his pay and desert. To be certain that he remained aboard, liquor and women were brought out to the ship, and the expenses were docked from his mythical wage. At sea, official ration lists to the contrary notwithstanding, his diet did not vary for months at a time from the old stand-bys of weevily biscuit, salt horse and lime juice, the latter to prevent scurvy. Flogging for spitting on the deck or lesser crimes was common. In a world at war his only sure rewards were sickness or death. It is hardly surprising, then, that, with the encouragement of a common language, he eagerly deserted to a berth on any American ship within jumping distance, for the pay, the more humane treatment, the food that could be swallowed. Less surprising still was the horror and hatred the British service engendered in American seamen among whom one true tale of impressment in all its brutal detail quite probably gave wings to a thousand fanciful ones which lost no meat in the retelling.

England, hard pressed for men, finally gave orders to the captains of all her warships to stop and search American vessels for English deserters. It was a right well founded in international law. Technically there should have been no trouble about it. The trouble was that the certificates carried by American sailors proving their nationality could be bought for a dollar apiece along the water front of any New England port, and when British authorities found out about it they paid no further attention to the certificates. Boarding officers simply looked over an American vessel's crew and picked the likeliest looking of the lot. The chances of justice in the procedure were about fifty-fifty. A good example of the mixed character of American crews of the time is that of the *Philadelphia*. When that vessel fell prey to the pirates at Tripoli half the imprisoned crew turned out to be ex-British sailors without naturalization papers.

When things grow tense between nations or between neighbors the platitudes of the argument are invariably reduced to an "incident." In 1807 such an incident was supplied by a fifty-gun British frigate, the *Leopard,* whose commander had the poor judgment to fire a broadside into a United States naval training ship, the *Chesapeake,* not ten miles off the American shore. The British were looking for deserters, as usual, but the attack killed three of the *Chesapeake*'s crew and wounded eighteen, most of whom were boys training to be seamen. Adding insult to mortal injury, the British boarded the American vessel and removed three of her people to flesh out her own crew. This was too much, even for the landlubber President, Mr. Jefferson. With angry talk fanning the humid Washington air he decided it was time that seventy economical little gunboats should be built to act as a sheet anchor, just in case.

Mr. Jefferson's gunboats amounted to little, however. The war talk died down, and he relapsed into his landlocked state of mind, expressed in the view that all a navy did was get you in trouble. "Were I to indulge my own theory," he wrote at about this time, "I should wish them [the states] to practice neither commerce nor navigation, but to stand with respect to Europe precisely on the footing of China."

This theory, it need hardly be mentioned, did not settle well on New England stomachs even though the last thing in the world they wanted was a trade-disrupting conflict with their best customer, England. But there was worse to come. Since ships were the cause of the mess, Mr. Jefferson decided to take the course any sensible farmer would take. He'd keep 'em home, tied up out of trouble.

A Newburyport newspaper in 1808 had this wry jingle to offer its readers:

> Our ships all in motion once whitened the ocean,
>   They sailed and returned with a cargo;
> Now doomed to decay, they have fallen a prey
>   To Jefferson—worms—and embargo.

This was no joke. The government's frantic desire to keep American ships safe at home and out of trouble had got all hands into a pretty pickle. The root of the trouble lay in the unfortunate state of mind of the British. For in spite of the beatings administered by the Americans to the French and

Barbary pirates, England could not forget the fact that the United States was an ex-colony, and, on the high seas at least, she continued to treat the Americans insolently. Perhaps she could not overlook the fact that once again the Americans had no navy worthy of the name to protect their shipping.

Napoleon, putting on the screws in the game of squeezing neutrals, had issued an imperial decree placing England under blockade, an act which in practice simply gave more leeway to French privateers enthusiastically plundering British and American vessels alike. It was the beginning of a series of retaliatory measures from both sides. The British issued what they called "Orders-in-Council," a high-sounding term for regulations subjecting any ship on its way to a French or French-controlled port—which in practice meant all Europe—to capture. Then more imperial decrees from the French, more Orders-in-Council from the British, until no legitimate neutral shipping could safely sail the seas.

Obviously this called for a show of force by the Americans—another Battle of St. Kitts, perhaps, or another William Eaton with a few navy guns and a handful of marines. But there was nothing doing. The flesh was willing but the spirit, as exemplified in Washington, was weak. The United States was going through one of those periods of wishful thinking about neutrality. Mr. Jefferson was nursing along what he called an economy program, and one resultant economy had been the reduction of the navy to some half-dozen ships, all of which were partly out of commission and undermanned. In any case he felt it was safer and much cheaper to keep the navy and merchant fleet at home.

Anguished howls rent the air of New England. Ships were beginning to rot at their docks. There was loud talk of seceding from the Union. Timothy Dwight of Connecticut packed his bags and set out on a preaching tour with this as the text of his sermons: "Wherefore come out from among them, and be ye separate, saith the Lord." And no wonder. The American merchant marine had been earning more than fifty dollars a ton annually, mostly by carrying food and supplies to war-torn Europe. Massachusetts ships alone were bringing home some sixteen million dollars a year in freight money, which amounted to more than the entire cash value of the fleet that was earning it. It was an income larger than the entire revenue of the American government for the preceding year. And the announced purpose of the embargo was to save from capture these vessels which had already paid for themselves many times over! In dollar terms it did not make sense. To the sailors, mates and even masters lined up at the soup kitchens in seaport towns it made less than sense. Some of those towns, like Newburyport, Salem, and Plymouth, their harbors jammed with idle ships, never regained their former prosperity after the Embargo of 1807.

Even the British were regretting their highhandedness. At least the shoreside crowd were. To the British Navy an order was an order: the Orders-in-Council were still in effect and so American crews were still fair game. But ashore most people were broke, and sick and tired of war, and everybody, even Parliament, regretted the trouble with the Americans. British foreign policy was in a bad way; there seemed to be two foreign policies, one for the navy and one for the people. The fisherfolk of Dover seized the occasion of the Fourth of July to compose a song to express their feelings in the matter:

> Dear Sirs, it is wrong
>> To demand a *New Song;*
> I have let all the breath I can spare go;
>> With the Muse I've confer'd,
> And she won't say a word,
> But keeps laughing about the EMBARGO.

I wish that I could
   Sing in *Allegro* mood,
But the times are as stupid as LARGO:
Could I have my choice,
I would strain up my voice,
   'Till it *snapt* all the *strings* of EMBARGO.

Lest Britain should take
A few men by mistake,
   Who under safe colors may dare go;
We're manning our fleet
With our tars that retreat
   From poverty, sloth, and EMBARGO.

To make the embargo stick, the American coasts were more
heavily guarded by Federal officials and soldiers than they were
to be later during actual war. Exports, which had been climbing
since the time of Eli Whitney's cotton gin when they had
amounted to twenty million dollars a year, had reached forty-
nine million before the embargo. A year later they had dropped
to nine million.

Those were the official figures, but there were many leaks.
Troubled times like these were the stuff on which Yankee
skippers had been bred. With sharp noses turned to the ill
wind for any possible good it might blow, they took to remote
bays and creeks and from there operated much like the contraband smugglers of colonial days or the rumrunners of the
1920s. On the other side of the Atlantic the British were only
too glad to oblige by admitting them without clearance papers.
Tales of the embargo breakers are legion. They run pretty
much to a pattern, like the experience of Captain Charles Doten
of Plymouth. One dark night, in a northeast gale that had
driven the water-front guards to seek shelter, Captain Doten
hastily rerigged the brig *Hope*, which had been stripped of its

sails and gear by the collector of the port. Hoisting sail as quietly as he could, he beat out toward the open sea under a hail of lead from the revenue cutter that had spotted him, and eluded it in the storm. He then set his course for St. Lucia in the Windward Islands, that happy hunting ground of all smugglers, and made his landfall with a cargo of fish. He sold both vessel and cargo for $25,000 and arrived back home again with a light heart and a heavy coat, there being sewed in the coat's lining all his profits in the form of Spanish doubloons.

The embargo was finally too much even for Mr. Jefferson, and fourteen months later, to the regret of no one, it was quietly junked. But it was too late. Like a ship running before the wind, the ship of state boiled through the gusty halls of a Congress dead set on war. A crowd of young men called the War Hawks was at the helm, led by Henry Clay of Kentucky, who was sure the British could easily be beaten and would pay for their loss with Canada. Another crowd of Southern hotheads had their eyes on the Floridas. Of course the windiest speeches were not burdened with these heart's desires; the popular cry was against the vile impressment of American seamen by the British. A list of six thousand names of sailors forcibly taken from American ships was got up to show the perfidy of the British; but the pleading, protesting New England shipowners, gnashing their teeth at the folly of it all, got up their own list showing they had employed over eighteen thousand seamen in the past dozen years and of these there were only thirty-five known cases of impressment, of which only twelve were Americans. The war, it seemed, was to be fought for their benefit, but the last thing in the world they wanted was a war with their best customer. If somebody had to be fought, said they, why not fight the French again? Napoleon, it was pointed out, was seizing and selling every American ship he could lay his hands on.

But Napoleon was too shrewd to be caught that way. In the hope of embroiling the United States with England in order to get the British off his own neck, he had long since proclaimed to the world that he was revoking his various imperial decrees restricting sea commerce, it being understood, he said, that England would in turn revoke her Orders-in-Council. The language of this noble gesture was vague and ambiguous and did not fool the British for a minute. They had had more experience with dictators than the Americans. But the gesture served his purpose. In a fine frenzy of patriotic fervor, not without its provocations, war was declared on England on June 18, 1812. On June 16 the hated Orders-in-Council had been hopefully repealed by the British, in spite of their mistrust of all parties concerned, thus removing the chief cause for conflict. Unfortunately there was no Atlantic cable in those days.

So the war drums again began their beating. Ships were hastily rerigged and their bulwarks cut away for guns. The tidings ran like wildfire among the veteran privateersmen scattered along the Spanish Main and other distant coasts. Joyously they swarmed homeward to sail once again for glory and lush pickings. Almost as an afterthought Congress looked around for the weapons with which to fight. It was found that the United States had sixteen ships against England's eight hundred. In the Regular Army there were seven thousand men. For a general staff there were the Secretary of War and his office force of a dozen clerks. The only bright spot on the otherwise gloomy horizon was the superabundance of trained merchant officers and seamen, men trained on the seven seas to fight with whatever weapons were at hand—a superabundance only because the ships were lacking.

It was a sorry beginning for war. On the day it was declared bells tolled dolefully throughout New England and flags were flown at half-mast.

12

SECOND BATTLE OF THE ATLANTIC

THE IRONIES of the War of 1812 make disheartening reading. Not only was the war declared two days after the main issues had been resolved, but the only winner was a man imprisoned on the tiny isle of Elba who was in no position to cash in on his winnings. Then, too, the idea seems to have got around this country that the United States won the war, due, perhaps, to Commodore Perry's glorious victory on Lake Erie and Andrew Jackson's heroic defense of New Orleans.

Furthermore, everybody at the time had a different notion of why the war was being fought. The War Hawks and their freshwater followers in the West saw it as a crusade against Canada; the Southerners aimed to acquire the Floridas; the superpatriots along the coast were out to avenge impressed seamen. Ironical, too, is the fact that New England shipowners, who opposed the war, made money out of it. And as a capping irony, the greatest land battle of the war, the defense of New Orleans, was fought two weeks after the peace was signed.

All this in no way dims the heroism and loyalty of the men who fought and died for their principles. A good many wars before and since have been fought for less reason than this one. The men of 1812 considered it a defense of their country, and, their country right or wrong, they were out to win the war.

To understand the merchant seamen's part in this mixed-up struggle it is helpful to keep in mind that the scene of operations was divided into three parts: the Great Lakes, the coast, the sea. To appreciate fully the supreme importance of American merchant ships and sailors in staving off utter ruin to the nation in this Second Battle of the Atlantic, it is well to have a look at what was going on in these areas of combat before their sails and thunderous guns hove over the horizon in telling numbers.

Hostilities opened with disaster. General Hull at Detroit made a weak-kneed surrender to the British and Canadians, in large measure because of the incompetence of politically appointed officers in the Regular Army. After that disaster the War Hawks' windy talk about taking over Canada had a very hollow ring, to say the least. It meant that all the region on the southern borders of the Great Lakes was in British hands and upper New York State was open to invasion.

The New Englanders were sorrier than ever they had entered the war. American wounds were partially salved when Captain Isaac Hull, nephew of the general, redeemed the family name by taking the *Constitution* and her green crew into battle against the *Guerriere* off the Nova Scotian coast and battering the British frigate into surrender. This cheering victory was followed up with another when the United States sloop *Wasp,* evenly matched in a fair fight, captured the British sloop *Frolic.* Then into harbor sailed Stephen Decatur of Tripoli fame, now a commodore, in command of the frigate *United States* and bringing with him as prize one of the best ships of the British Navy, the *Macedonian.* A few weeks later came word of the *Constitution* again: this time she had destroyed the equally powerful British frigate *Java* off the Brazilian coast. The *Hornet* sank the British *Peacock.* The navy was in its glory. The nation took heart.

In the first rush to battle, American naval vessels were proving superior. There was no doubt of that. They were of a tougher build, with heavier timbers and better armament, and they were speedier and more agile. Through the summer and fall in the first six months of the war they captured three British frigates and three sloops-of-war with the loss of only two brigs and the heroic little eighteen-gun *Wasp,* the latter having fallen prey to the seventy-four-gun frigate *Poictiers.* Unhappily the navy's day was brief. The alarmed British increased their Atlantic squadron on the American coast to ninety-seven ships. By the following summer the United States fleet of some twenty-odd vessels—if practically everything they had afloat is counted—had been swept from the seas by sheer weight of numbers. By fall, under the British blockade that reached from New Brunswick to Florida, there was not an American naval vessel offshore.

Around the Great Lakes, however, things began to look better. As American troops had been beaten on land, it was decided that a naval action might have more chance of success. So Commodore Oliver Hazard Perry was sent up to Presque Isle, now Erie, Pennsylvania, to see what could be done about building a fleet of lake boats to send against the British there. He arrived in March and found the ice giving way under spring rains. It was a desperate race against time and the enemy at Fort Malden. Local storekeepers boosted prices sky-high—not that it mattered much, since necessities like sails, rope, nails, anchor cables, anchors, cannon and muskets could not be had at any price. These, together with artisans and seamen, had to be brought through the wilderness from the seaboard. The shipwrights went on strike, and half of them headed back over the snow trails for Pittsburgh. There was no military protection for those who remained. The men grumbled. The job looked hopeless.

Commodore Perry persisted. He secured five hundred ill-trained militia from the interior. Then he declared the whole layout a military reservation and officially lowered food prices.

Racked with a raging fever, he even took time out, while the ships were being built, to join in the capture of Fort George on the Niagara River. It was largely due to this fighting commodore, sick as he was, and to the fleet marines that the British were defeated there, leaving some of their ships behind them. Meanwhile, it was getting on toward summer and the British were sailing up and down outside Presque Isle Bay, waiting for a chance to get at Perry's still-to-be-born fleet. Returning from Fort George, he brought with him five captured ships—a brig, three schooners and a sloop—and added them to his future forces. Even this operation was a struggle. Unable to sail them back to Presque Isle for lack of wind, he had them literally dragged along the shore by oxen, expecting any minute to be discovered by the English squadron, while he lay on deck, swathed in blankets, shaking with the ague.

At last, toward the end of the summer of 1813, Perry had his fleet. Despite the adversities of war, weather and human frailties, he had managed to get two brigs of twenty tons and three schooners built. These, together with the captured vessels, gave him a navy of ten. They didn't all get into the fight—one stuck on a sand bar on the way out to battle—but with the last-minute arrival of a hundred marine reinforcements, sharp-eyed Kentucky squirrel shooters all, he set sail in quest of the cruising British squadron. On September 10 he was able to send word to General Harrison: "We have met the enemy and they are ours; two ships, two brigs, one schooner and one sloop."

Detroit was recaptured. Perry was master of Lake Erie, and the British invasion of upper New York was headed off. These achievements did not win the war, by a long sea mile, but they were hard facts that were to count heavily at the peace table.

Wars cost money, as the Founding Fathers had been all too painfully aware not a generation before. This time there was more money to be had in the country at large, but on the other hand there wasn't the same unanimity of opinion about the need for raising it. New England shipowners and their friends and relatives, which meant practically everybody up there, were still talking loudly about secession. This is a little difficult to understand because by this time their privateers were bringing home fat profits despite the British blockade that had bottled up what was left of the navy. And as a side line, New England merchants were busy supplying the British army in Canada in wholesale lots. This latter piece of business became such a thriving one as the war went on that General Prevost of the British forces was able to write home the cheerful report that "two-thirds of the army in Canada are at this moment eating beef provided by American contractors." The New Englanders were doing all right by themselves.

But this put no money in the Treasury in Washington. Before the war only hard coin of the realm had been issued by the Treasury Department, but now a loan was needed and needed quickly. Hard-pressed Secretary Albert Gallatin reached what must have been a painful decision for his economy-minded Swiss soul and issued treasury notes bearing over five-per-cent interest. He managed to hedge a little on this by providing that all notes under one hundred dollars denomination would bear no interest at all, thus creating what could be called the first paper money issued by the United States Government, although it was not commonly used as such.

Gallatin's chief reliance, however, was on the sale of bonds, which must have hurt him even more than printing paper money did, because the bonds paid six to eight-per-cent interest. Even so, not many people bought them. In fact, so few bought them that they quickly began selling below their par value. Gallatin not only had to see his Federal securities selling at eighty and below, but he had to accept payment in state bank notes worth only sixty-five cents on the dollar themselves. These loans, finally, amounted to over eighty million dollars at face value, for which the United States Treasury actually got only about thirty-four million dollars in cold, hard cash.

No wonder the harried Gallatin slammed shut his ledgers, packed his bags and scuttled off to Europe to see what could be done about putting a stop to this extravagant war!

Meanwhile the English, too, were writhing from attacks on their pocket nerves. Peace negotiations had begun almost as soon as the fighting did. They grew more intense as British underwriters' charges for insuring vessels merely crossing the English Channel mounted rapidly to twelve per cent and finally fifteen per cent. These high-priced risks were due to the ravages of American privateers now beating down the sea lanes of the Western Ocean in their full glory.

It's high time we had a look at them.

A shot rang out at the village tavern. A bell tolled. By word of mouth the news spread that there was to be a "signing on" at the Sailor's Rest. No parades and drums of recruiting officers were necessary this time to fill up a ship with sea-hungry men still suffering the vicissitudes of Mr. Jefferson's embargo. The pay was small—nothing a month most likely—but a share in the prize to be taken was promised, and that was enough to fill the articles with scrawly marks, to sling a Long Tom aboard a pilot boat, a fisherman or even a pull-galley and get it to sea.

Names of these privateers tell their own story: *Orders-in-Council, Right-of-Search, Fair Trader, Revenge.* As the leathery lean-faced veterans of the trouble with the French and the Barbary pirates swarmed back to the beaches to put to sea in anything that would float, fat British merchantmen went foaming to cover. From the start it was speed, not power, that gave the Americans their strength—speed and a sense of revenge. For although not many seamen had actually been pressed into the British Navy, if the list of the committee of fifty-one New England shipowners is to be believed—or even multiplied by ten— there was a feeling abroad in the land that this was the common seaman's war, and their nerve and daring in the battles at sea were beyond all past experience. Crammed to the scuppers with fighting men who scarcely had room to lie down for an off-watch snooze, the Americans ran down their prey, grappled, and sprang aboard the enemy, shouting and swinging cutlasses as if loosed from the gates of hell.

Ranging farther to sea there were bigger ships too, and their plunder must have turned gray the hair of the gentlemen at Lloyd's. There was the *America* of Salem, which made six captures off Land's End of the British Isles; the *Anaconda* of New York, with her prize of $80,000 in gold and silver coin taken from His Majesty's packet ship *Express* after a battle off the Cape Verde Islands; and the *Lion* of Baltimore which, while ranging the Bay of Biscay, sold prizes worth $400,000 in the French port of Lorient.

In the English Parliament Lord Lansdowne observed bitterly:

Some time ago it was imagined on all hands that in the event of war with America the first operation would be the destruction of her navy. What the fact has turned out to be, I am almost ashamed to mention. If anyone were asked what had been the services of our own navy in this war, he would unfortunately find some difficulty in giving an answer.

That was the beginning of it. When the British Atlantic squadron was hastily increased to nearly a hundred ships and the blockade tightened along the American coast, the doughty pilot boats, fishermen and pull-galleys were bottled up in harbor to some extent, along with the ships of the navy. But it was like trying to clamp your thumb over the stream of a garden hose. Yankee traders, beset by wars all over the globe, had been building ships for years that could run away from anything they met—long, sharp vessels with a mountainous spread of sail and of moderate draft so they could run into lagoons where no British warship could follow. It was as if they had been specially planned for the war to come. They slipped to sea, north and south, in numbers beyond all British control.

By 1814 the desperate British Admiralty stepped up their reinforcements along the American coast to some two hundred ships. No use. A new type of privateer was putting to sea. These were the flashing little Baltimore clippers, forerunners of the greater offspring to come, which had been born along the shores of the Chesapeake to meet the stiff competition for freight and passengers in that region.

These Baltimore clippers were beauties, and they bled the British lion white. Their paper-thin hulls, clean-running as any racing yacht's today, with raked masts and broad spars for piling on sail, were baffling to the British. On the rare occasions when they managed to capture one of these will-o'-the-wisps and tried to convert it to their own service, the effort generally failed for lack of crews trained to handle it. And when they cut down the spars and reinforced the masts with heavy stays and the hulls with more planking, as any sensible sailorman would, then the skittish things behaved like birds with their wings clipped.

These were ships! Baltimore became the beating heart of the merchant navy. Frantically the English sent more men-of-war to join in the American blockade, but by now the American seagoing hornets were triumphing over anything that came against them, or making good their escape to fight another day. They even counterblockaded the English coast. The hit-or-miss cruising of the early days of the war was supplanted by planned naval strategies. By the time the British Atlantic squadron clamped down with their two hundred ships of the line, the Americans, always probing, daring, hunting the foe, discovered that English convoys were not holding formation close to home ports; rather, it was their custom to break up as the various returning merchantmen, rich with cargoes from India and elsewhere, fanned out in home waters heading for their various destinations.

Promptly American sails swung down like vultures all along the coasts of the British Isles. Flames by night and smoke by day marked the terrible courses of the impudent raiders, leaving funeral pyres of British commerce in their wakes. The war was brought to England's doorstep at last.

This notable understatement appeared in an English publication, the *Morning Chronicle*, in 1814: "That the whole coast of Ireland from Wexford round by Cape Clear to Carrickfergus, should have been for above a month under the unresisted domination of a few petty fly-by-nights from the blockaded ports of the United States is a grievance equally intolerable and disgraceful."

One wonders if Wild Tom Boyle may not have seen this particular item. His swift little Baltimore-built *Chasseur,* mounting fourteen guns and jammed with over 150 officers, seamen and marines all spoiling for a fight, had been making the English Channel its favorite hunting ground. In any case he soon had the British changing their minds about the pettiness of these "fly-by-nights," for the coastwise ravages of his *Chasseur* were thought to be worth the while of a squadron of seven ships to hunt him down. They never did get him; he got one of them, in fact. She was the British cruiser *H.M.S. St. Lawrence,* twenty guns, disguised as a fat merchantman to lure the *Chasseur* within range of her double-shotted cannon. When the British let go with a broadside the Americans replied in kind, then drove in, grappled and boarded, cutlasses swinging, and forced surrender.

The British had long made it a practice to announce a paper blockade of such and such a port; they didn't have enough vessels to spare actually to picket all the American ports at the same time, so a commanding officer would simply issue a proclamation that a certain port was under blockade anyway, a nice legal point which gave him the right to capture any neutral ships that might be hanging about. Then he would sail away on other business.

Captain Boyle, taking note of this, announced a one-ship blockade of his own. He drew up a formal proclamation of blockade with all the official trimmings, and while he was about it he made it good: he announced a blockade of all the ports of Great Britain and Ireland and had it posted at Lloyd's. He, too, then sailed away on other business. If Captain Boyle saw it, he must have read with deep satisfaction an item that soon appeared in another English publication, the *Annual Register,* announcing "a most terrifying reflection," that with a navy of more than a thousand ships "it is not safe for a British vessel to sail without convoy from one port of the English or Irish Channel to another."

There is always a little sour with the sweet. The American Navy complained that privateers, as in the Revolutionary War, were robbing them of men for the fleet. Offhand this might appear to be captious in view of what had happened to the navy even when it did have men—more men than ships to carry them—but, after all, the privateersmen were mixing business with pleasure, so to speak, whereas the navy's single purpose was to get on with the war. It was not as if the privateers were costing the government nothing. Congress was paying twenty-five dollars a head for all prisoners taken by them, and as an added inducement the import duties on captured cargoes were drastically reduced. Only the lucky ships were making huge profits, and many a privateer failed to take a worth-while prize for as long as a year at a time, which accounts for the government subsidies. It has been estimated that with government cash thus expended, together with the loss of revenues from import duties, a sum sufficient to keep at least twenty naval sloops-of-war at sea throughout hostilities could have been provided. Furthermore, naval authorities insisted, such vessels could have done far more actual military damage to the enemy than all the privateers put together. So ran the argument. But a bird in the hand is worth two in the bush, and the government, grateful for a merchant navy with teeth in it, backed it to the limit.

Napoleon arrived at Elba in May 1814. Before the summer was out the veterans of the Duke of Wellington's Spanish campaigns, free at last for duty in the American war, landed on these shores ten thousand strong. Under cover of their naval guns they could come ashore anywhere on the coast they chose, and they chose upstate New York and the banks of the Patuxent River in Maryland. General Sir George Prevost's idea was not so much to execute a pincer movement, apparently, as to create a diversion down in Maryland for the main attack on New York.

So nearly five thousand British regulars sailed up Chesapeake Bay in early August and poured ashore along the banks of the little Maryland river. The astonished Americans, on beholding such a warlike crowd, hastily blew up a few gunboats in the shallow waterways as a sort of rear-guard action and then ran for their lives toward Washington with the news that the British were coming. This mild reception encouraged Admiral Cockburn, in charge of the expedition, to keep right on going and see what could be done about invading Washington itself. His advancing forces were met in the little town of Bladensburg, on the hot, dusty road to the capital, by some seven thousand disorganized and wide-eyed government clerks, farm hands and what might loosely be called militia, backed up by a handful of marines from the destroyed gunboats. The ensuing debacle, heightened by a British display of skyrockets to add to the Americans' confusion, became known to wits of the day as "The Bladensburg Races," with the Americans leading the way—backward.

At first glance it might be thought that this unhappy scene and its flaming aftermath at Washington were too far removed from the sea to have any bearing on the work of the merchant navy in the war. But William Eaton and his marine veterans of the war with Tripoli could have testified that land and sea actions in the long run go hand in hand to victory or defeat. In this long view the invasion of Washington and its subsequent looting and burning was a senseless and above all a time-wasting spree for the British. It was the beginning of a series of events that were to be written in blood in the distant harbor of Fayal in the Azores and to end with the battle of New Orleans.

With the loss of Washington the year 1814 was coming to a close in deep gloom. The war seemed all but lost. The remnants of the United States Navy were bottled up in harbor tighter than ever. The public debt had spiraled to unheard-of proportions. From angry sounds on the cold winds blowing down from New England the Union seemed about to dissolve.

Meanwhile the victorious Admiral Cockburn dallied with his fleet in the waters around Baltimore for two months, seemingly undecided what to do next. Then at last he weighed anchor and set his course for New Orleans and new worlds to conquer. Had he but known it, he would have done better to sail a month or so sooner on a more easterly course with his watches doubled all around on the lookout for a small graceful brigantine called the *General Armstrong,* sailing to her rendezvous with destiny in the sleepy harbor of Fayal.

The British Navy was closing in for the kill. In London the great Wellington himself had agreed that the Americans should not be allowed to have Louisiana and the Floridas. To that end a rendezvous for the British fleet was agreed on. It was to be off New Orleans, and the force was to comprise some fifty vessels and ten thousand seasoned troops, with Admiral Cockburn in command of the fleet.

The admiral got there, but three of His Majesty's ships hurrying over from Europe with troops and practically all of the artillery needed for the attack made the fatal mistake of pausing in the quiet little Azores harbor of Fayal. Their purpose was to join up with two more British ships coming from Spain with more officers and additional gunpowder.

Easing in on the evening tide, Captain Lloyd, commanding *H.M.S. Plantagenet,* seventy-four guns, together with *H.M.S. Rota,* thirty-eight guns, and *H.M.S. Carnation,* eighteen guns, was delighted to discover a little American brigantine of some fourteen guns lying quietly at anchor. On closer inspection Captain Lloyd was overjoyed to discover she was the *General Armstrong,* the most hated privateer of the war by reason of her five victories over British ships in the past. She was owned by a syndicate of New York merchants and commanded by Captain Samuel Reid, an imaginative and versatile skipper who was later to invent the lightship and design the present arrangement of the American flag.

Fayal was a Portuguese-owned port, a neutral, but war is war. That night, by the light of the moon, Captain Lloyd quietly put over four boats with orders to take the pesky American and no nonsense about it. The moon was bright, and Captain Reid, seeing them coming, broke out his sweeps and edged in closer under the protecting guns of the decrepit Portuguese fort overlooking the harbor. It was a useless move. The Portuguese had no intention of getting mixed up in the brawl. As the British boats, down to the gunwales with armed men, approached his ship, Captain Reid warned them off. Still they came on. Sure, now, of their intention, Reid shouted a final warning, and, this failing, the *General Armstrong* boomed with a flaming broadside that made slaughter pens of the English boats.

In the confusion, while what was left of the English boats drew back to their mother ships, Captain Reid moved closer under the still-silent Portuguese batteries, thus placing the town behind him in direct line of fire from the British men-of-war. Toward midnight a second attack began, with twelve big barges from the three Britishers loaded with four hundred men and each barge mounting a howitzer in the bow. A crowd gathered on the beach, lighting the scene with bonfires for a better view. Captain Lloyd, aching to fire his guns but not daring to risk shelling the town behind his quarry, saw the *General Armstrong*'s men cut down and repel this second attack with savage cutlass fighting on her own decks.

By now there were over two hundred British dead and half as many wounded, to say nothing of the damage done to the British ships by the American's gunfire. Captain Lloyd was raging. The Portuguese governor, tearing his hair, pleaded for a cessation of the attack, but Lloyd could not stop now. Moreover, the Americans, although their ship was a ruin, showed every sign of preparing to continue the fight. Lloyd announced that, town or no town, he would destroy the *General Armstrong* by cannon fire in the morning if the Americans would not give up. The American consul hastily summoned Captain Reid ashore, pointed out the hopelessness of his position and demanded an end to the fighting. Captain Reid returned to his ship, adamant; but when the British opened up with their heavy guns in the morning he scuttled his ship and withdrew with his crew, of which only two had been killed, to an abandoned convent in the interior. There he prepared to resist capture.

But the British had had enough. As things turned out, they had had too much. Three weeks went by while they buried their dead, made repairs and waited for replacements. It was three weeks too long. Before the assembling British fleet was ready for its attack on New Orleans, General Andrew Jackson had descended on the town from the backwoods with his Kentucky and Tennessee sharpshooters to settle once and for all, on the plains of Chalmette, the question of the South's heart's desire.

The battle of New Orleans was a useless struggle in some respects, since the worried little Secretary of the Treasury, Albert Gallatin, and his confreres had at last put their names to a treaty of peace with the British at Ghent on Christmas Eve, two weeks before. But if it accomplished nothing else, it won for the United States a cordial acceptance into the family of nations.

FOR

SAN FRANCISCO

THE CELEBRATED CLIPPER SHIP

GREAT REPUBLIC

LIMEBURNER, Commander,

AT PIER 36 EAST RIVER,

Will have immediate dispatch.

This ship has been newly coppered, and put in complete order. Her short passages, and the perfect delivery of cargoes, entitle her to a preference with shippers. Having large hatches, she can take bulky freight under deck. Two-thirds of her capacity is already engaged.

For balance of Freight, apply to

A. A. Low & Brothers,

31 Burling Slip.

SAILING CARD FOR THE *GREAT REPUBLIC*

"Immediate dispatch" means she would sail whenever she was fully loaded. Later competition tightened departure dates.

SAILING CARD FOR THE *ELVIRA OWEN*

This vessel is announced to sail as advertised, fully loaded or not. Watch your daily paper.

PART *3*

The Golden Years

13

STEAM VERSUS SAIL

FOR TWO hundred years American merchant ships had been engaged in a struggle for existence. Now, at last, having fought four wars during the forty years since they had hoisted the American flag, they were free to sail the high seas unmolested and to enter the world-wide race for supremacy of the Western Ocean.

True, England had not promised to stop impressing seamen or to observe neutral rights according to international law. England had promised nothing, in fact, and changed nothing as a result of the war. The troublesome and stupid Orders-in-Council had been revoked, but they were revoked two days before the declaration of war. Nothing was settled on the books that couldn't have been settled years before with a little hardheaded diplomacy and a judicious use of the Long Tom at psychological moments.

Yet there was some salvage from the War of 1812. Like the new boy at school who has fought his way into a place of respect, the United States was accepted at last on equal terms among the international bullies and big shots. This new-found recognition of power, paid for in blood, served the useful purpose of giving the nation a degree of international maturity and assured it elbowroom at the dinner table.

Thus at war's end an era which has been called golden by many people was dawning for America's merchant ships.

Superficially, or perhaps it is more accurate to say temporarily, it was indeed a golden era which was to reach its magical zenith when the great clipper ships of this country were carrying three quarters of the world's overseas commerce and almost all of its own. But from the beginning there were adverse winds piling up a thunderhead that was to bring disaster to the merchant fleet. Just four years after the war of 1812 an awkward little 380-ton full-rigged ship, equipped with paddle wheels and a forty-inch cylinder carrying a steam pressure of twenty pounds, chuffed and sailed her way across the Atlantic from Savannah to Liverpool and by so doing quickened the maritime world's interest in steamships. The most noteworthy thing about this voyage was that the *S.S. Savannah,* in proving the venture practical, had already carved the headstone for the grave of the American clipper ships before they were born.

Farsighted people on both sides of the ocean thought the day of the sailing ship was done, right then and there; and so it would have been if great racing machines with inspiring names like *Flying Cloud, Sovereign of the Seas* and *Fiery Cross* had not delayed the end of the windships by sheer speed. There is a strong argument for the unpopular belief that those white-winged goddesses of the sea paved the way for America's maritime ruin. The clanking, smoking *S.S. Savannah* signaled the fork in the channel. American ships took the wrong tack.

First among the seducers were the Baltimore clippers. They came home from the wars with tales of their deeds on everyone's lips. Their fundamental influence on ship design became apparent from the moment the Long Toms were stowed away ashore and paying cargoes took their place. Strictly speaking, the Baltimore clippers were not clippers at all; they got their name from their ability to "clip" along, but they did have some of the basic characteristics of the extreme clippers to come. They had increased length in proportion to beam, which gave them greater speed, and they carried much lighter rigging in proportion to tonnage than anything anyone had ever seen before, which among other things meant greater economy in the number of paid hands to work the ship.

These early postwar Baltimore ships were vessels of three hundred tons or so, used around Chesapeake Bay in local trade and up the coast. They were well built and generously canvased; their lower sails were large, their topsails enormous, with three reefs, and very tricky to handle. Studding sails were carried for lighter winds. It was this complicated carrying of canvas, and carrying it to the last limit of safety, that made these original packets so fast. The word *packet,* by the way, was a term borrowed from the English to denote small swift ships carrying foreign mail on regular sailing dates. In the beginning the Baltimore packets carried no foreign mail, but they advertised regular dates for carrying freight, mail and passengers to specified American ports.

An overnight voyage was an adventurous occasion for most of the passengers, and the captain himself was careful to observe certain social amenities which undoubtedly served to foster his ship's popularity. His eye-catching rig usually consisted of a three-quarter-length blue coat and the traditional double row of brass buttons, with a *V* of white shirt front showing a wing collar and black bow tie. His trousers were of white duck, his blue cap was round and flat as a cake and visored with patent leather, and his face was usually garnished with chin whiskers running from ear to ear.

The crew, too, were no dull dogs, with their shiny black tarpaulin hats, red-checked shirts and bell-bottom dungarees, to make rolling them up easier for the morning scrubdown. For shoregoing there was plenty of black ribbon for a bow on the hat, and a black silk kerchief was tied in a loose sailor's knot around the neck. If the occasion warranted it, white ducks and black pumps also were worn. Fancy rig notwithstanding, these men were seamen in the fullest sense of the word, expected to handle the jungle of lines at the fife rail, though it be in the dark in a shrieking gale, with the sure skill of an organist at his stops.

On sailing day, glasses and decanters were broken out by the captain and placed on the polished mahogany saloon table. Toasts were drunk to master, ship and voyage in generous proportions; letters of greater urgency than those carried by coach were dropped in a box at the head of the main companionway; there were more toasts, more tearful farewells, and the voyager was off on his travels. Such an overnight trip would cost about ten dollars with meals. The ship arriving at its destination, the incoming mail was distributed to eager recipients who came aboard and the decanter ceremony was repeated.

It was a peaceful life and a gracious one—quite a change from the hardier prewar days. But there were other changes in the making, and some of them not so gracious, although inevitable. In New York a group of gentlemen, mostly Quakers, noticed with keen interest the performance of the Baltimore packets and determined to organize a shipping line to share in the harvest of the lush traffic by placing it on a grander scale. The run from New York to Liverpool was selected as having the most enticing possibilities. Naming their company the Black Ball Line, they scheduled sailings in 1816 with four 500-ton ships: the *Amity,* the *Courier,* the *Pacific* and the *James Monroe.* Sailing days were fixed for the first of each month, and the Atlantic ferry was under way.

Renowned all over the world for swift passages and fighting mates, the line's ships were easily identified by the large black ball sewed or painted on the fore topsail. In all kinds of weather, regardless of whether or not they had any freight on sailing day, the captains were under orders to keep to their announced schedules, thus causing them to drive ship and crew under mountainous presses of sail that sent the worn-out packets to the Nantucket whaling fleet in a few years and the seamen to early graves. Average time for an eastbound passage was twenty-three days; westbound, it was forty because of adverse winds and Gulf Stream drift. Record runs to Liverpool of fifteen, even thirteen, days often set the water fronts to buzzing.

These early Black Ballers were painted black from the water line, with a light band scraped and varnished along the strakes. As an added touch, the boats, deckhouses and bulwarks were painted green. They were vessels built to catch the passenger trade as well as freight, and their builders were no pikers. This is what an awed reporter for the Liverpool *Courier* had to say about the *Pacific* when she came into port on her maiden voyage:

Her dining room is forty feet by fourteen. A mahogany table runs down the centre, with seats on each side formed of the same wood and covered with haircloth. The end of the dining room aft is spanned by an elliptical arch supported by handsome pillars of Egyptian porphyry. The sides of the cabin are formed of mahogany and satinwood, tastefully disposed in panels and most superbly polished. . . . An arch extends over the entrance of each stateroom, supported by delicate pillars of beautiful white Italian marble exquisitely polished. The staterooms are seven on each side; they are fitted up with much taste, and with a studious regard for the comfort and convenience of the passengers.

The cost of these ships ran anywhere from $40,000 to $100,000 each. The passenger fares were pretty much standardized at

$140 for the crossing. There were accommodations for about thirty passengers in the earlier days, but as the ships were built larger they carried as many as eighty. Sometimes price wars lowered cabin fares to $100; but the owners counted on freight to bring them anywhere from $5,000 to $10,000 a voyage, and a good ship made six voyages a year. These vessels had flush decks, which is to say the top deck ran in an unbroken line from stem to stern, with the crew living forward in the fo'c'sle, the steerage living down in the 'tween decks and the first-class passengers living in the trim, comfortable cabins aft. Food was carried alive. For fresh milk a cow was quartered in a shed amidships over the main hatch. Eggs were supplied by the hens roosting, usually, in the longboat. Pigs, ducks and geese were penned near the galley somewhere amidships. Stores were stowed aft, handy to the watchful eyes of the officers.

What a far cry from the sanded, smoky holds in the leaky ships of not so long ago! Transatlantic business picked up. New lines were organized. The Red Star Line entered the New York-Liverpool trade with a ship a month, sailing a week ahead of the Black Ball ships. This would never do. The Quakers and their fellow stockholders pulled their noses, did some figuring and announced eight new ships with regular sailings to Europe on the first and the middle of each month.

That was only the beginning. Another line, the Swallow Tail Line, offered a weekly service. Other ships in other ports spread their sails for a share in the burgeoning transatlantic trade, and the race was on. In a few years over fifty ships, with as many as twelve sailing on the same day, were racing east and west, often arriving at the same port within hours of one another. When the vagaries of wind, tide and navigation in those days are considered, these transatlantic races ending in a hairbreadth finish are nothing short of miraculous.

Steam? The *S. S. Savannah* and her jointed paddles creaking over the same course in twenty-five days? Nonsense! The wind was free and there was plenty of it!

Speed and more speed was the order of the day. Meanwhile, times were changing; not ship design but the basis of trade itself was changing and with it the sailor's lot. Merchants were now trading on the ability of a vessel to get there first with a cargo already arranged for, rather than to be swapped for whatever was available at a profit. Ships came to be operated by shoreside interests almost exclusively. The owner and the skipper were no longer the same person, to say nothing of the crew's having a financial interest in the cargo as of old. Freight was loaded for a shipper at a given rate per ton; in other words, the owners would carry anybody's merchandise for a price, with no interest in whether or not it was bought or sold at a profit, and the captain, mates and crew became strictly paid hands. True, the captain often bought shares in his ship or in other ways participated in its profits; but by and large there was a new order in dealings ashore, and the fo'c'sle hand was naturally the first to feel it.

When Ralph Waldo Emerson sailed to England in the 750-ton *Washington Irving,* a Train Line packet from Boston, he wrote:

Our good master keeps his kites up to the last moment, studding sails alow and aloft, and by incessant straight steering never loses a rod of the way. Watchfulness is the law of the ship, watch on watch, for advantage and for life. . . . Jack has a life of risks, incessant abuse, and the worst pay. It is a little better with the mate, and not much better with the captain.

Some of the hard-driving packets held onto their crews, who showed a strong inclination to jump the ship the moment she nosed into the dock, by signing them on at a monthly wage of twenty-five dollars instead of paying them off at the end of each voyage as was the custom. Naturally a crew which was used to the foibles of one particular ship and its officers was more efficient than a new one, and "loyalty," with a consequent insurance of greater speed, was purchased by paying the men a bonus for winning a transatlantic race.

Mr. Emerson was a little off in his figures so far as they applied to a captain, however. Perhaps he got his information from that familiar type found aboard all ships of all ages, the "sea lawyer," who chronically takes the gloomy view and usually doesn't know what he's talking about. In any case, the captain's wage was only one item in his annual earnings and a relatively small one at that. Most skippers worth their salt in the larger packets made four or five thousand dollars a year by purchasing a share in the ship, usually an eighth, and were paid for carrying the mail at twopence a letter from the British government and two cents from the United States. Quite a nice little take! And, in addition to this, he could carry his wife free, which quite possibly meant a saving in rent.

For the common seaman, however, there were no such rewards. His work, though skilled and specialized, had already come to be regarded as cheap labor. Since the unsuccessful New York strike in 1803, about the only increase in his rewards for twenty-four-hour duty, seven days a week, had been the free Bibles handed out by the Protective This and the Beneficial That societies, more bent on assuaging the needs of his spirit than his stomach. Since the captain and perhaps the mates were usually the only ones who could read, it is doubtful if these served to alleviate even the spiritual side of life in the fo'c'sle.

There was a man up in Boston who did take a hand in doing something practical for the sailors. This was Father Taylor, as he came to be called. Having been a sailor himself, he at least made the free Bibles understandable to their recipients. Edward Thompson Taylor was an orphan who had been sent to sea at the age of seven as a cabin boy. He had learned to pray at an old-time conversion meeting in the Methodist Chapel in Boston, and when the British took him and his mates off a privateer called the *Black Hawk* during the War of 1812 and threw them in prison at Halifax he came into his own. The American prisoners did not relish having the prayers for the king read to them by the prison chaplain, and they arranged to have the orphan boy pray and preach for them. When they were released Taylor found himself back on the streets of Boston peddling for an Ann Street junk dealer; but his talents were not to be hidden under a pile of rags and tinware. After his discovery by the parishioners of the Bromfield Street Methodist Church, who encouraged him in his education, his rise in the church world was rapid.

But Father Taylor never forgot where he came from. He managed to establish the Seamen's Bethel, and from its pulpit for more than forty years he "walked the quarter-deck," looking more like a down-East skipper than a preacher, and so inspired the horny-fisted men who came to hear his salty sermons that his name was known wherever ships sailed. His convincing friendliness and ability to speak the seamen's language were conceded by all hands to have had a powerful and beneficial influence on the thousands of sailors dumped homeless and penniless on the town.

To keep the record straight, however, the ordinary seaman's pay, if the packet rat's bonuses are excepted, was still ten dollars a month.

In a span of twenty years since the nation had gone to war a shaky third-rate neutral bent on preserving its rights, American ships unsurpassed in speed, beauty and economy of operation had become queens of the sea.

Where were their age-old competitors, the English?

They were still fussing with laws and monopolies and ship-building methods that were a hundred years out of date. The United Company of Merchant Venturers of England Trading to the East Indies, better known as the East India Company, was bogged down in its own fat. It was costing them a quarter of a million dollars to build a 1,300-ton ship, a slow, ponderous tub whose design had advanced little in over two centuries—and nobody cared, because with the company's carefully controlled and legalized monopoly the profits of a single voyage paid for the ship's cost.

The sight of fleet, trim Yankee ships nosing into London and Liverpool docks, however, with records of two-or-three-week crossings, made a lot of Englishmen restless if not downright resentful. Public pressure was put on Parliament to withdraw the East India Company's charter and throw open the trade to other British lines, and, after much hemming and hawing, this was finally done—for English lines only. The world at large was still excluded from the rich trade with India. Meanwhile, the Americans, who had been building and improving their ships for a couple of hundred years, were holding them in leash like a pack of greyhounds, eagerly looking forward to the day when the trade with India would be thrown open and they could cut the pie.

Eventually even the British House of Commons, worried over the number of shipwrecks in the British merchant service, decided it had better look into all this talk about American packets ruling the Western Ocean. To their astonishment they found that "ships of the United States of America, frequenting the ports of England, are superior to those of a similar class amongst the ships of Great Britain, the commanders and officers being generally considered more competent as seamen and navigators, and the seamen considered to be more efficient." It was further noted that American ships were commanding better freight rates than English ships for the same runs and that insurance rates were lower. It might also have been justifiably pointed out to the parliamentary committee that the American packets' better food, higher pay and superior equipment were causing British sailors to jump ship and sign on with the American service in droves. But British shipowners were not yet inclined to face unpleasant realities. They seemed bent on the temporary comforts of self-deception. As late as 1856 the London *Nautical Magazine and Naval Chronicle* was to publish the following with a straight face:

Chief causes for the loss of ships at sea:

1. Teetotalism—the serving of tea instead of rum.
2. Presence of the captain's wife or other women.
3. Insanity.
4. Drunkenness and revelry.
5. Mutiny and insubordination.
6. Discord and dissension.
7. No devil being aboard.
8. The devil having been let loose.

As to the competence of American navigators in the early decades of the new century, that happy truth was due in large measure to the genius and labor of a former apprentice to a Salem ship chandler. Nathaniel Bowditch was a poor boy with very little formal education, but his passion for mathematics, fed by an Irish scientist's collection of books captured by a privateer during the Revolutionary War, set him on his course. He went to sea in 1796 at the age of twenty-three, as captain's clerk, and later as supercargo to Manila in another ship, the *Astra*. On this latter voyage he spent every spare moment taking observations and teaching a dozen crew members how to take and work lunars, the only method of getting the long-sought and mysterious longitude without a chronometer, which, it was felt, no Salem ship could afford.

Lunars were a tricky business, as any error in observation brought a thirtyfold error in the result. Young Bowditch discovered some eight thousand errors in the tables of the standard English work on navigation, and decided to write his own. On two more voyages he made detailed calculations that gave him the material for his first edition of the *New American Practical Navigator,* which he published in 1802. It was eventually translated into a dozen languages and passed through many editions, and remains today a standard American work on navigation. With the success of the *Navigator* he got himself a berth as master of the *Putnam* and sailed to Sumatra on a successful pepper voyage. But the great and lasting success of the voyage was when he gave dramatic proof of his navigational theories by sailing into Salem harbor in a blinding northeast snowstorm on Christmas Eve 1803 by dead reckoning after a single glimpse of Baker's Island light. After that, "I sailed with Captain Bowditch, sir!" became a Salem password for an officer's berth.

As a happy footnote to Nathaniel Bowditch's long and scholarly career it is pleasant to record that he was one pioneering genius who was not neglected by his contemporaries, for among his rewards was the presidency of the Essex Fire and Marine Insurance Company, of Salem.

After 1819, the year of the *S.S. Savannah's* first transatlantic crossing, the story of sail and steam runs parallel in a race for survival of the fittest. Although the *Savannah's* voyage stirred up much talk but very little do, the idea of crossing the Atlantic independent of the wind was never abandoned. Those in opposition to the idea grew rabid on the subject. Marine architects and mathematicians proved on paper that no vessel could ever possibly carry enough fuel to propel itself three thousand miles over water without a stop. One eminent British scientific authority was delivering a lecture in Liverpool proving this point when the *Savannah* came steaming into the harbor. Naturally the professor was quick to point out that the Yankee smokebox had run out of fuel on the way over and had been forced to resort to her sails. But the sight must have been somewhat disquieting. Even so, the quips going around the Liverpool docks were mostly to the effect that steamboats would be a success, provided they had fleets of sailing ships convoying them over to supply the fuel.

No doubt it was all very amusing. But a few years later there was a Dutch steamer, the *Curaçao,* plying the Atlantic between Antwerp and South America on a regular run with passengers, mail and valuable freight on steam power alone. Nobody seems to have paid much attention to her, but in view of all the huzzahs over the *Savannah* as the "first steamship to cross the Atlantic," it is puzzling why so many stories of the sea have passed the Dutchman by with scarcely a nod of recognition as the first steamship actually to make the entire crossing of the Atlantic on steam. Perhaps the oversight is due to the fact that South America was a long way off the transatlantic shipping lanes in those days and that few people spoke Dutch. In any case the upshot of it was that the two maritime nations most interested in bridging the Atlantic did not receive their impetus from the successful voyages of the *Curaçao.*

Regardless of the *Curaçao*, this steam business began to look pretty good to the British, wallowing in the wakes of the swift American packets. They commenced to take stock of the situation. It is difficult to know just how they approached the problem—whether the chicken or the egg came first—but with the perspective of hindsight it is obvious that they discovered several advantages over their American competitors for developing a good, profitable steamship. In the first place, they were not burdened with the smug self-satisfaction the Americans had in their sailing ships. Moreover, there were plenty of machine shops in industrial England for building the engines and boilers—as witness the firm of Boulton & Watt that supplied Fulton with the engine for his *Clermont*—and there was an abundant supply of coal for fueling them. These were two assets almost entirely lacking in the United States at the time. Then, too, while the North American continent had immense stretches of inland waterways, such water highways were conducive to the development of a type of steam navigation peculiar to river boats, whereas the choppy waters of the English Channel and the coasts had required from the start oceangoing vessels.

In spite of these natural motives for steaming to sea, it was left to an American to give the British a first push into the transatlantic trade. Dr. Junius Smith, a Yale graduate of 1802, had been pestering shipping men and financiers on both sides of the Atlantic for some time before they finally made it possible for him to organize the British and American Steam Navigation Company and lay a keel for an oceangoing steamer in 1838. Before he could get his ship launched, a rival group of shipbuilders at Bristol, England, were putting the finishing touches to another steamship, the *Great Western*. Dr. Smith, in a frenzy to beat them to it, chartered a little coastal steamer called the *Sirius* from the London-Cork run and hastily fitted her out for sea. In addition to her crew, seven hardy souls boarded her as passengers. She took on 450 tons of coal, and three days before the *Great Western* was ready to sail she set her paddle wheels spinning on the long haul to New York.

For eighteen days the 700-ton *Sirius,* wallowing in seas that nearly swamped her and her mountainous load of coal, clanked her way westward while her captain peered anxiously astern, watching for the telltale smoke of the *Great Western*. Her single-cylinder engine, probably as good as any extant, was imperfectly designed and machined, and since good lubricants were unknown, the parts wore out and squealed for mercy. Her boilers, like all boilers of the day, were crudely made of iron and riveted together by hand so that seams leaked copiously under any amount of pressure. Fire was a constant threat from embers out of the stack, or from the red-hot firebox, improperly insulated. Little wonder her captain had to quell a mutinous crew that was convinced they would never make it! But make it they did, with their coal supply all but exhausted before Sandy Hook was sighted, and on the nineteenth day, on a beautiful April morning, they steamed in triumph up New York Bay to the Battery.

A crowd swarmed to meet her in small boats. Flags waved, a band played. Then a lookout shouted that more smoke was sighted on the horizon. Soon the *Great Western,* fifteen days out of Bristol, hove into view. The excited New Yorkers fairly went wild. River steamers and tugs rushed to meet her, and a twenty-six-gun salute thundered a welcome. By the middle of the afternoon she was anchored off Pike Street with her bunkers still holding five days' coal supply. It was a triumph for both ships, but the *Great Western,* having been built especially for the trade, was a bird of a completely different feather. She carried nearly double the tonnage of the *Sirius* and cost a quarter of a million dollars to build, of which $67,000 was spent on the engines. She had covered over two hundred miles a day and consumed 655 tons of coal on the voyage—less than a good many ships today burn in twenty-four hours.

Facts, figures, records—nothing very startling from the viewpoint of the hard-driving American sailing-packet owners. Their ships were cheaper to operate, and by this time they, too, were often making the Atlantic crossing in fifteen days and less. Often but not always. The haunting fact they chose to ignore was that the *Great Western* and even the little *Sirius* continued to cross and recross the ocean at the same steady gait, reliable and on time, regardless of adverse winds and tides. The *Great Western* made the run seventy-four times before going into the West Indies trade, and her profits were as much as $30,000 for a single voyage. Even the *Sirius,* small and as incommodious as she must have been, was able to compete with a cabin fare of $140 including wines and food—the same as on a sailing packet—and the *Great Western* was able to charge $250 for a cabin reserved for one person.

From then on British steamers rapidly came into their own. New steamships were built. New lines were organized. Samuel Cunard, a Halifax shipping magnate who had gone to England to make a second fortune, was among the early birds, although a little slow to get started, as witness a letter of his to a Nova Scotian firm anxious to establish a steamship line:

DEAR SIRS—
We have received your letter of the 22nd. inst. We are entirely unacquainted with the cost of a steamboat and would not like to embark in a business of which we are quite ignorant. Must, therefore, decline taking any part in the one you propose getting up.
We remain, yours, etc. S. CUNARD & COMPANY.

But, cautious and slow as he was, after the *Sirius* and *Great Western* had been in successful service for a couple of years Cunard himself was well on the way toward his line's ultimate glories in the twentieth-century sea queens, the *Queen Mary* and *Queen Elizabeth*.

All this fuss over steam led the Americans to believe that if a good sailing ship could be built to beat the best speed of ships like the *Great Western,* and if such ships were equipped with more economical engines nearly as powerful, they could still keep a grip on the transatlantic trade. It looked reasonable enough on paper, but in practice it did not work out. It was the sort of scheme that was later to be tried in the First World War; but auxiliary sailing ships, even with efficient Diesel engines in them, never successfully competed with steam freighters. Meanwhile, trade was booming in the forties, people wanted to go back and forth to Europe and they were coming to prefer the reliability of regular steamship schedules.

Certainly the trade-wise Americans were aware of this steam-generated crisis, but mechanics and machine shops were still scarce, and what little capital there was available was being snatched up by the empire-building railroad men, to say nothing of the already proved river steamboat lines. Lest any exaggerated conclusions be drawn concerning English notions of maritime progress, it is interesting to note the British Admiralty's reluctant decision to conduct a practical experiment to determine the virtues of the screw propeller invented by John Fitch and improved and used successfully by Colonel Stevens and his son on their *S.S. Phoenix,* all of which had been accomplished nearly two generations earlier.

The propeller had been in use on both sides of the Atlantic for years, but not until the clamor of public opinion grew too much to bear did the Admiralty consent to try it out in 1845. Consequently a propeller-equipped craft was built, called the *Rattler,* which was a duplicate of another, the *Alecto,* except that the latter was a tried-and-true side-wheeler. In a test race at sea the *Rattler* proved the faster ship. But this was not proof enough. It was decided to secure the two antagonists stern to stern for a test of strength. In the ensuing tug of war, with both vessels threshing mightily at full steam ahead, to nobody's dismay (except perhaps the admirals') the screw-propelled *Rattler* triumphantly towed the *Alecto* and her wildly flailing paddles in her wake at a speed of two and a half knots. That was the convincer. To the everlasting credit of the British Admiralty, in another eleven years England had a screw-propelled fleet ready for the war with Russia.

Meanwhile, such trifles as the screw propeller were the least of American shipowners' problems. With their windships rapidly becoming outmoded they stood on the brink of economic disaster. But rescue was at hand. A solution to the struggle of steam versus sail was being produced on the drawing board of a young New York naval architect in the early 1840s that was to revolutionize ship design and create the swiftest sailing ships the world has ever seen. With them the doom of American shipping for years to come was sealed.

14

GOLDEN VESSELS

JOHN W. GRIFFITHS' ideas on how to build a windship so
alarmed marine critics of the day that they earnestly advised his
employers they had better discharge so dangerous a young
man. In the long view it might not have been a bad idea at that.

Basically, Griffiths adapted the lines of the fast little Baltimore
clippers to his plans for streamlining a hull that would leave
every despised coal mill on the ocean grinding helplessly in its
wake. He designed his ships "with a dolphin's head and a
mackerel's tail." More specifically, he carried the stem of the
ship forward on a curved line up from the forefoot so that the
bows along the water line became concave before they became
convex and had an overhang now familiar in racing yachts and
other modern-day vessels. With a sharp forward entrance to
the water, the hull was given a long, clean, tapering run. The
hull had dead rise—which is to say it was V-shaped in section—
and her main deck had a graceful sweep, or sheer, from stem to
stern. Then he topped it off with masts and spars to carry a
thunderhead of sail such as the world had never seen before.

To a generation familiar with the principles of aerodynamics
this may not seem like much, but in those days it had old shellbacks muttering in their beards.

As anyone familiar with John Fitch's frustrated career might guess, nobody wanted any part of young Mr. Griffiths' plans. Obviously he was crazy or, more charitably, a daydreamer. But down on the water front there were those confounded English smokepots cluttering up the harbor and robbing honest ships of their legitimate freight. The China trade was booming, too, and faster ships were needed there. Finally William Aspinwall, who was later to build the Panama Railroad, decided to take a chance and put up the capital for a 750-ton vessel to be constructed according to Griffiths' amazing design. The keel was laid and the experts gathered round, wagged their heads and predicted that the misshapen vessel would never stand up in heavy seas, if indeed she did not first turn turtle under the weight of her outsize spars at the launching. When she was ready she was christened *Rainbow,* sent smoking down the ways, and, failing to capsize as predicted, she went skimming over the water in the East River at the foot of Fourth Street as pretty as you please.

This was in 1843, five years after that tumultuous April morning on the Battery when a twenty-six-gun salute had welcomed the battered little *S.S. Sirius* and the *S.S. Great Western* on their triumphant arrivals from across the Western Ocean by steam.

At the moment of the *Rainbow*'s launching, the largest vessel afloat was being fitted out for sea on the other side of the Atlantic. Nobody was bothering with fancy rigging for her because she was an iron steamship 322 feet long, able to carry 260 passengers and over a thousand tons of freight. She was driven by a screw propeller, and she could cross the ocean in less than two weeks, regardless of the weather. Just to make sure, though, the *Great Britain*'s builders stepped six stubby masts into her as a final grandiose gesture, and, as seagoing names were lacking for so many masts, each one was named after a day of the week. Perhaps because there were no Sundays off soundings for the sailors, Sunday was omitted.

Disdainful of these smoky goings on, the *Rainbow*'s builders had their fondest dreams realized from the start. She was loaded with a cargo for the China trade, and on her maiden voyage made the run to Canton, discharged, reloaded and was back at her home port in six months and fourteen days. In order to get a bearing on what this meant, a good comparison is with the *Empress of China*'s voyage in opening the trade some sixty years before. The *Empress* had made what was considered excellent time in sailing from Boston to Canton—a one-way trip—in six months. On another voyage to Canton the *Rainbow* went billowing up the River of Flowers just ninety-two days out of New York. She returned from Canton in eighty-eight. No ship known to man had ever put so much water astern in so short a time. Here was the answer, speed and more speed, without the degrading business of depending on grimy mechanics and a pile of coal to achieve it. More of Griffiths' extreme clippers slid down the ways. More records were made.

And then, as if the gods themselves were in conspiracy, everything happened at once. Word flashed up and down the Atlantic coast that people were picking up golden nuggets on the streets in California. Workmen dropped their tools, ministers quit their pulpits and farmers mortgaged their farms to set out for the gold fields of '49. Ships, ships and more ships, with speed at any cost, were the order of the day. As if this were not enough to make a Yankee skipper rub his hands in anticipation, England decided in the same year to revoke her ancient and trade-strangling navigation laws and throw open the bursting markets of India to the world.

Promptly American shipyards went to work with the wondrous designs of John Griffiths' clipper ships. Men like Donald McKay, the greatest builder of them all, laid the keel for his first clipper to be just double the tonnage of Griffiths' first ship. Named *Stag Hound,* she slid into the chill December waters of East Boston in 1850, a pioneer in size and speed. Following her down the ways came the *Flying Cloud,* a miracle of copper-sheathed beauty, never to be surpassed by any sailing ship anywhere for perfection of design, for seaworthiness or for constant speed under every condition. This latter ship of McKay's was the fastest sailing vessel on long voyages that has ever carried the American flag before or since. On her maiden voyage the *Flying Cloud* logged 374 miles for a day's run, a good fifty miles more than the average day's run for an oceangoing freighter today. Or to look at it another way, eight knots is still considered a good speed for an America's Cup race. These clipper ships of McKay's and of other great builders like Samuel Hall, Robert E. Jackson and Edward and Henry Briggs were setting records like the *Red Jacket*'s 14.7 knots for six straight days in the Atlantic, the *Lightning*'s 15.5 knots for 3,722 miles, the *James Baines*'s Australian voyage when she logged 21 knots for an hour.

At full tide in this era of golden vessels there were only a handful of them, measured against the country's total merchant fleet, but their world-wide reign was supreme. Built solidly of the best oak, Southern pine, and hackmatack, they were copper-fastened and sheathed with Taunton yellow metal, and they were noted wherever ships sailed for the evenness of their seams and the perfection of their joiner work. Bursting into the new trade with India or flying up the China coast, their pine decks holystoned white, stanchions and fife rails gleaming with mahogany, rosewood and polished brass, they spelled bad news for their wide-eyed competitors wherever they docked.

The *Oriental,* eighty-one days out of New York to Hong Kong, was chartered to load a cargo of tea for London at six pounds per ton of forty cubic feet, while British captains fumed idly at anchor, waiting to pick up the leavings at three pounds ten shillings per fifty cubic feet. With sixteen hundred tons of tea in her holds she sailed off down the China Sea in the teeth of a strong southwest monsoon, crossed the Indian Ocean, skirted the African coast, and ninety-seven days out of Hong Kong she tossed her monkey fist onto the West India Docks in London. She had cost her owners $70,000 ready for sea, and that single cargo together with other Hong Kong freight netted $48,000. In just two days over a year she sailed 67,000 miles.

Not all this speed was confined to the open sea. At sailing time, when the wind was right, these master mariners would set all sail while still at the dock and drive stern first out into the stream, then turn around and go foaming off for deep water. And coming into port, sometimes still under sail, the vessel was eased into her berth unaided by a tug, not only as a matter of pride but also in consideration of the $140 tug bill involved. By dint of seamanship and brutal discipline these vessels actually capitalized on foul weather. As Captain Samuel Samuels once remarked after a record run in his semiclipper, *Dreadnought,* which to this day holds the transatlantic speed record for a sailing ship, "She was on the rim of a cyclone most of the time." No wonder his vessel was known as "The Wild Boat of the Atlantic." As long as a gale permitted these ships to hold a course they were driven with all possible sails set, even though the lee rail dragged through green water under the blast. To make sure that frightened sailors would not let any canvas fly free at night, unseen by the skipper, the sheets and halyards attached to the most important sails were made of chain instead of rope and locked in place with padlocks. But that was the least of it. Some skippers, among them Captain Waterman of the *Sea Witch,* were known to shoot men off the yards for the sin of handling the sails too slowly.

It was a gay whirl while it lasted. As in the days of the Nantucket whalers, the world was once again America's oyster. War hadn't done it. Certainly building cheaper ships hadn't done it. Cheaper ships were being built in northern Europe right along, and anyhow the ships that returned to American owners their greatest profits were the very ships that were costing them the most per ton to build. Even low wages hadn't done it, for, low as they were, they were still lower abroad. It's as obvious as the carved angel blowing her trumpet from the bowsprit of the *Flying Cloud* that America was able to gain and hold her supremacy at sea because builders, owners, shippers, masters, mates and crews had created a racing machine and a team to work it that was able to give more ton miles per dollar than anything else afloat.

American clipper yards spawned larger and larger ships to reap the rich harvest of tea and gold and human freight until at last the great McKay built the most magnificent of them all, the 4,556-ton *Great Republic.* She was a symbol and an augury of ill winds to blow, for this largest of the extreme clipper ships was doomed never to sail in her full glory. While she was being loaded at a South Street dock in New York on the day after Christmas in 1853, a warehouse fire sent sparks into her sky-flung rigging and sails. Bursting into flames, she burned for two days until to save her she was scuttled. A cofferdam was built to refloat her, but, before she could be refitted, freight rates, driven down by competing steamships, had dropped off to such an extent that it was thought best to fit her with stubby masts and a more conservative rig in order to reduce the size of her crew.

The handwriting was on the wall.

If a sailor of colonial times, used to sharing in the profits of his vessel, could have walked the water front in the 1850s to shoot the breeze with his mates, he might well have made some pointed comparisons. It is one of the paradoxes of America's story of the sea that in the era of its so-called golden vessels the ships of a nation dedicated to ideals of democracy and fair play should have earned for themselves in every port of the world the name of "blood boat." If the galley slaves of ancient times are excepted, and the poor flogged devils of Nelson's fleet, it is doubtful if the estate of the common seaman ever sank lower than during the days of the clipper ships.

To the ordinary seaman of those days, as in the time of Dana's *Two Years Before the Mast,* it was an era of hard-case after-guards, miserly pay and food, limitless hours of dangerous work and a life ashore which was always subject to the whims of the boardinghouse crimp. Americans built the clippers but they rarely manned them. Gone from the fo'c'sle was the typical Yankee sailor with his picturesque clothes and skillful seaman-ship. In his place were what were commonly referred to as the "squarehead," the "dago," the "frog" and the "limey," cowed, bullied and ignorant of their rights.

Incidentally, not all these ships were, strictly speaking, clip-pers. Most of the Western Ocean packets on regular runs, for instance, although influenced in design by the clippers, were not racing machines to the same full extent. They were built to ride deeper in the water and to keep as dry as possible on deck for the sake of the large numbers of immigrants they carried from Europe through the storms of the North Atlantic. But they were all a part of the scene in the struggle of steam versus sail.

Skippers in the clipper-ship era were as individually fash-ioned, as famous and as tough as their ships. Their names and feats at sea ranked as good newspaper copy along with the politicians and actors of the day, and their standings in the communities they called home were as solid as those of any pillar of the church. Men like Captain Samuel Samuels of the clipper *Dreadnought* could boast that nothing at sea had ever passed them in a strong wind, not even a despised steamship. And Captain Bob Waterman was considered by many to have discovered the secret of the trade winds, so fast were his China passages. Once, in a flat-bottomed ship, the *Natchez,* he made the voyage from Canton to New York in seventy-six days without ever tacking on his course. Captain Bully Hall of the *Splendid,* the largest merchant vessel in the United States at the time he commanded her, was famous for his courage and seamanship; but he hadn't earned the sobriquet "bully" for nothing, as evidenced by such playful habits as locking up his recalcitrant mate in a chicken coop one voyage and derisively clucking to him while he fed him with corn.

Perhaps the most notorious bully of them all was Captain Bully Hayes, pet fancier, lady-killer and all-around scoundrel. Bully Hayes's operations were largely in the South Seas, and yarns of his voyages, murders and escapades were the talk of every water-front bagnio and saloon from the Embarcadero to Wooloomooloo Bay. William Henry Hayes was born in New York and evidently learned his early sailing on the Atlantic coast. When he appeared in San Francisco in the receding wake of the gold hunters, a huge man with sparlike shoulders and deeply grooved, strong features, little was known of him—at first. His magnetic personality quickly earned him one command after another wherever he chose to stow his sea bag. But honest seafaring wasn't in Bully Hayes's bones, and soon he embarked on a long career of blackbirding—looting the Pacific islands of natives to sell as slave labor. The females in these human cargoes were called "squab," and Hayes made it a practice to keep the squab in his cabin for his pleasure, later selling them at fancy prices to the Chinese mandarins.

Although he was devoted to the spaniels he raised as a hobby, in a cruel era he was known as a cruel man, and on one occa-

sion at least his own crew tossed him overside just off the
Golden Gate. A missionary compelled to take passage in a vessel under Hayes's command described him this way:

He was apparently a perfect gentleman and host, with handsome face, bright blue eyes, strong nose, well-cut mouth, large
mustache, and long, clustering hair. In his not-infrequent un-
governable rages he was a madman. His face became purple
and his eyes jet black. Yet he was a man of considerable culture,
and spoke English, French, German and Spanish.

One favorite yarn concerning the prodigious amorous pro-
pensities of the man concerns a voyage he made in Japanese
waters. While ashore there, perhaps to relieve the tedium of
squab hunting, he invited a group of Japanese officials and their
wives aboard his ship in the harbor, where he lavishly enter-
tained them. At the height of the party he somehow managed
to get the officials aboard one of the longboats and set them
adrift. Then he raped their wives at his leisure, set them adrift,
too, and sailed away to other happy hunting grounds.

There are old-timers in San Francisco and Sydney today who
still swear to this story.

Life for the crew of a clipper ship, however, was no such
carefree affair as Bully Hayes's career might suggest. Wages
for a man before the mast were eight dollars a month—two dollars less than what the sailors of New York were being paid
when they struck unsuccessfully in 1803. The increase in size
of the ships was largely responsible for this low wage, because
as the tonnage rose from the modest 750 tons of the first clipper,
the *Rainbow,* to the more than 4,500 tons of the *Great Republic,*
more hands were required to work the ship than ever before.
Ashore, times were flush, and in a period of rising costs and
wages American boys took one look at the sailor's pay and hied
themselves off to the machine shops, the railroads and the west-

ern plains. This left the culls for the fo'c'sles of the golden vessels—the jailbirds, the misfits, the drunks. Especially the drunks. Said Judge Peleg Sprague of the District Court in Boston, in settling a court dispute involving a drunken sailor: "Masters hire them with this knowledge. Owners get their services at a less price for these very habits; year after year they serve at a mere pittance because of them."

Just why the skippers and mates were habitually so brutal on clipper ships and their more ponderous counterparts, the Western Ocean packets, is not easily understood. In view of the character of their crews they undoubtedly had to enforce severe discipline in the interests of the ship's safety, and there is no doubt there were the usual yardarm furlers, buntline reefers and those given to soldiering on the job, using ignorance of the language, perhaps, as an excuse. There were mutinous crews, too, on occasion, which of course deserved and received no mercy. But aboard most clippers there prevailed brutal methods that were certainly over and above the call of duty.

With crews understandably scarce, shipowners turned to the shipping agencies for their supply of seamen. The agencies in turn procured them through that low form of life known as the boardinghouse crimp. The crimp, by the time-honored and judicious use of a few floozies and a co-operative barkeep—the "boardinghouse" itself was often never reached at all—would drug and rob the seaman, then dump him aboard some outbound packet and pocket his three months' advance wages in settlement of his "debt." Once aboard, stripped of all his worldly goods save the threadbare gear he stood in, he had the choice of shivering his way around the Horn or across the North Atlantic, or else of buying a jumper, long sea boots and sou'wester from the slop chest at outrageous prices charged against future wages. From there the bucko mate took over. Since he was working out a dead horse, it was a matter of policy and pride with the mate to prove himself a tough customer. He did not hesitate to use any tool handy for a demonstration. There was the "persuader," a stick about a yard long with a nail projecting from its end, and there were iron belaying pins, capstan bars and mallets. These failing or being unhandy, there were always his fists and the gratings on which to lash a man up if he showed fight. With a crew of as many as thirty or forty shanghaied fo'c'sle hands and a couple of boys, not one of whom could steer and only a few of whom had ever been to sea at all, it was often necessary to have a standing rule of "all hands on deck from daylight to dark." This in addition to the regular night watches.

One thing about it, they finished the voyage as sailors. But once back in his home port, poor Jack usually tumbled ashore as broke as the day he sailed, there to be met by the welcoming arms of the boardinghouse crimp and Sadie and Kitty and Pearl, to begin the vicious circle all over again.

Oddly enough, there were seamen who liked the life. At least they preferred it to any other they knew. So in a general way there were two classes of seamen in the fo'c'sles—"them as likes it, and them as don't." The former, naturally, were the backbone of the crew and were peculiar to the transatlantic trade. These packet rats, sometimes called packetarians, seemed to glory in their ill-treatment and ability to take it; and although they usually shipped by the run, they turned up in crew after crew down the years, broke, starving, threadbare, with the Philadelphia Catechism on their blue lips:

> Six days shalt thou labor and do all thou art able,
> And on the seventh holystone the decks and scrape
> the cable.

Wise in the ways of the fo'c'sle, the packet rat would come aboard "flying light," as he was fond of calling his possessions-

less condition, but before the voyage was over he was no pack-
etarian worthy of the name if he hadn't rifled some rayneck's
or joskin's sea bag of blanket, donkey's breakfast and oilskins.

Raynecks and joskins were in a class by themselves. They
were generally boys in their teens or other shanghaied green-
horns who had wandered down to the water front to see the
sights, fallen prey to the blandishments of the crimp and been
tossed aboard dead drunk or drugged at sailingtime. Often
they were more welcome to the skipper than the more experienced packet rats because of their willingness and ability to
learn and to fight their way up through the hawsepipe to posi-
tions of responsibility. However, no joskin or rayneck willingly sailed on a Yankee packet. It was only the packet rats who
could appreciate the better food, as compared with European
fo'c'sles, that was dished up on the transatlantic packets—hardtack, fresh meat once or twice a week while it lasted, potatoes,
burgoo, molasses and pickles.

Perhaps few worth-while achievements in this world are accomplished without suffering. Certainly, if the lot of the seamen in most periods of our history has been characterized by
misery, their achievements, at least, have been worth while.
For all down the years America's march on the sea has served to
narrow the oceans, to make possible a continuing exchange of
goods and ideas with the other peoples of the earth and to make
this nation strong in war and rich in peace. In these achievements the sailing packets of the Western Ocean and the golden
clippers were no exception.

There were people other than the seamen who fared even
worse on the clipper ships and their windjamming competitors
in the transatlantic trade. These were the disinherited, the human scourings, the misfits, the ambitious and the castoffs of
Europe, who paid some sixteen dollars apiece to make the

A TRANSITION SHIP OF THE SIXTIES

The *Concordia* under sail and steam.

THE COLLINS LINE STEAMER *BALTIC*

When the *Baltic* broke the record for an Atlantic crossing in 1852 she became the last American ship to hold the championship until the *United States* won it again a century later.

TOO MUCH, TOO LATE

The S.S. *Quistconck*, first of the Hog Islanders, at her outfitting pier, October 1918. Note the camouflage.

SCHOOLSHIP BOYS OF WORLD WAR II
This picture was taken at Port Hueneme, California.

greatest voyage of their lives—the ocean crossing to the New World.

At the height of the immigrant trade in the fifties, a fair-sized sailing ship carried from half a hundred to three times that number of bewildered men, women and children in their stinking 'tween decks. Sleeping accommodations were usually in three tiers of wooden shelves with a clearance from deck to overhead deck beams of about six feet. Space between the bunks was limited to aisles three feet wide into which were piled baggage, food and cooking utensils. Portholes in these lower decks were usually awash and therefore closed against air and light, so that in the dull flicker of horn lanterns swaying in the fever-ridden gloom it is not difficult to imagine the stench.

Food rations were doled out once a week. In the beginning this consisted of rice, salt pork and hardtack, but later regulations required shipowners of both England and the United States to allow steerage passengers an additional ration of bread and potatoes. Later still, when nearly three million immigrants crossed in ten years, the weekly issue was increased by regulation to provide twenty-one quarts of fresh water, two and a half pounds of biscuit, one pound of wheat flour, five pounds of oat flour, two pounds of rice, two pounds of molasses.

Cooking was done by the passengers in the waist of the ship, open to the weather, in pots slung from hooks on a rail over the fires. On the larger ships the women often waited for hours to take their turn at the ovens and kettles to prepare the family meal. In all but the regular mail packets the westbound passage was often delayed for a week or longer beyond the announced sailing date while the skipper held his ship in port waiting to fill her up. Since no fires were allowed aboard, this meant that whole families, who had generally budgeted expenses down to the last penny, were left to the tender mercies of profiteering dockside tavern keepers for their subsistence until the ship was filled up and ready to sail. The British Protective Emigrant Board, and the Irish Protective Society, formed for the protection of emigrants going to the promised land, eventually improved matters some, but since they had no legal authority their efforts were pretty much confined to friendly advice and information concerning how to make the crossing as painless as possible.

In the gales of a midwinter passage no cooking was possible. Ports were sealed shut, hatches were battened down and the crowd below screamed all night in terror, praying, no doubt, for a quick and merciful end to it all. In the morning the dead were counted. At the end of a voyage, which may have taken as long as two months if the weather was particularly bad, the toll of dead would range anywhere from a dozen to as many as eighty, depending on the size of the ship, the time taken to cross and how many cases of smallpox and other contagious diseases had broken out. One of the worst epidemic years was 1853, when the *Washington* arrived in New York from Liverpool with cholera raging. Nearly a hundred had died during the trip, and over sixty more cases were found aboard. Other vessels arriving in New York that fall with dead and dying cargoes were the *William Tapscott,* sixty-five dead; *American Union,* eighty dead; *Corinthian,* from Havre, forty-one dead; *Statesman,* from Antwerp, twenty-five dead . . . and many, many more.

In the last half of the century over eighteen million souls crossed to the New World, some by sail, some by steam. They got here. They helped make this country the great nation it is today. But whether the clippers so many of them came in were blood boats, hell ships or golden vessels depends on the point of view.

On their record it is difficult to sympathize with the time-honored idolatry of these great windships, shared by so many, that helped to keep America's merchant fleet on its fatal course. Only the sailors seemed to sense what was in the wind. For while the merchants and shipowners were gravely assuring one another that tea and fruit brought in by steamers lost their flavor, and while the windship skippers continued to cut a swath along the water fronts with their yellow pongee suits and Malacca sticks as they regaled their awe-struck listeners with tall tales of record runs, the fo'c'sle hands, eying the comforts of steam heat and regular landfalls made on schedule, were improvising their farewell chanties:

> Oh, the times are hard and the wages low,
>   Leave her, Johnny, leave her!
> I'll pack my bag and go below,
>   It's time for us to leave her!

15

"It's Time for Us to Leave Her!"

STEAMSHIP PRESSURE on the American windship fleet was rising with the steam pressures in their rivals' boilers. No longer were the boilers the leaky affairs found aboard the gallant *Sirius* when she raced the *Great Western* across the Atlantic. With better boilers came higher speeds and lower fuel costs. Steam-gauge needles were rising from a paltry fifteen pounds to the square inch in the early vessels to twenty, thirty and forty pounds when the clippers were fighting for their lives. Such pressures made John Fitch's screw propeller even more efficient, and it was already beginning to drive paddle wheels from the high seas.

Onto this scene burst an angry and worried American sailing-packet owner, Mr. E. K. Collins, who had decided it was high time the battle of steam was joined. He announced that he intended to "sweep the Cunarders off the Atlantic." This was quite an order in view of Cunard's ten-year head start in 1839 with steamers like the 207-foot *Britannia* and two or three others, backed by hundreds of thousands of pounds of British government subsidies. Bolstering Collins' resolve, perhaps, was the fact that Congress had bestirred itself to pass an act in 1845, providing payment to United States ships carrying the foreign mails, for the declared purpose of encouraging Americans to build and operate steamships. By the time Collins persuaded Congress to grant him a mail subsidy—for that is what it amounted to—the gold rush was on in full cry. Anything that would float with a forward motion through the water was bound to get popular support. The Cunard Line was receiving from the British government $15,000 a voyage for a weekly transatlantic service of forty-four trips a year. Collins was granted $19,250 a voyage for twenty voyages a year, and the fight was on.

There were some strings attached to the Congressional gift. It was stipulated that the Collins Line ships must always make the passage between New York and Liverpool in faster time than the Cunarders. The object of the 1845 act had been made clear in its preamble: "To provide efficient mail services, to encourage navigation and commerce, *and to build up a powerful fleet for use in case of war.*" The italics are for the purpose of this story and were not, unfortunately, in the original. The words were there but the spirit, alas, was still weak.

Collins organized his line capitalized to build four steamships, and then, of all things, he hired a famous yacht designer to build them. Inevitably he gave these bark-rigged sidewheelers sharp noses and shaped them on clipper lines. They were beauties to look at. They should have been. They cost $700,000 apiece to build, had every luxury conceivable in those days, including the novelty of barber chairs, steam heat and electric-bell service, and were the fastest things afloat. But their designer also gave them keelsons under the engines that were only forty inches deep, while the keels were 277 feet long. There was enough give and sway under the bedplates to rack the engines to pieces.

As soon as these ships, named the *Atlantic,* the *Pacific,* the *Arctic* and the *Baltic,* raced to sea, that is exactly what happened. The engines were run at full speed, and at the end of each run when the last passenger was safely ashore a gang of machinists swarmed aboard and worked day and night in strictest secrecy, literally overhauling the shattered machinery to get it in shape for the return trip. Even so, Collins was making good on his contract to beat the Cunard Line ships. His ships were averaging eleven days and ten hours for the crossing, against twelve days and nineteen hours by the Cunarders.

The food provided aboard these luxury ferries was nothing short of elegant. It would hardly dazzle the twentieth-century traveler accustomed to the gustatory dream worlds created in the galleys of liners like the *S.S. United States,* but the saloon fare in the Collins Line steamers must nevertheless have called for ambitious appetites to weather a daily menu like this:

Soup

Croutons   Sherry   Relishes

Boiled codfish and Potatoes

Stewed chicken   Macaroni Pie

Roast Potatoes   Mashed Turnips

Rhine Wine

Plum Pudding

Cheese   Champagne   Fruit

Ices

Coffee

Porter, Madeira, Spirits

Nobody in England had done much about beating the grandiose Yankee clippers, least of all Cunard, but now Cunard and his stockholders sat up and took notice. This business of being outdone by Yankee steamships was quite another matter. Cunard succeeded in having the Admiralty increase his subsidy to $16,000, and new ships were built to meet the competition.

It was a losing game for Cunard. The throbbing, racking, floating palaces of the Collins Line continued to churn out the fastest passages, leaving the Cunarders in their wakes without a single victory to make it a contest. People began to lay bets on the relative times in the unequal races, and newspapers reported fast passages along with the other sporting news. English shipowners in general, and Cunard directors and stockholders in particular, were badly frightened by the speedy American steamers. Not only were the Collins Line ships drastically undercutting freight rates to as low as thirty and forty dollars a ton, but the American traveling public was giving them fifty per cent more business than to the Cunard ships, and even the English preferred them. From January to November 1852, Collins liners carried 4,306 passengers as against 2,969 carried by Cunard ships. Fares were the same on both lines: $130 first class, $75 second class. English public opinion was reflected in *Punch* in this fashion:

> A Steamer of the Collins Line,
>   A Yankee Doodle notion,
> Has also quickest cut the brine
>   Across the Atlantic Ocean;
> And British agents, no way slow
>   Her merits to discover,
> Have gone and bought her—just to tow
>   The Cunard's packets over.

This probably referred to the *Baltic*'s remarkable run from New York to Liverpool when it set the transatlantic record of nine days, thirteen and one-half hours, with an average speed of 13.34 knots in August 1852—the last American-built-and-owned ship to hold the record for a hundred years. But *Punch* was indulging in poetic license. Nobody was buying Mr. Collins' steamships. They were costing everybody so much, including the taxpayers, that nobody, least of all the canny Scotsmen of the Cunard Line, dreamed of buying them. They merely wanted to get rid of them.

To keep them going, Congress raised the subsidy to a flat $858,000 a year for a voyage every two weeks. Even at that rate they were losing almost $17,000 a voyage. In addition to the continual and extensive repairs necessary for the tortured, ill-housed engines every time they docked, the coal bill alone was running to $8,612 for two thousand tons of coal consumed each voyage. Admiral Porter, rendering a post mortem to Congress in later years, reported:

I knew the Collins Line very well. . . . They had large crews, a large number of officers and a large number of engineers, for they had most powerful engines. . . . They had very large buildings in New York, a great many officers and a great many people connected with them. All these had to be paid. Then there were a great many deadheads, so that I used to be astonished how they kept running at all.

But more than money was involved in this last phase of the Third Battle of the Atlantic. There was also pride involved. When pride went, everything went.

Steaming through a dense fog whipped by a gale forty miles off Cape Race in September 1854, the *Arctic* with no safety devices, no red and green running lights and only a seaman blowing the customary tin horn from the fo'c'slehead, was rammed full tilt by the French steamer, *Vesta*. Panic gripped passengers and crew. In the wild confusion only two boats were launched. The *Vesta,* kept afloat by her collision bulkheads, was able to save only fourteen of the *Arctic's* passengers and thirty-four of the crew. The *Arctic* sank with over three hundred people, including the wife, son and daughter of Mr. Collins.

It was a disaster that shocked the nation. Worse, it marked

the beginning of the end for America's eighty-year reign on the high seas.

When the *Pacific,* a little over a year later, racing to redeem the line's prestige, went grinding onto an iceberg (it was assumed) and was lost without trace, it was only an anticlimax. The nation lost heart and its faith in steamships. The struggle became hopeless. The battle was all but over.

Collins tried to pick up the pieces and go on with the fight. As is usual in disaster, everyone and everything turned against him. People did not want to travel on Collins Line ships any more. Extravagant financing, combined with one of those money panics that periodically sweep Wall Street to the mystification of ordinary people, hampered his operations. Then Congress, with its ear to the ground for public opinion objecting to the cost, cut the line's subsidy in half. Wrote a cheerful English partner to Mr. Cunard: "The Collins people are pretty much in the situation of finding that breaking our windows with sovereigns, though very fine fun, is too costly to keep on." Closer to the basic trouble, however, was an observation in the *Scientific American:* "The great cause of our unsuccess in our Atlantic steamers is owing to our short acquaintance with the building of marine ships. There is a science and genius among our nautical engineers, but they want experience."

True enough. The death of the windships was proving too slow for the health of American shipping. Steam navigation had long ago passed from the experimental to an established fact in the fifties when the greatest maritime nation on earth actually "wanted experience"!

Nobody, it seemed, had a kind word for Mr. Collins and his steamships. At last Congress gave up the ghost and decided to abrogate all contracts for foreign-mail services, which was another way of saying no more subsidies. After an eight-year struggle starting with the launching of its first ship, the Collins

Line was through. With it perished all hope of the United States holding its own on the high seas.

It must have been a bitter pill for Mr. Collins to swallow, while knocking down his remaining vessels at bargain prices to satisfy creditors, to see the Cunard Line, which had also lost two of its large vessels during this period, having its subsidy raised to $900,000 by the British government. Worse, the *Adriatic,* largest and newest of the Collins Line steamers, was among the bargains acquired by his erstwhile British rivals, who promptly put her in regular service. For years she continued to hold the transatlantic record of five days, nineteen hours for the shorter crossing from Galway to St. Johns.

If the impression is gained here that America's part in this Third Battle of the Atlantic was a one-man affair, it is largely correct. There were other lines, like the Pacific Mail carrying the gold seekers to California and our old Quaker friends of the Black Ball Line making a feeble attempt to stay alive with their side-wheeler, *United States,* but certainly the Collins Line put up the stiffest and most spectacular fight. When it was over, America's maritime hopes were hull down on the horizon.

It has been frequently claimed that the Civil War was to blame for the wreckage, but consider that in the year 1855 over half a million tons of shipping were built in American yards, whereas only four years later—a year before the war started—American yards were building a scant 156,000 tons. Or another way to look at it: the proportion of total commerce carried in American vessels after 1858 fell off immediately from seventy-six per cent to sixty per cent, and the English proportion increased from twenty-four per cent to thirty-four per cent. It was after this time that British-Confederate cruisers were to complete the job of destruction on the remains of the merchant navy.

PART 4

The Doldrums

16

SWAN SONG

A POUND of coffee in 1863 retailed in Charleston, South Carolina, at eighteen dollars. Pins cost thirty dollars a package. Toilet soap was seven dollars a cake; ladies' gloves, thirty-three dollars a pair. And a good toothbrush could be bought for eight dollars. The monthly pay of a Confederate soldier was eighteen dollars. Most people in the starved and faltering South agreed that this was a rich-man's war and a poor-man's fight.

Conscription was being openly defied by armed bands of draft evaders in the poor hill sections of North Carolina, South Carolina, Georgia and Alabama. Sometimes these bands were numerous enough and determined enough to stand off whole detachments of Confederate cavalry on the prowl to round them up. In some country districts the lives of members of the draft board weren't worth a Confederate dollar bill. A dollar bill would still buy a drink of redeye.

When the war began, practically all the ships were owned in the North. What few merchant ships were owned in the South were bottled up by the Union blockade. And yet huge fortunes were being built up in the Confederate States of America. Running the blockade had become a princely enterprise. A successful run by a swift steamer was sure to pay back the cost of the ship several times over. Take the case of the *S. S. Herald* making eighteen trips to England with cotton which netted her owners three million dollars. What she earned on her return trip with such choice items as pins and toothbrushes is left to the imagination. And there was the *Banshee* making only eight trips before falling into Union hands and still able to show her owners a profit of seven hundred per cent. The list is long and glittering.

Steam, or, more exactly, sail-rigged steamers, were by this time accepted by North and South—even the navy accepted it along with the screw propeller—and Confederate commerce raiders as well as blockade runners came into their own with the enthusiastic support of English shipyards. It is interesting that the term "commerce raider" was the name applied to these British privateers, now that the tables were turned; and it is interesting to note, too, the outraged tone assumed by the government at Washington in referring to the depredations of Anglo-Confederate raiders committed on Union commerce, as compared with the official view taken of the havoc wrought by American privateers on British commerce in the brave days of '76 and 1812.

England had her own reasons for getting as many Confederate raiders to sea as possible. Not the least of these was the fact that over half a million of her textile workers had been thrown out of work for lack of Southern cotton. Over and above that was the traditional British policy of achieving and maintaining supremacy on the high seas. It was the same old story. From beginning to end, the rise, triumph and defeat of the American windships were closely related to this long struggle between England and the United States. When brother fell upon brother in her ex-colony across the sea in 1861 it cost England fifteen and a half million dollars in gold, as a result of the *Alabama* claims settlement, to maintain this policy. But the return paid dividends for two generations, until the United States built a new merchant navy for the First World War.

Shipbuilders like the Messrs. Dudgeon of Liverpool, who launched twenty steamers fitted with twin screws turning up fourteen knots, especially built for the blockade "trade," prospered beyond their fondest hopes. But the British went much farther than that. Commerce raiders, as well as blockade runners, were built in English yards or purchased from English firms by "private interests" and were manned by British sailors in flagrant violation of all the rules of neutrality. Some of them, flying Confederate flags without even bothering with the technicality of entering at any time a Confederate port, hunted down American merchant ships all over the ocean. Men-of-war, rechristened in England with Southern names like *Alabama, Florida* and *Shenandoah,* roamed the high seas, cutting to ribbons the dwindling American merchant fleet until scarcely a ship dared sail in foreign commerce.

Toward the end of the conflict Nassau, a British Colony and important way station for the blockade runners, was host to a dozen steamers a month. Nassau's annual imports had amounted to about a million and a quarter dollars before the war. In three years they jumped to over twenty-seven million. Overnight the quiet little tropic paradise became a boom town, indulging in the luxuries of iced champagne, rampant syphilis and a solvent government which paid off its debt of over two million dollars on the first flush tide of the war.

Flanked by fleet steamers and handy way stations like Nassau for coaling and exchanging cargoes en route to and from England, the United States Navy had its hands full. Even so, naval vessels managed to corner and destroy, among other British-built-and-manned commerce raiders, the deadly *Alabama,* an iron-hulled, screw-propelled raider of fifteen hundred tons, and in the end tightened the fatal knot of the blockade.

But in four years the American merchant fleet, fighting for its life at home and battling steam abroad, lost over a million tons of shipping. If only for sentimental reasons, it is interesting to note that among the Union's steamers to survive was the former Collins Liner, *Baltic*. She served the War Department under charter throughout the war, and one of her first duties had been to go to the relief of Fort Sumter, where she evacuated Major Robert Anderson and his command to New York.

When the conflict was over, when the wreckage was cleared away and the nation turned to the task of reconstruction, the victory at sea was England's. As the young men of America turned away from the sea toward new horizons on the western plains, English skippers pacing their bridge wings could truly sing:

> Far as the breeze can bear, the billows foam,
> Survey our empire and behold our home.

For the Yankee Clippers there remained to be administered only the *coup de grâce*. If steam had not taken the wind out of their sails, if British-Confederate cruisers had not shattered them and if coal, iron and skilled mechanical labor in England had not overwhelmed them, then most certainly their doom was sealed at eight o'clock one balmy November morning in 1869 when the French imperial yacht *Aigle* slipped her moorings in the new harbor at Port Said and, ringing her engines full ahead, steamed into the Suez Canal. Aboard her was the gorgeous Empress Eugénie, languorously inspecting this new bauble for her empire as she led a procession of sixty-eight gleaming, flag-draped vessels steaming in the *Aigle*'s wake toward Lake Timsah. No tall Yankee masts and great spars cut the bright-blue African sky that day, for the sky was windless. This was a waterway between two continents, built for the ex-

clusive passage of ships and men who were independent of
vagrant shifts of the wind. It was only a hundred miles long,
but for American windships it might as well have been ten
thousand.

The *S. S. Savannah*, fifty years before, had laid the headstone
for the grave of the clipper ships. The Suez Canal was its foot-
stone.

From Suez the story of America's merchant marine recedes
on an ebbing tide. The great tea clippers drifted into the Australian wool trade, leaving the fabulously rich China run to
foreign steamers that had not to sail around Africa to get there.
Symbolic of the times was the humiliating fate of Mr. Collins'
gallant old *Baltic,* which survived the Civil War and its aftermath only to be sold to Boston shipowners who promptly had
her engines removed and converted her to a sailing ship. In
the end she was broken up, in 1880, at Apple Island in Boston
harbor. Out on the Pacific coast the gold-rush steamers of the
Pacific Mail Line were already threshing helplessly in the
tentacles of the "Octopus"—the great Southern Pacific Railroad—and their whistles wailing in the San Francisco fog were
drowned out by the businesslike rattle of strings of boxcars
spanning the continent. America had turned in upon herself.
The oceans, once her highways to the world's markets, became
her Chinese wall.

Like a wallflower at the ball, the nation sat by with scarcely
a shy glance at the handsome ships and the fancy capers they
were cutting. There were watertight bulkheads and double
bottoms, bilge keels to lessen rolling and boilers that no longer
had a tendency to leak or explode. Steam pressures were higher
than ever, which meant that speeds were greater. The com-
pound engine, originally patented by an American forty-seven
years before, had given way to the triple-expansion engine
patented by a Frenchman in 1871. The basic idea of this engine

was so sound that it was to be used clear down to the time of the Liberty ships built to fight in the Second World War. By expanding steam from a high-pressure cylinder through a second and third cylinder, full use is made of otherwise wasted power, and fuel costs are greatly reduced. This engine in turn made the screw propeller more efficient than ever and drove paddle wheels off the ocean. It was a generation of mechanical change, a generation that saw the last of the transition ships, the steam-sailing ships of Conrad's time, while in the United States, land of mechanical and inventive genius, the dwindling shipping news was being replaced in the daily papers with accounts of the whisky-ring scandal, the back-pay Grab of Congress, the Union Pacific bribe case and other rascalities of the dazed administration of General Grant.

If John Fitch could have sat on a dockside bollard in Liverpool to watch the world go by in the seventies, he would have had the satisfaction of seeing the despised windships gathering barnacles in the back reaches of the harbor, their places taken for the most part by steamships. Some would still be burdened with cumbersome paddle-wheel boxes, but many would be sporting screw propellers, or even twin screws. Strange talk would fill the air and he'd have seen some strange sights, for most people even yet did not fully understand the relationship of the changes from sail to steam and from wood to iron and steel. Fitch would have seen smoking down the Mersey wooden steamers churning a wake with screw propellers, and ships built of modern steel splashing seaward with paddle-wheels or even atilt in the wind with auxiliary sails.

Dockside talk would have been confusing to him too. Marine architects were still viewed with suspicion as dreamy-eyed mathematicians, and few honest shipbuilders would pay any attention to them. Shipmasters and builders were still stubbornly fighting the transition from wood to steel. They simply failed, or refused, to understand the principles of flotation and were not convinced that an iron or steel ship would float at all, much less carry more cargo than a wooden ship of equal displacement. Fitch would have heard some windy talk about compasses going wrong in an iron hull, and endless explanations of how and why an iron ship would simply go all to pieces if grounded. In a burst of impatience he might have been moved to point to the case of the *Great Britain*, built of iron nearly thirty years before. She had lain a wreck in Dundrum Bay for eleven months while the Irish Sea pounded her in her cradle of two detached rocks; yet when she was refloated her iron hull was found to be still serviceable, and she brought home profitable cargoes for years to come.

There were other cases, too, as plain as the noses on their faces. Perhaps, after all these years, poor John Fitch would have found more willing listeners to whom he could point out the folly of their prejudices. Perhaps.

In the United States in the eighties the tide was on the ebb in full strength. . . .

A gusty March wind swept the Folsom Street Wharf on San Francisco's water front in 1885 where a group of bitter men were gathered around a notice tacked to a shed announcing that henceforth offshore sailors would be cut to twenty-five dollars a month. A man named Sigismund Danielwicz, no seaman, was talking union. A union of sailors? More Bibles? A couple of hundred joined up. During the summer a strike was called. No money. No leader. No jobs. No strike. Wages were cut again.

In 1893 permission was asked of Congress by the American Line, an organization formed out of the previous power of the Inman Line, which had withdrawn, beaten, from the Atlantic, to place under the American flag two British-built steamships.

Permission was granted and the ships were brought over. Shades of John Griffiths and Donald MacKay, the great builders of the clippers! What a comedown!

Meanwhile, on the West Coast, the wild and woolly San Franciscans were striking again. There was a man out there, Andrew Furuseth, whose Sailor's Union of the Pacific had somehow become the strongest union local in the country, with nearly fifty thousand dollars in its treasury. Fifty thousand dollars in a sailor's union? Reporters on the water-front beat looking for a fiery-eyed ungrammatical labor agitator were disappointed in the long-limbed, loose-jointed sailor they found there. His weathered face was thoughtful, his roving blue eyes purposeful, but the wrinkles that gathered at their corners when he spoke of the sailors' bondage hinted at a conciliatory disposition. Not much of a story there.

Furuseth, it turned out, was a man in his late thirties who had come to America from Norway over a dozen years before by way of Calcutta in a British ship. He had been up on the Columbia River with the fishing fleet when the Folsom Street sailors had formed their union and gone down to defeat, but he had come on down to San Francisco to join them. Now he was their secretary. Few knew it then, but he was more than that. He was their leader, their voice, their hope. Andrew Furuseth was ready to fight for the rights of the men at sea as few men were willing to fight for anything.

But fifty thousand dollars wasn't enough. Times were lean for the shipowners too, and by summer the strike collapsed. Wages were cut again—fifteen dollars a month this time.

A sailor who could read and write? No liquor, no women? They were calling him Saint Andrew now. But Andy Furuseth wasn't concerned with name calling or what people thought of him. He had no friends. He had only principles. For the sake of them he had long ago decided to put aside all those things most men count dear—wife, children, cronies, material goods.

He had laid off his course, and this was to be a long and bitter fight. In the corridors of Congress he was recognized on sight. In 1895 he was showing them the *Red Record,* a document with a blood-red cover displaying a hand gripping a belaying pin, which told the story of the seaman's brutal treatment. Occasionally he disappeared, shipped out to sea to keep his hand in, but he always came back to take up the fight.

And still the ebb tide flowed.

At the turn of the century fourteen steamships flying the American flag were carrying the nation's foreign commerce. Except for coastwise craft, fourteen ships made up the American merchant navy. Soon ninety per cent of America's overseas trade was being carried in foreign ships—easy pickings which had more than doubled since the Civil War.

At last the Shipowners Federation of the Pacific recognized Furuseth's union. In Washington a few laws were finally passed: in 1904, "An act to prohibit shanghaiing in the United States. . . ." The boardinghouse crimps were beaten. Legally, anyhow. No more collecting the sailor's wages before he sailed. No more working out a dead horse.

1906.

Slack tide.

Kaiser Wilhelm had taken a few nautical swipes at a good neighbor on the United States' own doorstep, Venezuela. The Japanese were hissing not so politely at California's exclusion law. President Theodore Roosevelt fingered his Big Stick. The odds on war with Japan were quoted at Lloyd's at even money, then jumped to two to one, and Mr. Roosevelt decided that a good-will world cruise by the navy might help to clear the air. So the Great White Fleet sailed forth from Hampton Roads, Virginia, in all its splendor, bound round the Horn.

But, lacking a merchant marine, the United States fleet's auxiliary and supply ships were a handful of chartered Italian and Norwegian tramps.

17

TOO PROUD TO FIGHT

In PHILADELPHIA President Wilson, tired, gaunt, but still hopeful, rose to make a speech. He said:

The example of America must be the example not merely of peace because it will not fight, but of peace because peace is the healing and elevating influence of the world and strife is not. There is such a thing as a nation being so right that it does not need to convince others by force that it is right. . . . There is such a thing as a man being too proud to fight.

This was not the kind of language the Germans understood. Too proud to fight! To them it was obvious the Americans could not fight. They weren't ready yet, and even if they did dare to tackle the great German Army, where were the ships to bring the Americans over?

One of them, the peaceful freighter *Gulflight,* was on the bottom of the Atlantic, the first American ship to be sent there by a German torpedo. But more than a German torpedo had sent her under. A good deal of cynicism on both sides of the Atlantic, and a great deal of bungling, had started the torpedo's blades spinning on that May morning in 1915.

More than ever before, this was a battle of food. In the beginning England had swept the Germans from the high seas with a naval blockade that was soon felt at every German family's dinner table. If Germany instead of England had had a vast merchant navy backed by an invincible battle fleet, English dinner tables would have been feeling a similar pinch and German victory would have been inevitable. But ships the Germans did not have. Countering England's disregard of neutral rights, they resorted to the even more unlawful tactics of sinking without warning England's and everybody else's ships with submarines. The Germans clothed this type of murder with a pretense of legality by proclaiming a war zone around the British Isles.

Trouble for the United States, as usual, had come from the sea.

As in the time of Napoleon's ravages of Europe, once again the United States found itself the world's most important neutral. There were the ingredients for a War of 1812 all over again. Even the old familiar and irritating Orders-in-Council were there. This time the British announced a long list of contraband, based on an agreement called the Declaration of London signed a few years before by most of the leading maritime nations. England had not signed it, but now it was useful. She added to it thirty-two articles of contraband, including food, which no ship sailing the high seas dared carry without risking a shot over the bows by a British cruiser, followed by confiscation. Furthermore, while they were about it, the British took to capturing the mails. It was a war-born necessity. No doubt about that. But as American shippers and businessmen, howling their protests, pointed out, what if the position were reversed? Suppose the United States warships were hauling British vessels into New York, piling their cargoes high on the docks, open to the weather, while it was decided whether or not they were contraband, meanwhile opening and perusing letters that often contained competitive prices and trade secrets which would make most interesting reading to American firms? The howlers could howl all they wished. This was the beginning of a new era of realism. The plain facts were that the United States did not have the ships to carry her own goods to other neutral countries, and even if she had had them there was no navy powerful enough to back them up.

While owners and sailors fumed against British highhandedness, the homefolk read their morning papers and hoped for the best. The Germans were quite right in assuming that the American people sought no fight.

Why should they? America was the greatest storehouse of food and supplies in the world. Already factory wheels were beginning to turn twenty-four hours a day. Everyone had money in his pockets. Goods were glutting the docks for lack of ships to move them. True, a great deal more money could have been made if there had been enough ships to carry the stuff away. To this end Congress, with noteworthy alacrity, had made it possible in August, the month the war started abroad, to bring ships of foreign registry under the American flag. These vessels, together with the handful already in operation, plus lumber schooners and other coastwise craft, served as a merchant marine of sorts totaling about a million tons.

This helped a little. How little is better understood by comparing it with England's fourteen million tons which were already proving inadequate.

Offsetting this Congressional prescience was the sad case of another shipping bill also introduced during the first month of the war. It provided for the government to buy what neutral ships it could lay hands on and to start building new ones while the cost of construction was still a modest forty dollars a ton. Forty dollars a ton meant that a good oceangoing freighter could be built for a quarter of a million dollars or less. But the shipping bill never became law. The ships were neither bought nor built. Frightened shipowners, outraged at the idea of the government owning a merchant fleet, fought the bill to a standstill. One of the loudest voices raised against it was that of J. P. Morgan, who happened to be financially interested in the British-controlled International Mercantile Marine Company. He said there was no need for the government to meddle in shipping, that a government-owned fleet would be a menace to the interests of private owners. In view of the skyrocketing freight rates in which his line was sharing he certainly had something there. So the shipping bill was gassed to death in the United States Senate in one of those talking marathons called filibusters.

In spite of German submarines, and in spite of British seizures, things were looking up for American seamen by 1915. Not that a million tons of creaking, rusting, leaking ships amounted to much in the way of more or better jobs, but Andrew Furuseth—old "Saint Andrew"—still haunting the halls of Congress, was finding more willing listeners. Backed now with a membership of 3,500 sailors and a financial rating for his union of over half a million dollars, he had already seen sailors' wages start moving up instead of continuing down. Then in 1915 President Wilson signed Senator La Follette's bill, the Seamen's Act: "An act to promote the welfare of American seamen in the merchant marine of the United States...." Among other things, the act provided that a seaman could claim half his due wages in a foreign port. More important was the requirement that sixty-five per cent of a ship's crew must be able-bodied seamen. Since the law also required that to get an A. B.'s ticket a man must have been to sea for three years as an ordinary seaman, it meant that shipowners could no longer round up landlubbers and send them to sea to break a strike. Henceforth, to sign on a ship a man had to produce his necessary qualifications and discharges.

Working hours in port and at sea were cut to eight hours a day. Instead of eating in the same quarters where he slept, the sailor now ate in a separate messroom. His quarters were better lighted, airy and clean. No longer did he bed down on the proverbial donkey's breakfast; each man had his own mattress cover, pillow and blankets. Steadily the demands were made, and steadily they were met. Wages rose to thirty-five dollars a month . . . forty dollars . . . fifty dollars.

Shipowners and business groups turned the air blue with their protests. The Seamen's Act, they predicted, would drive American ships from the sea. Andrew Furuseth, they said, was more dangerous than the Germans' torpedoes. But Furuseth's critics were dealing with a breed of sailor they had never run afoul of before: a self-trained economist, sometimes described as belonging to the classical school, who met their arguments with dispassionate facts, figures and cogent reasoning. He could talk with them sensibly of what proportion wages bore to the total cost of running a ship and of what wage rates prevailed at San Francisco, Seattle, New York or Newport News. "The Seamen's Law is not a labor law at all," he said. "It affects labor only insofar as it liberates the action of supply and demand for labor."

Startling words from the fo'c'sle! A seaman-economist applying the age-old doctrines of industrial freedom to the peculiar case of the sailors!

In any case there was little time and less need for worrying about the Seamen's Act driving American ships off the Atlantic. German submarines were taking much more effective action in that respect. The German counterblockade was still weak in spite of mounting sinkings of Allied and neutral ships, and the Germans were becoming more desperate, more daring. Still convinced that the United States would not fight, they held American lives and American ships cheaper than ever. Finally a German submarine committed the greatest mass murder on the high seas that any nation had yet dared.

On a late-spring afternoon in 1915 the ocean mammoth *Lusitania,* a Cunard Line passenger ship unable to defend herself, was steaming off the Irish coast on her eastward run from New York with nearly two thousand noncombatant men, women and children aboard. Suddenly the wakes of two torpedoes knifed the water. There was a shattering double explosion amidships, and the vessel's side lay open to the sea. The decks rapidly steepened with a heavy list. Most of the lifeboats were useless. There was no panic. Women and children were taken off first. In twenty minutes the *Lusitania* plunged below the waves, dragging with her to their deaths over eleven hundred people. Of these, 114 were United States citizens.

The German government claimed the *Lusitania* carried munitions. She did. There were a few hundred cases of cartridges mixed in with her general cargo, but the amount was trifling. The charge was a technicality. The *Lusitania* was primarily a passenger ship, unarmed and loaded with noncombatants.

Today it is difficult for a new generation in which international law has vanished, with only its shadow remaining as a weapon of propaganda, to understand the horror that swept over the United States at news of the *Lusitania's* sinking. Before the tragedy about half the country had no particular feeling about the war in Europe, one way or the other. There were no scientific, professional polltakers in those days, but it is safe to say that the remaining half was pretty evenly divided between those favoring the Allies and those favoring Germany. Even as late as the fall of 1916 President Wilson was to be re-elected on the slogan, "He Kept Us Out of War."

After the *Lusitania* the scales were heavily tipped against

Germany. In spite of President Wilson's policy of neutrality the road to war was clearly marked. Mr. Wilson hated war as did most of the American people, but his idealistic statements about being "too proud to fight" and "peace without victory" simply did not make sense to German realists whose submarines were by this time sinking over half a million tons of Allied shipping a month. To understand what half a million tons of ships means, consider that six, eight or even ten steamships, depending on their size, with their carefully machined engines, laboriously riveted hull plates, their holds jammed full of desperately needed foods, and their trained, experienced crews —consider that all this treasure was being consigned to the ocean's bottom every twenty-four hours, seven days a week, month in, month out.

American shipowners and Congress were beginning to be impressed by the mounting toll at sea. It was agreed that something had to be done about it. Finally a shipping act was made law on September 7, 1916, creating a board to regulate and make additions to the merchant marine. By this time the price of a ship had risen from forty dollars a ton to anywhere from $150 up. Mostly up. The United States Shipping Board thus came into being as a creature of peace legislation amidst a wartime boom. It was not contemplated that the board would operate ships—not even contemplated that it would build many of them. It was simply authorized to organize a corporation for ship construction capitalized at fifty million dollars, and the money was not to come from the United States Treasury but from the sale of Panama Canal bonds. This whole amount was less than the cost of one wartime shipyard-to-be. About all the members of the board could do was write urgent memos back and forth to one another and lay plans for the operations ahead.

Meanwhile, Admiral von Tirpitz was promising the Kaiser

that when the United States came into the war he would sink a million tons of shipping a month, and he would have England licked. It looked as if he would make good on it, too, because in two and a half years of war, while all the Allies, including England, France, Russia, Italy and Japan, were building two and three-quarters million tons of ships, the German Navy succeeded in sinking over three million tons.

Thus encouraged, the Germans went all out with their submarines. They had flatly announced early in 1917 that they would sink all neutral ships, meaning principally American ships, found approaching the British Isles. Now they heaped one deliberate insult on the other, feeling sure that England would be starved into surrender before the United States could get ready. Meanwhile, so went the reasoning, it was better to have the Americans worrying about war preparations than concentrating on feeding England.

Another German admiral, Von Holtzendorff, "guaranteed" the German Imperial Council that even if war were declared, not one American soldier would ever set foot on European soil. He had it all figured out with German mathematical precision. He could point to the example of the Dardanelles campaign of 1915 when Sir Ian Hamilton, begging for British reinforcements in May and June, finally obtained about a hundred thousand men between July 10 and August 10. It gave a hint of the amount of time required to transport an urgently needed military force on a two-week voyage. And this at a time when German submarines had not yet seriously damaged England's ships and shipping facilities.

As a clincher that finally brought the Americans into the slaughter, the German Foreign Office sent a radio message to its representative in Mexico authorizing an alliance with that country in case the United States came into the war. Mexico was to attack the southern border, and for her effort would be given Texas, New Mexico and Arizona as her reward at the peace table. The British intercepted the message, and their fondest prayers were answered. Diplomatic relations between the United States and Germany were broken off. The German ambassador, Von Bernstorff, was sent home. War was declared on Germany on April 6, 1917, by a large majority of Congress.

In the Regular Army of the United States there were 77,000 men, none of whom had ever buckled on a gas mask or thrown a hand grenade from a trench knee-deep in mud. Piled on docks and railway sidings and rolling from factories was enough war material to fill most of the world's ships. American factories were ready, but the ships were not. Foreign vessels were long gone on other business. Virtually all of America's merchant navy was with the vanished fleet of yesteryear.

18

THE BRIDGE OF SHIPS
TO FRANCE

ONCE AGAIN America's merchant seamen swarmed to sea in anything that would float. From the back reaches, from the saltings of decaying ports and forgotten bays and inlets, the ships came down to the sea. Windjammers, lake boats, river steamers, coal barges. So scarce were ships in the spring of 1917 that fly-by-night operators were bidding for new ones while they were still on the ways. The first bidder would often sell his ship before it was launched. Up, up went the price of each sale—two hundred thousand dollars, five hundred thousand, a million, two million—before the ship was launched.

They were cheap at the price. Cheap at almost any price. Shipowning had become one of the most profitable investments in the world. A tramp steamer could pick and choose her cargo from the mounting piles on the docks like a finicky express liner and clear her cost in a single voyage. Typifying the dazzling prospects for a nine-knot ocean tramp, one of them built for $280,000 was sold twelve months later for $1,375,000. Less than six months after that the vessel had earned $2,124,000.

The crying need was for ships to run the submarine gauntlet of the North Atlantic. That was the dramatic, primary need,

underscored with blood and booming guns from Sandy Hook
to Lizard Head. But in the excitement it is sometimes over-
looked that in this period the United States also had a desperate
need for imports. Over a thousand ships, including those of
our allies, were engaged in bringing to this country such indispensables as chromium, manganese, iron, nickel and copper
ores, to say nothing of rubber from the other side of the world,
and coffee, tea, rice and sugar, to name only a few. For the
most part this large chunk of the Allied merchant navy was
entirely removed from the scene of hostilities.

A windfall that helped to make up the deficiency were the
interned German ships that were confiscated in the United
States. These ships alone greatly exceeded in value and tonnage
the entire American merchant fleet thrown into the Atlantic
bridge of ships.

Not until June 15, 1917, over two months after war was
declared, did Congress confer on the President sufficient authority for the requisition, construction and operation of vessels
without limitation or conditions. On July 11, President Wilson,
in turn, delegated his authority to the Shipping Board to acquire
vessels already built and to operate them. To the board's offspring, the Emergency Fleet Corporation, was given authority
at last to begin building.

The greatest launch of ships the world had ever seen was
under way.

In three small rented rooms occupied by a handful of shirt-
sleeved executives and six clerks in the summer of 1917 the
phones began to jangle. Over the door was a sign: EMERGENCY
FLEET CORPORATION. Through the open windows the heat came
in waves while stenographers hammered their typewriters and

THREE C-TYPE VESSELS

At the top is a C-1, S.S. *American Packer;* in the center a C-2, the refrigerator ship *Blue Jacket;* and at the bottom a C-3, the cargo vessel *Sea Fox.*

Courtesy of the U.S. Maritime Commission

THE TIRELESS LIBERTY

The workhorse of World War II needs no description.

THE VICTORY

Something has been added; not much but something.

the adding machines set up their incessant rattle. The talk that filled the humid Washington air was as fantastic as the figures reeling out of the machines.

Two thousand ships . . . Three billion dollars . . . A thousand shipways . . . Half a million men . . . Now!

There was nothing in which to anchor facts, nothing to tie to. The Emergency Fleet Corporation, a child of war, had no roots, no parentage from which it had sprung, except in the log shipways of an ancient breed of fighters who had always got their ships, somehow, in time to meet the enemy. There was no one to whom the President could say, "Build a thousand ships," or a hundred ships or even one ship, and be told the order would be filled. What few shipyards there were on the two coasts and the Great Lakes capable of building an ocean-going steamship were already filled with hulls being completed mostly for foreign interests. These ways would not be available for months.

On the day war was declared there were in the United States thirty-seven steel-ship yards with 162 ways. Now over two hundred yards were needed with at least a thousand ways—three times as many as there were in all the rest of the world.

A desperate order finally went out commandeering all seagoing hulls and materials intended for foreign account. Cries of protest went up from the builders and their foreign customers. The term "total war" had not yet been invented, and a customer was still a customer. Settlement was made on a cash basis, but there was no provision for giving the ships back after the war. Neutral countries were especially outraged. Norway, who had no intention of getting into the war, had her eyes fixed on distant horizons of postwar commerce and was particularly stubborn about it. Final and satisfactory settlement with the Norwegians was never made during the war.

In the end, however, the commandeering order produced over four hundred ships of some three million tons which were put under the Stars and Stripes and sent to sea.

Still this was not getting new ships built. Ships meant steel and a place to build them. Ships meant lumber and machine tools, freight cars and cement, paint, wire, canvas, rope, glass. Above all, ships meant men. Finding enough men with the know-how for building these ships, who didn't already have their hands full, was out of the question.

Up in Maine, cradle of the American merchant navy, there were a few, and they went to work building 250-foot coal-burning wooden freighters. Their old sailing ships had already been hauled up on marine railways, scraped, painted, fitted with new canvas and sent to sea. They could, and did, also build auxiliary craft for the navy like trawlers, mine sweepers and submarine chasers. In the Pacific Northwest the Norwegian fishermen took the lead in building ships for the wooden fleet. But according to a Census Bureau estimate, there were no more than 44,000 men in the United States engaged in shipbuilding, ranging from battleships to rowboats.

Blueprints were drawn by the bale. Contracts were let in batches. The call for men went out, and campaigns for "Shipyard Volunteers" blared over the nation. There were "Four-Minute Men" and pretty girls and movies and State Councils of Defense with their enrollment centers. Shipyard workers were deferred from the draft. Those already in the army were given furloughs to return to the shipyards. Returned soldiers made speeches. There was even some talk of conscripting labor, but the need was averted as the volunteers poured into the yards 380,000 strong. To house and feed them entire villages went up overnight. Not tent villages. Families had to have homes. Children, perhaps, would have to grow up in them. Nobody knew how long the war might last. This meant sewers, schools, hospitals, electric lighting, stores, shops, fire engines, playgrounds and police.

Wages rose for all hands. In the yards a calker, a shipfitter, a chipper or a boilermaker had his pay raised from fifty cents an hour to eighty cents. A forger was paid twelve dollars a day. A longshoreman, with work now available in steady shifts, had his pay increased from fifty cents an hour to ninety cents.

And the sailors, even the sailors, were riding the golden crest. There were no parades through village streets, no merry recruiting officers enrolling "gentlemen adventurers" with promises of loot and bowls of punch in water-front taverns, for this was the new era of realism. Instead, seamen soberly signed on at the corner drugstore. The Sea Training Bureau enlisted the services of nearly seven thousand United Drug Company stores for the purpose, and American youths, 32,000 of them, signed up for a six-week schoolship course before being sent to sea.

They boarded the ships in a ratio of four new hands to six experienced A.B.'s. What the recruits found there was not to their liking. Demands were made. Wages were raised. The fo'c'sles, formerly three-quarters filled with foreign crews, were again manned by American citizens at a wage of sixty dollars a month plus bonuses in the war zone. They were given their own hiring halls, too, and at mess they were given knives, forks and spoons to eat with—quite an improvement over the old method of scraping the black pan with a sheath knife. The Seamen's Act humanized the merchant navy, but it was the Sea Training Bureau that Americanized it.

"Schoolship boys," the old shellbacks called them in more polite moments, but they turned out to be sailors, too. Said Admiral Sims, commander of the naval fleet:

The skill and seamanship of these sailors was something that amazed naval officers, and they proved themselves to be seamen in a sense that naval officers never have the opportunity to become. Courage, initiative, a sense of responsibility, skill in handling ships of all types, and noteworthy seamanship characterized the merchantmen.

As for the ships themselves, old ideas had to be junked. Cheap ships were needed to feed the bloody maw of the Atlantic. Cheap ships, standardized ships, *quick* ships. Building a ship had always been regarded as an individual undertaking, like a tailor-made suit of clothes or a carefully bred horse. Now they were to be mass produced, prefabricated, one just like the next, a steel tube pinched in at the ends with a boiler in the middle. Plans and drawings had to be made so any garage mechanic could read them. The parts were built in shops and vacant lots from Puget Sound to Key West, numbered, lettered and put on an assembly belt extending across the nation. Ninety-six per cent of the total weight of the hulls was manufactured outside the actual shipyards from coast to coast.

The bridgebuilder, using ordinary commercial steel, became the shipbuilder. So did the washing-machine manufacturer, the lumberman, the building contractor. The wartime fleet was built by the men who had built the country itself. Their goal was three thousand ships.

Eight and a half months after signing the first contract for a twenty-eight-shipway yard in September 1917 the yard was completed and from it the first ship for the new merchant navy was launched, a feat without parallel in the world's history of ship construction. She was the *Agwam,* 5,300 dead-weight tons. Taking the water in May 1918, she led the parade of half a million tons of her prefabricated kind to follow in her wake. These vessels, among the most successfully and economically operated during the war, were 335 feet long, powered by reduction-gear turbines, with coal or oil burners using water-tube boilers, and capable of a speed of ten and one-half knots.

Eight and a half months to build a yard and launch a ship—a ship that formerly required a couple of years to build ... Not fast enough. With each new ship the pace quickened. Out on the golden slopes of California a 12,000-ton ship, the *Invincible,* breasted the water of San Francisco Bay just thirty-one days after her keel had been laid. In New Jersey a 5,000-ton collier, the *Tuckahoe,* slid down the ways within twenty-seven days of her keel-laying. Two weeks later she was fitted out and at sea with a cargo of coal. Up on the Columbia River at Portland the 8,800-ton *City of Eureka* was delivered *ready for sea*—not merely launched to lie for weeks in a fitting-out basin—fifty-two days after her keel had been laid. At Seattle thirty-one ships like the *City of Eureka* were built in an average time of 119 days, with many exceptional records. A yard at Oakland, California, launched six ships on a single tide. The Pacific Coast, which scarcely two generations before had been a raw, wild land of gold seekers, lumberjacks, Chinese railroad workers and sleepy wine makers, was leading the country with more than half the merchant navy a-borning on its shores.

In the heat and noise and nerve-twisting bedlam that was Washington, the three rented rooms of the Emergency Fleet Corporation had spawned nearly eight thousand hired hands. The adding machines and shirt-sleeved executives and clerks had spread like a flood tide into twenty-one different kinds of buildings that included everything from the best-equipped office building in town to a five-and-dime store and a converted livery stable. They had their money now, nearly two billion dollars of it, and it looked as if they would have their ships.

Americans like things big, and the biggest, the most colossal monument to their epic trek back to the sea was reared on a swampy island in the Delaware River, south of Philadephia. The Delaware Indians had called the place Quistconck. *Quis-*

quis meant "hog," and *onck* meant "place for." Thus a place for hogs was Hog Island. But the hogs that came from there would have exceeded the red men's wildest speculations about the white men's magic, for these hogs belched smoke and steam and carried the white men's goods over the earth's waters.

The tale of Hog Island is a statistician's nightmare, a fantastic example of too much too late. With the exception of the ill-conceived Liberty airplane engines, it was the most reviled and most praised, the most glorious success and the most spectacular failure of all the homeland efforts of the war. As with so many great American monuments, it became fashionable to sneer at it. But one bright and shining fact stands out in all the calumny heaped on its builders' heads: it told a message in language the Germans could understand. In the cacophony of its riveters' hammers was a challenge to the Kaiser's submarines that meant ships, ships and yet more ships for as many weeks, months, years as the Potsdam gang would be able to prevail on boys and old men to go hunting under the sea amidst the rising crescendo of Allied depth bombs, mines and shellfire from which there was no return.

In the fall of 1917 Hog Island was a swamp. Twelve months later, in spite of one of the worst winters in history, nervous breakdowns and Congress, the swamp was a never-never land of towering cranes arching over fifty shipways stretched out along a two-and-a-quarter-mile water front. Somebody had figured out that it would cost about $27,000,000 to build, but when all the bills were in that guess turned out like most building estimates. The cost was $66,000,000. There were eighty-two miles of railway track. There were thirty-six warehouses and seven piers, each a thousand feet long and a hundred feet wide, and eighteen miles of roads. There were forty thousand workers at peak production, with a monthly pay roll of four million dollars. It was geared, finally, when the need no longer existed, to produce a 7,500-ton ship fully equipped for sea duty every seventy-two hours.

Musing in retrospect, Edward N. Hurley, chairman of the Shipping Board, estimated that the amount of steel bought for Hog Island was enough to build thirty Woolworth Buildings. The timber used in these steel vessels would have built comfortable homes for a city of twenty-five thousand people. Everything was on the grand scale, even the catastrophes. Because of the lack of planned decentralization, mass orders for lumber from the Pacific Northwest at one time had the railroads hopelessly blocked all the way from Philadelphia to Chicago. The ships themselves, squat tubs incapable of grinding out more than nine or ten knots, ran up a bill of $235,000,000. It was the sort of achievement, magnificent in failure, that could have been dreamed up only on the shores of the New World.

Into the creation of Hog Island and its production of ships was poured the greatest single treasure of the new merchant fleet. From it sailed not a single ship in time to fight the First World War.

Even so, there is no doubt about it: old Quistconck gave the Germans something to think about.

Such an extravagant war was enough to raise the ghost of Albert Gallatin. It would have been interesting to observe the reaction of that penny-pinching Swiss who held the purse strings during the War of 1812 could he have sat in a quiet corner of Secretary of the Treasury William Gibbs McAdoo's office in 1918.

Financing this Fourth Battle of the Atlantic to maintain America's freedom of the seas was costing the Treasury a pretty penny. To maintain Mr. Gallatin's credulity perhaps Mr.

McAdoo would have avoided the mouth-filling phrases of so many millions for this and so many millions for that in explaining the demands of his job. Certainly, had he mentioned the actual sums involved in building so much as one ship, it is doubtful if Mr. Gallatin would have believed his latter-day colleague was in his right senses. To simplify the figures Mr. McAdoo might have truthfully told the ex-Secretary that taxes were paying for about one third of the war's cost. The rest was being raised by the sale of bonds. Mr. Gallatin would more than likely have shaken his head sympathetically over this. He had tried bonds, too. But these bonds, Mr. McAdoo might have pointed out, were being sold by means of slogans, and nobody so dearly loves a slogan as John Q. American. There was a First Liberty Loan Drive, and there was a Second Liberty Loan Drive, and there was a Third. It was quite simple once you got the hang of it. In fact, there were six Liberty Loan Drives, and by that time every man, woman and child in the United States had invested an average of four hundred dollars each toward making the world safe for democracy.

Had there also been present at this mythical interview a reporter from the *Wall Street Journal,* Mr. McAdoo might have remarked in a quiet aside that direct expenditures for running the war were coming very, very close to twenty-two billion dollars. In a still quieter voice he might have added that this did not include the loans being made to England, France and the other Allies. At this point, had he overheard such fantastic remarks being made by a presumably sane official of the United States Government, Mr. Gallatin would more than likely have been on his feet with considerable color showing on his rosy Swiss features. But—and here Mr. McAdoo might well have thought twice before confiding the information—these loans of some ten billions were loans for credit to finance food and supplies and munitions bought in America with which to fight the war. And of course they would all be paid back later. . . .

On the rising tide of new ships there was indeed a financial bustle in the land. From forty dollars a ton at the outbreak of the war in 1914, the cost of a ship had risen to $264 a ton in 1918. The sailors were now being paid eighty dollars a month and more, plus sixty cents an hour overtime, with bonuses in the war zone. The selective-service draft, finally broadened to include all men from eighteen to forty-five, had brought into the army four and a quarter million men, of whom about half were sent to France. The bill for ships to get them there and supply them, paid by Mr. McAdoo, was close to three billion dollars. For his money he got 875 ships, good, bad and indifferent, in time for the war. As an incidental item there was a bill rendered by the British for transporting about half the American Expeditionary Force to France at eighty-five dollars a head. A rather odd charge, all things considered. In addition the British ran a sort of tourist concession whereby they purchased subsistence items on credit in the United States and sold them to the American troops aboard ship for cash.

Since strikes cost money, Mr. McAdoo might also have pointed out to Mr. Gallatin, assuming the poor man were still able to listen, that the sailors of the merchant navy were the only sizable group of workers to serve their country throughout the war without a strike.

To get the army to France the British were at long last prevailed on to tolerate convoys. Unbelievable as it seems today, the British Admiralty had opposed them throughout most of the war, endlessly pointing out to the Americans that convoys simply would not work. Herding ships together in frightened flocks was another of those unsound Yankee notions with which the admirals were constantly being pestered, like the nonsensical depth bombs the Americans were talking about—and using successfully—and the hydrophones they were beginning to use to listen for submarines. But convoys! Whole fleets of clumsy merchant ships of varying speeds zigzagging over the ocean helter-skelter, running one another down and running down valuable destroyers, of which there weren't enough for convoy duty in any case. Rank naval amateurism. Ridiculous!

Nevertheless, Admiral Sims of the United States Navy had his way about convoys after things got desperate on the North Atlantic. Virtually from the day the first convoy sailed, sinkings dropped sharply. Through 1918 the monthly average of ships lost was only two hundred thousand tons as compared with the half-million-a-month losses and higher of 1917, when the Germans had cut the British food supply to a point where there was left only enough to feed civilians for six weeks. By the use of convoys, contrary to Admiral von Holtzendorff's "guarantee" to the Kaiser, two million American troops crossed the North Atlantic in a steady stream, and German submarines were never at any time able to stop any of them.

Ships of the United States Navy supplied eighty-three per cent of the escort vessels for the convoys. Ships of the American merchant navy carried ninety-five per cent of the supplies. British ships carried half the troops. Except for a few rechristened German ships like the *Leviathan,* which carried some ten thousand troops each voyage, and a few home-built passenger vessels, the United States did not have the transports to carry her own fighting forces to the battlefield. By the summer of 1918 a million men had landed in France. By fall there was another million. But time, greatest enemy in battle as always, had slipped away before the bulk of America's merchant fleet was ready.

The bill for ships at sea and ships-to-be was still mounting when, on November 11, 1918, the generals of both sides sat down together in a French railway dining car in the forest of Compiègne to sign an armistice. Twenty-two days later, after sixty-five million men in uniform around the world laid down their arms, the *S. S. Quistconck,* properly snouted with champagne by President Wilson's wife, was officially turned over to the Emergency Fleet Corporation.

The first Hog was ready for sea.

19

EBB TIDE

LIKE A vast engine turning over of its own momentum after the switch is pulled, American ship factories spewed forth their vessels. At the launchings the glory and the glamour were gone. There were no more pretty girls and champagne and flags and bands. Now, instead, a hoarse whistle blew, the blocks were knocked out, and with a squirt of tobacco juice as a blessing, one more unwanted ship slid down the ways.

During 1919 six million tons of ships took the water. The United States was getting a new merchant marine, willy-nilly, of over two thousand vessels, three quarters of which were steel oceangoing freighters. For the first time in the nation's peacetime history there was coming into being an adequate merchant fleet backed by a powerful navy.

The glory and security were not to last. America's greatest naval disaster was in the offing. The balanced scales of merchant and naval sea power were again to be tipped.

The defeat did not occur at sea. The scene of the disaster was in Washington over a conference table. The core of the trouble was that the United States had come out of the war with a larger, more powerful, more modern navy than anybody else. This was understandable. The British had fought the naval battles of the war, five great battles in which they sank 160 German submarines, among other war vessels, and had lost fifty thousand men at sea. When it was over, the United States was completing a giant navy of battleships and cruisers incorporating everything learned in the sea war, while England had no first-class fighting ship that had been designed after 1914. It was a bitter pill for the mistress of the seas to swallow.

To make matters worse, the war-rich Americans were cooking up an even bigger pill with their loud talk about collecting war debts. For the British Admiralty, at least, it was too much to bear. Four giant battleships were dreamed up by their naval architects, the keel for one of them was laid, and another armaments race was in the making.

Before much else was done an attempt was made to head it off by Charles Evans Hughes, the American Secretary of State, who anxiously summoned all parties concerned, including Japan, France and Italy, to Washington to talk things over. Russia, still in the throes of revolution, was not included. The Washington disarmament conference of 1922, advertised by Mr. Hughes as a plan for ending naval building competition "for all time," lasted twelve weeks. When it was over, England had agreed to swap her obsolete war-worn battleships and her paper battleships still on the drawing boards for those already built or nearing completion in the United States. Japan agreed to tear up her paper battleships, too, if England and the United States would stop building naval bases and fortifications in the Pacific. France and Italy agreed to reduce their naval armament proportionately. British cruisers were to be left untouched. They were necessary to preserve England's foreign-trade routes.

If the battle was a paper one, the gunfire, at least, was real. In accordance with the terms of the Washington agreement this is part of what happened to the United States fleet:

One first-line battleship converted to a target ship and sunk.

The *U.S.S. Washington,* another first-line battleship practically completed, sunk by shellfire.

Two first-line battleships in active service, sold and broken up for scrap.

Six first-line battleships in various stages of construction, broken up and scrapped.

Fifteen second-line battleships in active service, sold and broken up for scrap.

Four first-line cruisers under construction, scrapped.

Only a naval expert could say how many actually battleworthy ships were lost in the Battle of Washington, but when it was over the United States Navy had put thirty-two of its warships permanently out of action.

Meanwhile, the blossoming merchant fleet was all dressed up with no place to go. There were war-born lines galore, all managed by private operators on behalf of the Shipping Board with fine patriotic names like the American Republic Line to South America, the American Export Line to the Mediterranean, the American Scantic Line to Baltic ports and the American Pioneer Line. As for the vessels themselves, contrary to popular opinion the bulk of the war babies were pretty good ships, sturdy cargo carriers able to grind out only nine or ten knots, but superior to the old-time European freighters. They had geared turbines and oil-burning, water-tube boilers; for the crews there were showers and steam heat in the fo'c'sles, electric lights, larger ports for ventilation, modern plumbing, and berths built of piping as protection against vermin.

The only trouble, or at least the overriding trouble, was that after the war there were not more than two or three American steamship services established for essential trade routes. A Merchant Marine Act had been passed by Congress in 1920, directing the Shipping Board to sell off these lines and ships as soon as possible to American buyers on easy terms. The wording of the act was certainly taken most literally, and there followed a bargain-basement sale that disposed of some of the choicer ships at least. The Dollar Line, for instance, bought five passenger ships for a little over half a million dollars apiece that had cost the government over four million dollars each to build. Henry Ford bought two hundred steel vessels for eight hundred dollars apiece, to convert to scrap. And there were other purchasers, but not enough of them, even at these knock-down prices.

Schoolships can produce seamen in a pinch, but no way has yet been found to produce shipping men able to master the intricacies of the countinghouse except through the tried-and-true method of experience. From the colonial days of merchant adventurers down through the years the surest way to have a ship show a profit has been first to have one that showed a loss.

Governments, however, are not run on a profit-and-loss basis. On that premise it is more easily understood why the United States Shipping Board was manned by swivel-chaired red-tapists instead of men who had sailed and owned ships. In the shipping ministries of Europe, where the long view generally prevails and where the national interest is traditionally considered first and foremost, regardless of war or peace, hardheaded shipping men must have smiled when Mr. Hurley of the Shipping Board made this postwar statement: "From the purely American point of view, which it is now permitted to hold, the importance of supplying vessels for the essential import trades is more acute today than it was during the war."

Unfortunately, at this late date it required considerably more than an "American point of view" to find men willing or able to send the rusting, idle merchant fleet back to sea. The government wanted to get out of the shipping business, but the plain truth was that there simply were not enough steamship operators of sufficient experience who could efficiently manage the

newborn fleet in the fierce world-wide competition for markets.
Trade routes were not only jealously guarded by European
syndicates, but the American people had lost contact with the
sea. Manufacturers, merchants and travelers were not "sea-
minded." They had no particular interest in patronizing American ships to make possible sustained service and permanent
trade connections between their firms and specified foreign
markets.

The Japanese were loading Japanese cargoes on their own
ships, the British on British ships and the Norwegians on
Norwegian ships. Those countries, like others, were building
ships cheaper and running them at far lower costs than the
Americans could do. To give them still further advantage their
governments were throwing in subsidies to be sure they would
have plenty of seaway. The operating subsidies ranged from
three or four million dollars a year in Japan to twenty or thirty
million dollars a year in France, depending chiefly on relative
costs. And this did not include loans to shipbuilders for new
ships. A Japanese ship could be built for less than half the cost
of the same type of vessel in an American yard; an ordinary
seaman was paid ten or twelve dollars a month; and a Japanese
ship running between San Francisco and Tokyo could make
the voyage for about sixty per cent of the cost to an American
vessel on the same run. Some shipping men claimed the
Japanese cost was closer to forty per cent than sixty, but it is
difficult to translate all the costs. Even the British and Scandi-
navians, accustomed to higher standards but always stiff competitors, with wages less than three quarters of American wages,
were operating their vessels at about sixty per cent of what it
was costing American operators to keep their ships running
between New York and Liverpool.

Ships of our former allies and of neutral nations, new and
faster since most of their old tonnage had been sunk, rang

their engines full ahead and steamed back into the shipping lanes to resume sea trucking on trade routes carefully preserved throughout the war. American ships, with no tradition of business relationships or that will-o'-the-wisp, good will, built up in South America or the East Indies or anywhere else, floundered helplessly in the wakes of foreign vessels. On a basis of speed alone, American ships ranked fifth on the world's sea lanes. Only a few vessels, including the seized German liners, could do better than twelve knots.

Despite the Shipping Board's efforts to charter its ships to anybody willing to gamble on running them, there were no takers, and the Board was forced to run the ships itself. From the beginning it was a losing proposition. The board's worst year was in 1921 when its efforts cost the taxpayers fifty million dollars. Every year it was in business showed a loss. Meanwhile, the ships were growing older. Twenty-five years is judged by the Bureau of Internal Revenue as the economic life span for a productive ship; in fact, after a dozen years of hard usage, in many cases, earnings begin to drop off. England, Germany, Japan, France, Italy, Norway and Holland were all building new, modern ships; and the Shipping Board, when it began to sell off the ships to anybody willing to sign a mortgage, was forced to let them go at prices that started at two hundred dollars a ton and rapidly dropped to ten dollars a ton. Over the next few years the American merchant navy was knocked down ship by ship to the highest bidder—as long as there were any bidders—for some $350,000,000, about ten per cent of what it had cost the people to build it. Of the original 2,316 ships the government had started with, less than two hundred remained in the laid-up fleet by the middle of the next decade.

In view of all this it is hardly surprising, though certainly it is ironical, that there was actually a serious shortage of sugar in the United States, to name one overseas import, *after* the war was over. Conversely, the industrial war colossus built and operated on credit for four or five years was splitting at the seams. Warehouses were overflowing for lack of foreign markets. Grain elevators were choked. Factory wheels slowed and stopped. In the confusion of shortages amidst overproduction, returned soldiers tramped the streets looking for work, for food.

Within a year after the war ended shipowners were talking feebly about cutting wages now that the party was over, but the hang-over hadn't really set in yet. Furthermore a sailor is not an economist. The nature of his calling is not conducive to worry over shoreside affairs unless he finds himself face to face with them on the beach. All he could see was that domestic and intercoastal trade was keeping at least some of the war fleet busy. Ports like New York, New Orleans and San Francisco were boom towns with ships anchored in the stream waiting their turn at the cargo-laden docks. Thus finding himself still riding high on the tide even though the whole economy ashore showed unmistakable signs of breaking up, he kept right on demanding things. Seamen's wages were raised to ninety dollars a month, with sixty-five cents an hour overtime both at sea and in port.

When at last the glittering superstructure came crashing down in 1921 the talk about cutting wages grew sharper. But in San Francisco the sailors cast a doubting eye at the still-opulent scene along the Embarcadero and turned a deaf ear to anything the shipowners had to say. A lockout was threatened. Andrew Furuseth called his men onto the beach. Ashore they found the puzzling situation of ex-soldiers, shipbuilders and factory hands apparently starving in the midst of plenty and willing to work at any price. The postwar boom had many paradoxes and that was one of them. The shipowners carried out their threatened lockout and opened their own hiring halls along the docks where seamen could come in and register under police protection. Boys and men who had signed on at the corner drugstores during the war, Shipping Board- or Navy-trained and now desperate for work, took the ships to sea.

Bitter war was waged on both coasts. The longshoremen, not on strike, continued to load the ships. It was a devastating blow to the strike's effectiveness. The sailors, baffled and alarmed, deserted the union in droves. During the summer the Seamen's Union met final defeat when Justice Van Fleet of the United States District Court issued an order preventing any union from interfering with water-borne commerce in United States ports. The strike was broken. Wages were cut to $62.50 a month. The eight-hour day was abolished. Many sailors worked four hours on and four hours off, watch and watch. Mates and engineers were deprived of their night reliefs in port, and at sea they were required to occupy their spare time with red lead, paintbrush and chipping hammer. Worse than all this, the grade books came back. Copied after the British system, they were a sea record carried by each seaman in which were registered his conduct and ability according to the shipowner's point of view and without which no man could get a ship.

This broke the union's back. Wages were cut again. Living conditions aboard ship grew worse. At the dawn of the "new era," beginning in 1923, amidst the debris of a navy destroying itself while people ashore were keeping cool with Coolidge, foreign crews bred to low standards were again taking over the fo'c'sles of American ships.

For the sailors the ebbing tide was in full strength.

There is more, much more, to the long, devious and harrowing tale of what became of the merchant fleet on the ebb tide of the twenties. The effects make clearer reading than the causes. The effects in this period were painfully clear: six out of every ten ships carrying America's overseas trade were foreign vessels. A desperate Congress passed a new Merchant Marine Shipping Act in 1928 providing, among other things, subsidies in the form of ocean mail contracts, as had been done so many years before for the ill-starred paddle wheelers of the Collins Line. Every sort of rehabilitation scheme was tried to get the patient on its feet. Loan funds were set up by the government totaling a quarter of a billion dollars for building new and faster ships; small down payments were arranged; low interest rates—but nothing could remedy the fatal illness, not even direct gold transfusions from the United States Treasury.

Then at last the trade itself vanished. With Europe's economic depression becoming our own in 1929 the graphmakers took to pasting strips on the bottoms of their charts to make space for the downward-plunging curves, and the jig was up.

It was the beginning of an era that saw East Coast crews being paid thirty-five dollars a month—when they could get it—and it was ushered in by the second great naval disaster for the United States Fleet in less than a decade. Again the scene of action was on dry land, where this nation's greatest naval defeats have taken place. Once more the trouble was that, from the viewpoint of other nations, the United States had too many warships still afloat or building, that some were too big and others too numerous or had too many guns; and anyway Messrs. Kellogg and Briand, of the United States and France respectively, had agreed there were to be no more wars. In fact they had outlawed war as an instrument of foreign policy.

The list of United States losses following the London Conference of 1930 would have caused a Congressional investigation of the admirals in time of war: two first-line battleships in active service scrapped; another first-line battleship destroyed in target practice; five first-line cruisers in active service scrapped, another sunk; forty-four submarines scrapped; eighty-eight destroyers, four light cruisers, one heavy cruiser scrapped, junked, sunk. A total of 223 naval craft of all types were lost at the Washington and London council tables.

Ten years after the creation of her greatest merchant and battle fleets, America's maritime hopes lay rusting at anchor, piled in the junk yards or rocked on the ocean's floor.

20

"As I Was A-walkin' Down Paradise Street"

As I was a-walkin' down Paradise Street—
    Aye, aye, blow the man down!
A big fat policeman I chanced to meet—
    Oh, give me some time to blow the man down!

IN THE days before Hitler's hooked-cross bombers Paradise Street was a thoroughfare down by the old sailing-ship docks of Liverpool numbering among its dingy buildings the Sailors' Home. The chanty with its endless verses must be sung to be appreciated, and appreciated it most certainly was when Jack scrambled ashore off a Western Ocean blood boat, sick, beaten and half-starved, into the waiting arms of a well-heeled crimp. It is a song that was known wherever sailors spent a night ashore, for Paradise Street was also every unbeautiful waterfront mecca from Limehouse to Zamboanga; it's what old shellbacks are talking about when they nod wisely and say they've seen every port in the world.

Paradise Street is also a state of mind. A good many school-ship boys today have never heard of the street or the song either, and care less, but the state of mind and the things that engendered it they would instantly recognize.

All through the twenties the American merchant marine suffered a depression in which some fifty thousand men were competing for twenty thousand berths. Many of them were willing to work without pay just to get food and lodging. As the tide continued its outward flow, sweeping the rest of the country's economy with it into the early thirties, the sailor's lot became more hungry, more desperate than any living seaman could recollect. Which is saying plenty. Paradise Street was called the Slave Mart. Shipowners, equally desperate, went to any lengths to keep what ships they had at sea in the losing struggle with foreign competitors. As one result, star gangs handling cargoes ashore were employed over long, steady periods in the interests of efficiency and consequent lower costs, which meant that favored workers were paid as much as fifty dollars a week, while the rest took the crumbs at ten and twelve dollars a week when they could get it.

Morals and morale ashore and afloat collapsed. It was the age of realism with a vengeance. What a shrewdly placed handful of cigars or a bottle of whisky wouldn't buy, cash money would. On the streets outside the company hiring halls from coast to coast an A.B.'s ticket could be purchased from a hungry seaman for ten dollars. The market was flooded. Any landlubber with five dollars and an inside track on a job could come into possession of a qualified lifeboatman's certificate and ship out on passenger liners up to and including the rechristened German mammoths *Leviathan* and *George Washington*. College boys, fruit pickers, song-and-dance men, anybody with a little loose change and a yen for a trip to sea could shoulder aside the helpless professional seaman and take his place in the fo'c'sle. With more seamen than ships to go around, there were instances in the other extreme where vessels were sailing in which every man jack aboard, from ordinary seamen up, held a licensed officer's ticket.

At sea, with some notable exceptions like United States Lines ships, the aging merchant navy jammed aboard larger crews of untrained men and boys rather than sign on smaller crews of skilled and more highly paid able-bodied seamen, crowding them into fo'c'sles so ill-equipped and neglected that all hands were crawling with vermin before the land birds were out of sight. Filthy toilets opened directly into messrooms. Sheets on the bunks, a hard-won luxury of wartime days, were changed once a month, if then. There were occasions when hospital beds were sold for additional passenger space, causing sick or injured seamen to be cared for in the fo'c'sles. Back ashore to begin the long hunt for the next ship—a hunt that would likely take from two to three months—there were instances of crews being paid off in I.O.U.'s instead of wages.

Along San Francisco's Paradise Street, the Embarcadero, there were hungry men in 1932 who were learning new, stronger words than any they had ever heard at sea. In the blurred mimeographed pages of a new sort of seaman's manual called the *Waterfront Worker* they found a voice, and old-fashioned talk of crimps and hard-case skippers and mates gave way to strange new epithets. Now there were scabherders, goons, beef squads and finks, and there were hot cargoes and quickies and phonies and whing-ding artists. In the *Worker* the bemused sailors found their own unreasoning hatred and fear of the company hiring boss, who for the most part was now not hiring. Andrew Furuseth, getting pretty old now, had spoken their hearts in an earlier day when on one of his not-infrequent consignments to the city prison he said, "You can put me in jail, but you cannot give me narrower quarters than as a seaman I have always had. You cannot give me coarser food than I have always eaten. You cannot make me lonelier than I have always been." They were words the wanderer on the earth's horizons, the rootless, the homeless, the eternally unmoneyed sailor could understand. On them Andrew

Furuseth had helped to build, brick by brick, the International Seamen's Union of America, and in those words lay the power of reason while reason prevailed.

But an empty stomach knows no reason. At the Sailor's Hall on Clay Street in San Francisco, old Saint Andrew's power was gone. He was being called "a tool of the shipowners" now, and the voices of a new crowd were demanding something stronger than words and reason. The *Waterfront Worker* urged revolt against the company union—the hated Blue Book union controlling the San Francisco Bay region—and railed against the speed-up system, the favoritism of the star gangs and the constant threat of layoffs. Perhaps Andrew Furuseth never grasped the new complexities of sea trucking in a world fighting for its economic life. A sailor to him was still a sailor, not a longshoreman or any other sort of landlubber, and the deep-rooted implications of what it meant to work a ship in these times was more than he could, or would, understand. Cargoes were brought into port by seamen, but they were unloaded by longshoremen, piled into temporary shelter by warehousemen and hauled away by teamsters. Break one link in the chain and you have broken the power of all its links. This had been demonstrated beyond the shadow of a doubt in 1921 when the longshoremen's failure to strike with the sailors had carried them all down to bitter and lasting defeat.

Over the rising gale of angry voices along the Embarcadero rose the twang of a man from "down under." Alfred Renton Bridges, an Australian seaman dubbed Harry by his shipmates, who had sailed through the Golden Gate some dozen years before in a South Sea Island barkentine called the *Ysabel,* had liked what he found here and quit the sea for the docks. Dark-haired, droop-lidded, his sharp nose shrewdly turned to the prevailing winds, he was a new breed ready and able to offer the baffled men on the beach a new union. Into the International Longshoremen's Association they swarmed. If their Marxist associates had their own private aims beyond the aims of the rebellious rank and file, few, if any, cared, for they had found an audible voice at last.

In March 1934 they felt strong enough to talk things over with the Waterfront Employers' Union. Through Bridges they demanded the right to their own hiring hall, which would mean rotation of jobs, *i.e.,* hiring from a union list. They demanded also higher wages and better working conditions ashore and afloat, and the right to negotiate for the entire Pacific Coast. Their demands were met with blunt refusal. The men voted to strike. More negotiations followed. Finally, early in May, the ships were tied up along seventeen miles of water front, the winches stopped their pounding and the sailors, with all to win and nothing to lose, poured ashore. Inside of a week the Pacific Coast, north and south, was strikebound. For the first time in their lives operators beheld from their office windows in every port from San Diego to Seattle a motionless harbor from which not one cargo vessel stirred.

It was a new and shocking experience with no precedent for finding a solution. But if there had been any doubt that this was a finish fight, the Waterfront Employers' Union promptly allayed it with this advertisement for strikebreakers:

LONGSHOREMEN WANTED

Experience desirable but not necessary
Apply Navy Landing Pier
Foot of Howard Street, San Francisco
85c an hour straight time
$1.25 an hour overtime
Strike conditions prevail
Waterfront Employers' Union
By W. J. Petersen

Hoboes from the outlying jungles, farmers, factory workers, college boys, anybody willing to take a chance on getting his head cracked, were brought in and put aboard the ships as "maintenance men." Every expedient was seized on to get the ships to sea. The new hands were armed with ax handles to negotiate the picket lines, and laid-up ships were taken over and fitted as temporary quarters.

Sea and shore workers, united in a Joint Strike Committee with Harry Bridges as their chairman, were agreed not to make a separate peace. Bridges thumbed rides to outlying union halls of truck drivers' locals and told over and over again the sea and shore workers' story until the truck drivers, imbued with the rank-and-file spirit of the movement, voted over the protests of their old-line union officials to join the strike.

In the picket lines were mates and engineers as well as seamen and dockworkers, for the Masters, Mates, and Pilots Union had joined the strikers. Not many licensed officers were members of the union, however, and, as the shipowners confidently predicted, only a handful of them left their posts. Ships anchored in the bay were thereupon forcibly boarded by the strikers, and mates and engineers loyal to the owners were dragged off them. Even captains were carried bodily from their commands, a blow to authority both legal and traditional from which it would take years to recover.

Newspapers stormed against the strike, giving voice to the operators' charges that it was Communist-led, but so many accusations were being shotgunned in all directions that the charges were dissipated by too many targets. In any case San Francisco knew sailors. Its people knew that a sailor was the most independent worker in America, that four out of five of them had no wives, that three out of five had no address. They were aware, too, that few sailors followed any organized political line, that a fo'c'sle hand was willing to take anything anybody would give him, always keeping his weather eye on the main chance regardless of what the ideology of his union leaders might be. So far as a sailor was concerned one hard fact stood out above all else: when he lost a strike his wages were cut, his working hours were increased and his food became worse; when he won, his wages were raised, his working hours were reduced and his food became edible.

This is not to suggest that San Francisco liked the strike. In one month, it was estimated by its merchants, the strike had cost the city three hundred million dollars. As the third month began with no settlement in sight the operators decided to move freight at any cost. The National Guard was called out by Governor Merriam, a pitched battle with police on Rincon Hill ensued and on a day to be remembered in San Francisco as "Bloody Thursday" the pickets had two of their men killed as their lines were shattered with tear gas, guns and clubs. Court records show that the police fired in self-defense. But by this time few people were interested in anything as dull as court records. One of the dead was an overseas veteran of the war, and when the strikers led a funeral procession up Market Street to the strains of Beethoven's Funeral March the weight of public opinion was with the sailors. The rank-and-file union men, sweeping aside their old-line leaders of Andrew Furu-seth's time, jammed through the Central Labor Council a call for a general strike. Eleven days after the Battle of Rincon Hill, San Francisco, with nearly 150,000 workers idle, was a dead city.

The streets were muffled in the eerie quiet of the general strike for three days. On the morning of the second day, however, the municipal streetcars were rattling again, at the request of the General Strike Committee. This broke the log jam. Four days later the teamsters returned to work. The shipowners decided to talk things over further with the seamen. Both sides agreed to submit to arbitration.

When the talking was over, the sailors took a look around and found their wages were up to forty-five dollars a month, with seventy-five cents an hour for overtime work. Aboard his ship on sailing day a fo'c'sle hand found his bunk made up with clean sheets and blankets. In the lavatory there were showers with hot and cold running water, his next meal was being prepared out in the galley, and in the messroom there was an urn of hot coffee ready for him when he came off watch. Three regular watches were established on those lines where they had been discontinued, meaning the return of the eight-hour day. And there were no grade books. They had been publicly burned in front of the Ferry Building. Down on the docks the longshoremen were paid ninety-five cents an hour for a six-hour day, with $1.40 an hour for overtime. Hiring halls were jointly controlled with the operators.

Those were the material rewards. But there was a larger gain foreshadowing a new era in relations between the men who worked the ships and those in the countinghouses. For the success of the strike gave shipworkers and dockworkers a feeling of unity for the first time. With it came a heady sense of power. The sailors had at last got their horny hands on the pendulum of events, and—understandably, all things considered—they set about giving it a heavy swing indeed.

At sea, discipline vanished. The officers, their careers at stake, who by tradition and instinct had for the most part remained loyal to the shipowners during the strike, came to the bitter realization that they had only the sailors to thank for their improved lot. Rarely had their wages or working conditions been voluntarily bettered for them by the shipowners. It was only through the affiliation of their own union with the striking sailors that they had received such benefits as increased wages, overtime pay and relief in port. Despised, now, by the crews, their authority gave way to the power of the fo'c'sle. Everything was done to discredit authority of the officers and even the captain himself. Fire and boat drills, always regarded by the foremast hand as a nuisance, now became a joke. No part of the ship was inviolate to the crew, including the passengers' quarters, where their occasional effrontery, lack of courtesy and not-infrequent drunkenness played a large part in discouraging Americans from using their own ships. In showdowns between officers and crew it was generally the officer who got his orders from the front office to pack his gear and seek another berth. Masters and mates who got into "beefs" with crew members were regarded by the harassed operators as costly troublemakers, better left on the beach.

No grievance, real or fancied, was too petty to cause a brief local strike, called a quickie. Ships were prevented from sailing for no better reason than a lack of Worcestershire sauce in the crew's galley. On one occasion the Secretary of State, on an official mission, was held up in port for eight hours aboard the Munson Line ship, *American Legion,* because there were not enough sailors available who belonged to the right union. Volumes have been filled with these harrowing incidents, and the story is a familiar one. The seamen had at last succeeded in turning the tide of their own misfortunes and were riding the current for all it was worth.

Trade-starved ships, laxity in safety regulations, labor strife, greed and ignorance—all these were a part of the flotsam and jetsam on the outgoing tide. Symptomatic of the ailments that had laid hold of the decaying merchant fleet is the fate of the *Morro Castle*.

Steaming through choppy seas one September night in 1934, this Ward Liner was inbound from Havana to New York with over three hundred returning vacationists. Earlier in the evening, like an evil omen, her captain had died and his body lay sealed in his cabin. Chief Mate William Warms had taken over. In the small hours of the morning Warms was startled by the cry of "Fire!" The fire-patrol watchman came pounding down from the boat deck to report smoke pouring from a ventilator. On the bridge the automatic alarm bell had failed to go off. The ancient electrically controlled detection system and smoke-reporting device showed nothing. By the time the mate and watchman reached the promenade deck the lounge was a sheet of flame. It was too late to close the fire screens. Up on A deck the passengers were raving, trapped inside.

Finally the "automatic" alarm added its din to the panic. While men, women and children scrambled for the boat deck the lights went out, the alarm bell stopped its clamor and the engines went dead. The *Morro Castle* lay wallowing in the trough of the sea, her leeside lifeboats hidden under a screen of wind-driven smoke. A few passengers, their hands and faces black, eyes running water, were shunted to the boats while most of the unskilled crew looked out for themselves. At last eight boats pulled away, none of them full. One lifeboat with a capacity for seventy-eight people contained but two seamen.

Of the 318 passengers aboard, ninety-one died that night. Of the 231 crewmen, thirty-one lost their lives. In the morning, after attempts had failed to tow the burning hulk to New York, the *Morro Castle* was allowed to drift ashore off Asbury Park, a charred monument to the dying merchant marine.

In the next three years more bloody seamen's strikes followed. Out of one of them in New York in 1936 the National Maritime Union was formed under the leadership of Joseph Curran, an Irish-American from the lower East Side who had come ashore after fifteen years in the fo'c'sle to head what became the world's largest trade-union of sailors. Curran, no Communist, nevertheless managed to use to his advantage the Marxist politicians who would have liked to control the tough, restive and cynical seamen of the National Maritime Union. He finally earned for it a description in a United States Maritime Labor Board report in 1939 as "the most fiercely independent segment of labor to be found anyplace in the world." Its members made up the crews of grain and ore ships on the Great Lakes, of stern wheelers on the Mississippi (even more active than in Mark Twain's day), as well as of American oceangoing merchant ships and tankers.

Curran himself, a massive, fractured-nosed giant of a man whose formal schooling didn't take him beyond the fifth grade, came to look on his union as considerably more than a bargaining agent for higher wages. The union's weekly newspaper, *The Pilot,* said:

We feel that the same spirit which fought for religious liberty and political freedom in the past is today fighting for industrial democracy in the guise of the N.M.U. Our bloody fights for meetings in company towns have protected the right of assembly. Our insistence on our right to speak our mind, even when what we said and what we stood for has been misunderstood, has protected the right of free speech. Our fight to distribute handbills and union literature has buttressed the freedom of the press. . . .

To Joe Curran, as to many others caught up in the tide of social change sweeping the country, trade-unionism became something like a religious sect. "The unions," he said, "have made it possible for thousands of men and women to participate in decisions governing their own lives. Participation is what makes the difference. That's democracy." In the registration room for new members off the main lobby of the National Maritime Union's six-story headquarters building at 346 West

A POSTWAR MARINER-CLASS FREIGHTER

On her trial run off the Delaware Capes the *Keystone Mariner* exceeded her design speed of 30 knots by a substantial margin.

A CLASSROOM ON A SCHOOLSHIP OF WORLD WAR II

Seventeenth Street, New York, he caused to be erected a large
sign bearing an excerpt from the union's standard contract with
128 shipping companies:

THERE SHALL BE NO DISCRIMINATION BECAUSE
OF RACE, CREED, COLOR, OR NATIONAL ORIGIN

America's merchant fleet had claw-hauled its way off many a
wind-lashed shore in the past, but, driven on the death-laden
winds of the great social wars in Europe and Asia, blowing in a
rising gale down the decade of the thirties, it seemed headed
for permanent disaster.

Three quarters of the offshore merchant fleet still carrying
the flag, and now numbering little more than four hundred
vessels, was rapidly approaching obsolescence. The government
was pumping gold into its failing bloodstream—nearly four
billion dollars in the past twenty years—but the rescue attempt
seemed hopeless. Of the original twenty-three hundred vessels
the Shipping Board had started with, less than two hundred
still remained in Federal ownership. The rest had been sold,
junked or lost. In travel to Europe, one out of every four
Americans crossing the Atlantic went on an American ship.
The rest spent, in round figures, a hundred million dollars
annually to cross in more modern, more efficient British,
French, Italian or German ships.

Old age and sailor trouble were not the only reasons why
American vessels were sailing half empty. There was also
money trouble. For if the sailors' hands were deep in the
pockets of the shipowners, there was still one place where they
could not get them—the United States Treasury. That long-
familiar poaching ground was still the private preserve of the
shipowners. In Washington a Senate committee buzzing with
the perennial question, "Where in hell did the money go?"

agonized through a tedious investigation of the twenty-six-million-dollar-a-year subsidy which had been doled out to the operators for years and finally came up with the answer. To nobody's surprise, except perhaps the operators', it developed that nobody knew. It took a long, long time to reach such a painful conclusion, officially, at least, and in the fitful squalls that swept Congress one of the early casualties was the old Shipping Board. It was banished under an alias to the Department of Commerce, to be quietly interred.

At last, in March 1935, President Roosevelt recommended to Congress that a new, honest form of shipping subsidy be instituted forthwith. Considering the squabbling, the throatcutting, the drafting and redrafting that dragged on for over a year, which was finally topped off with a steaming filibuster during the hottest summer anybody in Washington could remember, it is a tribute to legislative gestation that the Merchant Marine Act of 1936 was born at all. That it turned out to be a healthy child, able to revitalize America's ships and the men who sail them, is nothing short of miraculous.

The child did not turn out to be the hot-eyed reformer that many predicted. When it made its debut in 1937 in the charge of a five-man commission headed by Joseph P. Kennedy, it soon became evident the act meant what it said: "To further the development and maintenance of an adequate and well-balanced American merchant marine, to promote the commerce of the United States, to aid in the national defense, to repeal certain former legislation. . . ." In the next thirty-six pages of its maiden speech there was some pretty fancy language better left to the attention of statisticians and future investigating committees. By and large the act's simple purpose was to get new ships to sea. There was no loose talk about "achieving supremacy" or "regaining our place in the sun." That chance had passed years before. But at least it could be planned to launch a modest two hundred thousand tons of shipping. How modest these initial plans were are understood by comparing the building going on in other parts of the world at that time. England and Ireland, for instance, were building a million tons more than this; the Germans were building a quarter of a million tons more, and the Japanese were building over a hundred thousand tons more than was planned by the United States.

At least it was a move in the right direction. The frank subsidies called for by the President to be substituted for the old concealed mail-pay subsidies meant an honest aboveboard payment of the differences in the cost of operating an American ship as against operating a foreign one. For a company planning to build a ship there was similar encouragement. Above all, among other approvals required for the ship's plans were those of the navy. *All agreements stipulated the navy had to be satisfied that there was provision for quick conversion of the vessel into a naval auxiliary in case of war.* It had taken 160 years to learn the lesson, but now at last the merchant and battle fleets, if not legally wedded, at least had an understanding.

The anchor was tipped and coming up. The United States Maritime Commission had hoisted the Blue Peter.

PART 5

Battle of
the Seven Seas

21

NEW SHIPS, NEW WAYS

WHEN THE American people picked up their Sunday-morning papers on September 3, 1939, to discover that the world had again run amuck, the United States for the first time in its history had the nucleus of a fighting merchant navy.

The privateers of '76 and 1812 had been hastily and successfully thrown into the breach to save their days, as had the knocked-together fleet of the First World War, but in each of those crises they had started from scratch without organization, without plan or equipment for a sustained military effort. Now, as the Nazi war machine rolled into Poland, American cargo and transport vessels were still largely on paper, the plans were incomplete and scattered, but the organization for creating a permanent fighting merchant fleet was in flesh and blood. In its two years of existence the United States Maritime Commission had rigged up a skeleton blueprint from which to build merchant ships for the future, come war or peace.

The job had not been easy. By comparison with today's arithmetical dream world where half a dozen ciphers are added to all public projects, the ambitious work sheet laid out in 1937 by the Maritime Commission's new chairman, Admiral Emory S. Land, seems more like plans for a yachting regatta. To get a bearing on what the commission was up against, it should be remembered that in the fourteen years prior to 1937 not one oceangoing cargo ship in foreign trade had been built in an American yard. The ship factories of the First World War were gone. Great shipyards like the Cramp yard at Philadelphia had lain idle, stripped of their tools and equipment, for ten years and more. The biggest of them all, Hog Island, had been sold to the city of Philadelphia for use as a municipal airport. In the entire country there were just ten shipyards, with a total of forty-six ways capable of producing a vessel over four hundred feet long. On a basis of speed and earning capacity the American merchant marine trailed in eighth place in the world-wide race for markets, behind England, Germany, Japan, France, Italy, Norway and Holland.

A checkup made by the Maritime Commission before the war showed that the largest merchant fleet they could reasonably hope for by 1942 was 117 ships. Such ships were not to come off an assembly line like so many steel boxes. Planned as ships of the merchant navy in the truest sense, they were shrewdly designed in three general classes to do battle on the world's commercial sea lanes in time of peace and to be readily convertible for naval purposes in time of war. With time and economy of operation urgent considerations, fuel-guzzling giants with their thousand-men crews like the *Normandie* were thought to be as dead as Jason. So-called "C" ships were laid out to meet combined cargo and passenger demands comfortably, efficiently and, above all, economically. The three standard designs were for C-1 cargo ships of about 7,500 dead-weight tons, turning up a speed of fourteen or fifteen knots; for C-2's of 9,000 tons with a speed of fifteen knots or over; and for C-3's of about 12,000 tons, capable of speeds ranging from sixteen up to twenty-one knots.

Fifty of these ships a year for the next ten years was the goal set in 1937. They were to be a streamlined challenge to a stream-lined and deadly businesslike world.

Admiral Land's job was to rebuild not only the merchant navy but to call back somehow the vanished skills to the ship-yards and to re-create a seafaring class. To build the ships, training schools for shipworkers were set up with the help and advice of private builders. To sail them a cadet corps was or-ganized for training youngsters as deck and engineer officers under the guidance of the United States Coast Guard. Seaman training on a nonmilitary basis was also provided in Maritime Service Schools on both coasts and the Gulf.

The proof of the pudding was in the eating. When the first new ship in service, the *Challenge,* a C-2 vessel, matched per-formance with an ancestral Hog Islander it was plain that the Maritime Commission was on the right course. On October 11, 1939, a Hog Island freighter, the *Crown City,* built for the First World War and assigned to the Pioneer Line, sailed from New York on the long voyage to India. Nearly a month later the *Challenge* sailed on the same voyage in the service of the same line. On the morning of February 24 the Hog came wallowing up New York harbor on her return run. In her wake, less than an hour behind, came the *Challenge.* Both ships had returned with capacity cargoes from an identical voyage—the *Crown City* with six thousand tons, the *Challenge* with seven thou-sand. The new ship had proved fifty per cent faster than the old and had used half as much fuel on the voyage. In dollar terms it forecast a saving of some $35,000 a year for ships of the *Challenge* type in fuel costs alone.

This, then, was the new breed of ship at sea and on the draw-ing boards which, together with the organization behind it, constituted the bedplates for building a resurgent merchant navy. The remnants of America's old merchant fleet, stirring to answer the call of Europe's war needs, had aged beyond its allotted economic span of twenty years, but the *Challenge* and her kind following her over the horizon gave hope for the future as dimly envisioned in those early days of the war in Europe.

Again the Battle of Food. Again in 1939, as in 1914, foreign ships withdrew from United States ports to feed and supply their homelands. And again, for lack of ships, there loomed shortages in such indispensables as rubber, tin, chromium, manganese, to say nothing of coffee, tea, rice and sugar, while the products of America's factory-rich but ship-poor industrial colossus commenced to glut the docks and railway sidings.

Promptly the wild scramble for ships began. Any ship to float a cargo. Gone on the winds of necessity was cautious talk of fuel costs, speed and maintenance. The Hog, at last, was in its glory. A tramp ship that had gone begging for lack of takers at eight or ten dollars a ton before the war was now being fought over at prices of fifty, sixty, seventy dollars a ton and no end in sight. To old-timers it was the same old song with new words. A Hog cleared port in January 1940 under charter to carry motor trucks, copper and blankets to France. The only expense to her owners was the cost of fuel, the charterers to pay the rest. When she returned she had grossed $132,000 for her owners, with only her fuel costs to come out of the profits. And there was the *Bellflower,* another old Shipping Board vessel built in 1919, now selling for over $300,000. Her new owner spent another $150,000 reconditioning her, and sent her to Italy with a cargo of coal. Gross profit, $85,000. In the spring of 1940 cargo rates averaged twenty dollars a ton or more. A 7,500-ton tramp could gross $125,000 on a single voyage. Even taking out a round hundred thousand for the skyrocketing costs of insurance, wages and bonuses to the crew, this left a net profit to the owner of such a vessel, for the round trip, of some $20,000.

"Tons," by the way, no longer had any connection with Captain Popham's reference to the "tons burthen" of the *Virginia*, launched on the Kennebec three hundred years before. These modern figures referred to dead-weight tons, which represent the carrying capacity of a vessel, including fuel, fresh water and stores. Thus a 7,500-ton Hog Islander like the old *Quistconck* and her relatives could actually carry about six thousand tons of freight. Unfortunately it became a confusing wartime custom to refer to dead-weight tonnage while a ship was afloat and to list her gross tonnage when reporting her a victim of the enemy. Perhaps this was because in reckoning gross tonnage about one third is knocked off the dead-weight figure, thus making all hands feel a little better about the loss.

And losses there were. The undersea pig boats from Kiel were on the prowl again. As the Nazi conquest thundered into its second year, England alone was on her way to losing one third of her merchant fleet. Worse, under the pounding of enemy bombers many British shipyards already lay in tangled ruins. Hastily the British sent a Merchant Shipbuilding Mission touring from Maine to California to look for likely builders of emergency cargo ships to keep her life lines open. It placed an order for sixty ships, all patterned after a standard coal-burning British tramp. The United States Government, struggling with a new scheme for financing an old problem, this time under the name of Lend-Lease, followed Britain's lead by ordering two hundred vessels of the same general type with certain refinements such as equipping them to burn oil instead of coal. Soon the United States order was raised to over four hundred, and finally, as the crescendo of mine, bomb and torpedo rose at sea, to nearly a thousand emergency-built ships.

From the Propaganda Ministry in Berlin came hoots of derision. "Paper ships!" "The Americans," said Herr Goebbels, "have gone mad. The more hopeless their goal becomes, the more grandiose their plans!" To more than one hardheaded American shipbuilder in 1940 it looked as if Herr Goebbels might be right at that. How could a nation of landsmen which had found difficulty with a program to build five hundred ships over a period of ten years hope to build a thousand ships *now?* Were there more Hog Islands with their too-much-too-late ships in the offing? Had Admiral Land and the Maritime Commission, as Goebbels suggested, indeed blown its collective top?

Faced with the terrible necessity of building a fleet of cargo vessels in months instead of years, the prewar plans, ideas and hopes were scrapped. The immediate need was to build a single emergency type of ship for ourselves as well as for the British on a schedule of five or six months per ship.

It was decided that these would be EC-2's, popularly known as Liberty ships, "the work horse of the sea," adapted from the Sunderland-built British northeast tramp under the skilled hand of an American yacht designer and naval architect, William Francis Gibbs, who was later to design the ocean queen *United States.* With an eye to avoiding, as far as was practical, the boxlike Hogs of yesteryear, these new vessels were given sheer, meaning a graceful dip and rise from bow to stern, and camber, meaning a rounded weather deck to carry water shipped in heavy seas to the scuppers. This meant extra labor in molding and furnacing the hull plates, but also a better ship and fewer regrets in the future. Four hundred and twenty feet long, with seven main watertight compartments and five holds capable of carrying some ten thousand tons of freight, the Liberty presented a surprisingly trim figure with her raked stem, compact superstructure and cruiser stern. To avoid an inevitable bottleneck in turbines, gears, electrical equipment and intricate machining, it was decided to propel her with a simple old-time, two-story-high, triple-expansion engine burning oil, unlike her coal-burning British counterpart.

"A five-year ship," commented Admiral Land, admitting they were obsolete before they were launched. "But this time we're building ships for *this* war." The Maritime Commission was determined that old mistakes would be avoided. Instead of concentrating shipbuilding in a few vast yards with consequent congestion of railroads, housing and supplies, the commission planned new yards purely as assembly points, laid out on a nation-wide scale so as to tap as many available supplies of industrial capacity and labor as possible. As the bulldozers, pile drivers and dredges bit into back-bay swamps and mud flats, readying the ground for shipways, a spread-the-work policy was put into execution, farming out contracts for the thousands of items that go into a ship.

With the Liberty's design rigidly frozen, parts were interchangeable. The flow of parts and supplies was regulated and dispatched to the shipyards from one master control at the Maritime Commission. The commission paid the bills; the single function of the yards was to fit the pieces together and launch the ships. Orders for parts went out to manufacturers in over two thirds of the states. Slowly, fumblingly at first, shipbuilding from hull plates to binnacle became a country-wide industry as the gargantuan assembly belt commenced to grind across the nation. Training schools for three quarters of a million shipworkers were completed or nearing completion in 1941. With practice the know-how came easier, yards picked up speed. The dimly remembered plan to build five hundred ships by 1947 seemed trifling in the face of an order reducing the standard contract time for a 10,500-ton Liberty to 105 days from keel-laying to delivery, ready for sea. Already some of them were nearing completion on a faster schedule than that. Even the long-range program of "C" ships—the modern "tailor-made" beauties designed before the war—were now being built on a schedule calling for a hundred a year instead of fifty.

To man the merchant fleet, men were trained in schools geared to produce over six thousand licensed officers and twenty-five thousand seamen within the next two years as the ships came off the ways.

On September 27, 1941, the first Liberty ship was launched. Named *Patrick Henry,* this first-born of the wartime merchant fleet was the cynosure of all eyes in the shipping world as she steamed to sea to keep a promise. The promise was based on an estimate that supplies and equipment required for each soldier landed abroad weighed fifteen tons and that a Liberty could normally load nine thousand tons, depending on the cargo. This was enough for six hundred men. The promise was kept when the *Patrick Henry* gave heart to her sponsors and the doubters as well by making a 7,600-mile voyage with a back-breaking load of eleven thousand long tons at an average speed of eleven and a half knots. This didn't compare with the record of a "C" ship like the *Challenge,* which had halved a Hog's time on a voyage to India and back; but, measured against its First World War counterpart, the Hog, which carried seventy-five hundred tons at a bare ten knots, the *Patrick Henry* looked pretty good, particularly when pencils were sharpened and it was figured out that Liberty and Hog had each consumed about the same daily amount of fuel.

To the military planners it was a clear demonstration that the Liberty ship would live up to its promise of more carrying capacity per ton of construction, per man power of labor, per horsepower of machinery and, most critical of all, per ton of steel than anything like it ever built.

In the half-real world of 1940-1941 the idea of total war for everybody everywhere, as carefully charted, explained in advance and then being conscientiously demonstrated by the

ex-house painter of Vienna, was consigned in the United States
to the realm of never-never land. To most Americans the war
in Europe was still a long way off. The stubborn resistance to
a new idea, as poor John Fitch could have testified, is exceeded
only by the resistance to abandonment of an old idea. And the
old idea of all aid short of war—and short of running in the
red—was enjoying its time-honored esteem. Of greater moment
to most American shipowners were their fiscal ledgers being
closed in mid-1941 on a year of feasting after the long, long
years of fasting.

United States shipping had not looked so good since the
golden years of the clipper ships. For the first time since the
Civil War American ships were carrying the bulk of American
cargoes in overseas trade. Contributing to the miracle were
ghosts of the past which had been dreaming away the years in
the back reaches of old bone yards. The laid-up merchant fleet
of the First World War, swinging at its weed-hung anchor cables in the James River in Virginia, at New Orleans and on the
Pacific Coast—over a hundred ships in all, classed hopelessly as
a war reserve years before—had at last come into its own.
Emerging like blowzy prima donnas from a shady past, they
joined the march down to the sea. With foreign trade nearly
double the size of anything seen in the preceding few years,
shipowners saw their first ray of hope to accumulate a surplus
for future operations. As in the days of the privateers, there was
the dual satisfaction of serving the nation in its moment of
extremity while at the same time reaping a rich reward. From
an American point of view based on past experience, this was
the way a war should be run. Let the warring world fight in
its own back yard while peaceful homefolk gather in the spoils.
All through this period of the European war ran a deadly parallel to events of 1914-1917. To many there was the eerie feeling
of reliving an old nightmare.

Even our unofficial allies, the British, were having difficulty rooting out old ideas in which the fight for trade and the fight for existence were badly confused.

On the complaint of American ship operators the House Merchant Marine Committee found evidence that the British were crowding American shippers out of a share in Lend-Lease business. Lest this seem a rather hoggish worry in view of the shipping boom being currently enjoyed by all hands, it should be remembered that speculators, fly-by-night operators and anybody else who could lay hands on a ship were figuring largely in the business. Their overhead was usually nil, with their offices in their hats, and most of them, as Admiral Land remarked, put their operations on a basis of "we'll furnish the ocean if you'll furnish the ships." Old-line operators, battered into caution over the lean years, took a longer view of things. It was this group who were thinking of the war of trade that inevitably follows the war of guns when they complained to the committee. They pointed out that the Lend-Lease Act gave England title to war materials at the American docks, which was fair enough, since they owned the goods acquired by the British Purchasing Commission in the amount of some four billion dollars; but the British had designated the Cunard Line to handle the freight, excluding American shipping firms from their own docks. As a clincher to the complaint it was shown that Cunard Line stock had gone up four hundred per cent since the beginning of the war.

The *New York Journal of Commerce* reported that testimony on the O'Leary Bill, aimed at remedying the trouble, revealed that every ton of freight leaving the United States, loaned or leased to England, was first passing through the hands of the British Ministry of War Transport. Furthermore, it was brought out, there was a gradual infiltration of British control "not only in the freight forwarding business, but ultimately over the operations of the entire American merchant marine." Control was being gained by Cunard on the Atlantic Coast, by the Harrison Line on the Gulf and by the Furness Line on the Pacific—all British lines. It amounted to the power of life and death over a rapidly growing competitor, the American merchant navy.

Months later the problem was to be partially solved by the establishment of an Office of Supervision of Cargo Clearances through which export bookings on some routes were placed under joint Anglo-American control. But American shipping men had had a sharp reminder that theirs was not the only long view being taken in a world falling apart. A great deal about total war in all its ramifications was yet to be learned by Americans and British alike.

For the United States a tragic lesson was not long in coming. When word flashed from the Pacific that bombs were falling on Pearl Harbor, on another Sunday morning two years and three months after the German invasion of Poland, the nation found itself once again plunged into a struggle for existence. The Battle of the Atlantic had become the Battle of the Seven Seas.

22

HOW TO WIN A WAR

WHILE SALVAGERS were still probing the tangled ruins of Pearl Harbor, President Roosevelt and Prime Minister Churchill, sweeping aside the old jealousies and frustrations of the past, laid off a course for fighting this new kind of war with a new kind of weapon—an internationally unified merchant navy.

Before the United States entered the war the Allies had been fighting at sea with about twenty million tons of merchant ships, two thirds of them British. But this was a misleading figure. To reach an honest one they faced the fact that only about a fourth of the cargo-carrying fleet was available at any one time. Among the reasons for the shrinkage were the desperate need of arming some ships as merchant cruisers for convoy duty and of using others as transports, particularly the big passenger liners which were worthless for anything else. Still others, mostly Dominion ships, were required to supply war industries in the Dominions themselves. Then, too, crippling damage by air attacks on European repair yards and docks, together with the time required to assemble convoys and travel on zigzag courses, cut the shipping available at any one time to five or six million tons.

With the United States now engaged in combat there were eleven million more tons available for the shipping pool. Two boards were set up, one in Washington, the other in London, with representatives of both countries on each board. Their purpose was to "adjust and concert in one harmonious policy the work of the United States and British shipping of the United Nations." The prime function of these boards, later to be known as the United Maritime Authority, was to allocate ships where they were most needed at any given time. Not only British and American ships were pooled but the great majority of ships under the flags of other of the United Nations were also requisitioned by their governments and chartered for the duration of the war to the British Ministry of War Transport or its opposite number in the United States, the War Shipping Administration.

As for deciding the ticklish question of who got the ships and when, assent to the allocation of ships under American control to British service could be made only by the United States member on the Washington board; conversely, British ships for American service had to be cleared by the British member on the London board. Decisions of the two boards carried weight because they represented the concerted opinion of the heads of the shipping agencies of both nations. Unlike so many international agreements in the past, this one had teeth in it. The teeth were ship warrants, documents authorizing a ship to use certain port facilities and to purchase such necessities as stores and fuel. Without a warrant it was impossible for any ship to avail itself of these necessities in any port under Allied control anywhere in the world. Thus the United Nations were able to restrict the maritime operations of any nation unwilling to co-operate. This world-wide pool of ships was one practical answer to the oft-expressed Nazi doctrine of divide and conquer.

Nor did the teamwork end on the international level. Ashore, in the United States, one of the brightest pages in the record is that of ship operators, longshoremen and government working together to get the ships to sea. It was a triumph of private enterprise working within the framework of government, in which every pound of the two hundred million tons of cargo eventually to be moved to the far corners of the earth by the American merchant marine was cleared through the offices of American ship operators, acting as agents for the War Shipping Administration. Without the experienced supervision and team play of the shipping industry the merchant fleet would inevitably have lain idle in harbor months on end or gone to its death at sea, victim of an unsolved tangle of misdirection and confusion.

A year after Pearl Harbor submarine wolf packs were still sinking American merchantmen, many of them as yet unarmed, almost at will. It was common practice for an enemy submarine to surface when it was out of torpedoes and sink them by shellfire. At Atlantic Coast ports attacks began from the moment the open sea was reached and continued without respite all the way to the shores of Britain and beyond. The Jersey beaches were black with oil from sunken ships. Death and destruction dogged their wakes in the Caribbean, the Mediterranean, the Baltic, the Persian Gulf and the Pacific and Indian oceans. Later, as deck guns became available and gun crews of the navy armed guard were put aboard to man them, some semblance of self-defense was established. But in the North Atlantic alone, in spite of diminishing losses, a year-end average for only American vessels showed that the enemy was sinking more than a ship a day. The merchant fleet was fighting for its life.

By the spring of 1943 American shipyards were delivering five merchant ships a day. Convoys became more frequent. Ships were scheduled to be loaded for their next crossing weeks before they reached port. As the convoys grew into vast armadas greater than had ever maneuvered as single integrated oceangoing units before, they were scheduled with clocklike regularity to sail twice a week from ports like New York, Boston, Norfolk and Charleston. Before the year was out a ship was sailing from the United States with a war cargo every thirty minutes, night and day.

A war cargo, one single cargo, was something to reckon with. A Liberty ship, the work horse of the sea, could carry a cargo equal to the capacity of four railroad trains of seventy-five freight cars each. Or to take a long sight back down the seaway of history, the fifteen active ships of the United States Navy at the outbreak of the War of 1812 had a combined tonnage of just slightly over that of one Liberty ship. As for tankers, from D-Day to the collapse of Germany enough gasoline and oil was shipped across the Atlantic to drive from New York to Chicago every automobile, truck, tractor and bus existing on the face of the earth in 1941.

As never before in America's history, military pressure against the enemy was again demonstrating the direct relationship between strategy and ships. While the blows fell heavier on a crumbling Germany, while the Allies advanced ever nearer to the Japanese homeland, each new success was written in terms of ships. The striking power of the army and navy depended directly on the merchant marine. So vast, so complex is the saga of the war at sea that it is doubtful if this generation will have the perspective to view it in its entirety.

To get some kind of bearing on the scope of operations imagine a city the size of Wichita, Kansas, being dismantled and crated for sea. Organize the cargo so that it can be stowed aboard a fleet of freighters, ready to be set up again complete with houses, hospitals, theaters, machine shops and warehouses, together with enough supplies to feed and clothe every citizen. Make provision for an ample water supply, communications facilities, athletic fields, a highway network, a police force, a fire department and a complete system of government. Then move the whole thing six thousand miles across an ocean patrolled by the enemy and you have a fair idea of what the task was to establish one Pacific island outpost—Okinawa.

To build the ships, the nation's forty-six prewar shipyards had been increased to three hundred. Instead of sixty-six thousand workers there were now seven hundred thousand of them trained in their trades. As the demands of the armed forces cut into the ranks of the men, more than a hundred thousand women took their places. The women shipbuilders proved exceptionally able where manual dexterity was requisite in such jobs, for instance, as welding. In a shipyard with one of the highest production records, the Kaiser yard at Portland, Oregon, over a quarter of the workers were women. By the time the books were closed on 1943, the peak year of the building program, the United States alone had enlarged the United Nations shipping pool to the point where all merchant-ship losses had been replaced. In spite of higher pay scales, in spite of building larger and faster ships than in the First World War, the cost of building them was less. Ships built during and after the first war had cost about $210 a dead-weight ton; now, by reducing multiple production methods to a fine art, the cost was about $160 a dead-weight ton. Furthermore, these new ships were not only from thirty to forty per cent larger, but four times as many of them were built, and they were built in time for the fighting.

The bumblebee cannot fly. According to recognized aeronautical tests the bumblebee cannot fly because the size, shape and weight of his body compared to the total wing area makes flying absolutely impossible. But the bumblebee does not know this so he goes ahead and flies anyway.

—From a Bell Aircraft Co. cartoon

Henry J. Kaiser's "bumblebees" were ships. On production he said this:

I never saw a ship launched, let alone built one, until after the war began. . . . Man works with rhythm and material flows. The material flows as it passes the man and the man should do as little to it as necessary and do it with rhythm. It sounds poetic, but it has a tremendous effect on building in assembly-line production.

This master builder, whose bald head has been compared to the symphonic dimensions of the Finnish composer Sibelius, became, in the space of months, the symbol of a struggle in which speed and mass production were weighting the scales for victory or defeat. As a boy, Henry Kaiser was no bollard-sitter in a sailor town, dreaming of strange places below the sun. He was born in Sprout Brook, a fresh-water village on the banks of the Mohawk River in New York State, fifty-nine years before he was to build his first ship. He went west to work as a builder, first in paving the streets, then in building the highways, bridges and eventually the dams of the lusty young country on the Pacific slope. But like John Griffiths, designer of the first extreme clipper ship, and Donald McKay, builder of the *Flying Cloud,* Kaiser was a man of innovations, a trait evident from his first modest one of putting rubber tires on wheelbarrows to make possible more loads wheeled per man-hour. At no time was his imagination proscribed by the limits of the job at hand. He thought of himself simply as a builder, whether it be dams, wheelbarrows or ships. Donald McKay would have shuddered to hear him refer to the "front end" of a ship, but he would have approved of his dream to build them with new, lighter, stronger metals to lighten them in the future world race for trade.

As the necessities of war turned its spotlight on Kaiser, he became a man whom the press delighted in describing with superlatives. He had built the largest or highest dams in the world, he built and operated the largest cement plant in the world, he was building more ships faster than anybody in the world. Starting in 1941 with his first shipbuilding contract, his seven shipyards with fifty-eight ways on San Francisco Bay and on the Columbia River at Portland reduced their over-all man-hours by one third, and in some subdivisions of the work by as much as seventy per cent, until by mid-1943 his yards alone were launching and sending to sea one ship a day. They reduced the standard time of 105 days for building a Liberty ship to twenty-nine days by late summer. Foreseeing that Eastern steel mills were not going to be able to supply steel fast enough to keep the West Coast yards operating at full capacity, he remedied the situation by building a completely integrated steel plant in Southern California to produce steel plate and structural members as well as shell steel. Ground for the plant was broken in April 1942. Eight months later the blast furnace was blown in to start producing pig iron. The steel produced by this mill served not only his shipyards but other West Coast shipyards and war industries as well.

Kaiser's shipyards became the pacemakers for the nation. His launch of ships for the war—1,490 of them, including tankers and military vessels, totaling over fifteen million dead-weight tons—became the yardstick wielded over other builders by a Maritime Commission fighting to outbuild the mounting toll at sea.

Since Liberty ships comprised over half the merchant fleet, they became the most popular target of both the enemy at sea and critics at home. These were the ships that were to launch Eisenhower's men in Europe, that were to defy the Nazis by the murderous Murmansk run to support the Russians on the march to Berlin and that would put MacArthur's men in the

Philippines. Yet almost from the beginning a hue and cry was raised that the Liberty was an unseaworthy vessel. The fact that a few of them had broken up at sea was used to substantiate the charge. But from the launching of the first Liberty, the *Patrick Henry,* to the launching of the 2,710th and last one, during which time they were constantly overloaded with everything from locomotives and bombs to ungainly cargoes like airplanes and mules, and driven hard in convoy through heavy seas in all kinds of weather, to say nothing of those under frequent enemy attack, less than five per cent of them suffered serious fractures.

Faults of the Liberty were for the most part deliberate faults, committed in the interests of volume production and wartime needs. "Ships are bullets," said Admiral Land of the Maritime Commission, "and in war they are made to be expendable." To save brass, the portholes of a Liberty were made of malleable iron, and as that grew scarce a new type of fabricated steel was devised. Exhaust pipes from the main engine were changed from copper to steel, stamped and prefabricated. Cast aluminum, bronze, rubber and other hard-to-get materials all found substitutes in the Liberty. The miracle is that they proved to be good ships, that their performance was excellent. On this latter point, the only one to be considered in time of war, the men who took them to sea and brought them home again—deck officers, engineers and crewmen—were generally agreed. The files of every ship operator in the nation bulged with the records of their staying qualities.

One classic example of a Liberty that would not die is that of the *George Clymer,* built at Portland, Oregon. Loaded deep below her marks, as usual, with a cargo which included that most desirable wartime freight from a sailor's point of view, lumber, she was blasted by two torpedoes, one in the engine room, the other in the bulkhead between No. 1 and No. 2 holds.

But she would not sink. A British auxiliary cruiser came up with orders to sink her as a menace to navigation and pumped thirty-three six-inch shells into her. Fire from her cargo gutted the vessel, and she turned bottom side up to float like a huge gray whale. Still she would not sink. A dozen hundred-pound bombs dropped from the cruiser's diving plane only dented her bottom. Five days after the cruiser had picked up the *Clymer's* crew she was still afloat, spouting water through holes made in her bottom by the shells but refusing to break up and go down. Said the baffled captain of the cruiser to the *Clymer's* skipper, "We can't waste any more bloody ammunition on her"—and forthwith sailed away. Her lumber cargo may have done it. But anybody who has witnessed a lumber schooner break up and sink might have his doubts.

And there was the *Patrick Henry* herself, flagship of the Liberty fleet. Her log reads like a page torn from a geography book. Soon after Pearl Harbor she made her first voyage to Aden. Then, with occasional return voyages to the United States, she plowed her way to Mombasa, Durban, Cape Trinidad, Natal and other African ports; to the Red Sea, the United Kingdom, Murmansk in northern Russia, where she was a target during sustained attacks on a convoy both at sea and in port; and then back to Casablanca. She shuttled from supply bases to the war fronts in the Mediterranean for a while, where depth-bomb explosions did some damage to her cargo, and later she suffered minor damage from bombs and machine-gun bullets. Then back to the South and East Africa run, and again to the Mediterranean. At war's end she was still at sea.

When her operators, the Lykes Bros. Steamship Company, of New Orleans, were asked why their reports of enemy action involving this and other vessels were so infrequent, the reply was that "masters have become so accustomed to operating in danger zones that they seldom report attacks on their vessels unless serious damage results."

Neither speed of construction nor economy of materials used in these ships seriously affected their performance. For like the *Patrick Henry,* whose prewar building time was a matter of months, the Liberty ship *Robert E. Peary,* built at Richmond, California, by Henry Kaiser and delivered for sea duty in one week flat, was still on the job, rounding out two years of front-line war service when the bomb was dropped on Hiroshima. Ships like these were the answers to critics of the mass-production methods which sent to sea a wartime fleet of nearly six thousand merchant ships totaling fifty-one million tons.

Thomas McTaggert, chief engineer of the *Esso Bolivar,* a vessel of the tanker fleet, was awakened in the middle watch by the sound of shellfire. The following dramatic account of what happened is from an official report of the U. S. Maritime Commission:

The first order from the bridge was for full speed ahead in an attempt to outrun the submarine, and the engine-room crew under McTaggert's direction strained to squeeze every ounce of power out of the engines. Fireman Lauman was on watch in the fireroom when the attack occurred. Chief Engineer McTaggert asked him if he could stay at his post and keep up steam for the attempt to outrun the submarine. The sixty-year-old fireman replied that he certainly intended to. A few minutes later a shell went through the smokestack casing, cutting off a ten-foot section of six-inch copper pipe and some smaller piping. Pieces of steel crashed down into the lower fireroom, which was already filled with live steam escaping from the ruptured pipes. The chief engineer hurried in to check on Lauman and found him calmly going about his duties. Then another shell tore into the uptake and sprayed the room with pieces of metal. Fireman Lauman cleared the foot plates of the broken pipes and trash and kept the steam up until ordered to his boat station. By this time all the exits from the fireroom were afire and it was necessary for him to climb through the engine-room skylight to get on deck.

First Mate Hawkins Fudske found himself in command when the captain was shot down. For two hours, under a hail of shells and machine-gun bullets, he had been attempting to escape the submarine. Then a torpedo was sent into the vessel's side. Several members of the crew were killed before the order to abandon ship was given. By that time all but one lifeboat were battered beyond use, and the crew launched emergency life rafts for their escape.

Seaman Charles Richardson was assisting the gun crew during the attack. When the abandon-ship order came he found that two of the gun crew had been seriously wounded. Richardson hauled both men to the ship's side and tossed them over. Diving into the water after them, he placed one man on his back and told the other to cling to his neck. In this manner Richardson began swimming toward the lifeboat. Then they were attacked by sharks. Drawing his knife, the seaman struck out with the blade. After a few seconds of struggling, a shark pulled the man off Richardson's back and made away with him. Richardson suffered lacerations of one hand in the battle but finally made the lifeboat with the other wounded man, and both were taken aboard.

With the second engineer, Chief McTaggert remained behind in the engine room and methodically made every adjustment necessary to insure operation of the machinery later in case the ship should remain afloat and salvage should prove possible. Then the two made their way to the one usable lifeboat which was under the command of the first mate.

As the enemy fire continued, the boat was lowered while shells exploded on the side of the ship overhead. An exploding shell badly mangled one of First Mate Fudske's arms. Despite this severe and painful injury he grasped a line and assisted in loosening the falls. Another shell exploded and fragments from it hit Fudske again, this time mortally wounding him. In his dying condition he realized that the safety of the men depended entirely on getting the lifeboat away from the ship. His final words to those who anxiously bent over him were "Never mind me, fellows. Try and get the boat away."

Chief Engineer McTaggert took command and directed the men to lie down in the bottom of the boat. The submarine had the lifeboat in such perfect range that McTaggert finally ordered the entire group into the water, and directed them to hold the boat between them and the submarine until the shellfire ceased. McTaggert kept the lifeboat in the vicinity of the tanker until daylight when he spotted and picked up a number of men floating in the water.

After reaching port where the injured were placed in a hospital, McTaggert at once set about salvaging the ship. With a crew of Navy men he returned to the vessel which was listing badly and still burning. Although the engine room and fireroom were badly damaged, the engines, he found, could be operated. Finally getting the ship into a near-by foreign port under her own power, McTaggert then supervised emergency repairs sufficient to permit taking the ship to a United States port where complete repairs were made.

The acts of heroism and devotion to duty of Fudske, McTaggert, Lauman and Richardson have won them the Merchant Marine Distinguished Service Medal. All three survivors are back at sea.

One ship and a handful of men . . . These and the quarter of a million other officers and crewmen who manned the merchant fleet were doing a professional job under war conditions. In the excitement and distortions of war it was sometimes forgotten that the merchant marine was the only transportation industry to be engaged one hundred per cent in war operations. Its wartime management reposed in the hands of trained private operators who had spent their lives in the business. The men who sailed these ships through every peril were civilians, serving voluntarily, and though often under enemy action they had no military status. They ranged in age, officially, from seventeen to fifty. Actually they ranged from boys to old men.

The pay was good. Ashore, the average wage in the ship-yards was $248.04 a month. On a merchant ship an ordinary seaman's base wages were $82.50 a month, with war-zone bonuses increasing it to an average of $215 a month. A captain's pay on a Liberty ship was about $415 a month, plus similar bonuses. In addition there was insurance by the government without charge up to $5,000 for death and up to $7,000 for disability from war or marine risks. Additional insurance could be purchased up to $15,000 at low rates.

This compares favorably with the lot of the privateersmen of '76, who also were carrying on their business under hazards of war and who, upon signing on a vessel, were guaranteed, "If anyone shall first discover a sail which shall prove to be a Prize, he will be entitled to Five Hundred Dollars. . . . If he loose a leg or an arm he shall be entitled to Four Thousand Dollars . . . an eye, Two Thousand Dollars. . . . "

Discipline aboard ship also had its parallel with the merchant fighters of old. In that early struggle at sea, as in this one, they were under no compulsion to remain in service. The chief weapon of the captain in enforcing discipline then, as in the later war, was an economic one. For where an unruly "gentleman seaman" of the days of the cutlass and Long Tom was subject to forfeiture of his rights in prizes taken, modern skippers used the traditional method of levying fines, based on entries in the ship's log, deducted from the offender's pay. Both means to the same end were fairly effective. In the case of the merchant fighters of the Second World War, a Government Committee on Crew Disciplinary Matters reported that it found no indications of broad conflicts of interests between officers and crews. Only three tenths of one per cent of misconduct cases concerned economic questions and disputes arising out of collective-bargaining matters. Principal sources of shipboard difficulties, the committee reported, were "clashes of personalities, cases of individual intransigence, incompetence and negligence"—the sort of derelictions that might be expected in any cross section of hastily trained civilians doing a wartime job.

In this war, as in all the wars of our history, there were no strikes by the merchant marine. As for staying with their ships, at a time when the toll at sea was heaviest the War Shipping Administration reported:

There has been an absenteeism of less than six and one-half per cent of all officers and men. . . . The majority of those who did not go back to sea after concluding a voyage were prevented from doing so because of reasons of health. When Americans consider the risks these men took and the conditions under which they sailed they will fully understand that such a low rate of attrition can only mean extreme loyalty and courage beyond the line of duty.

It is a curious phenomenon of seafaring that the vast majority who manned the merchant fleet came from inland states— from the plains, the mountains, the fresh-water towns, where the lure of the sea has always been the strongest. Perhaps it is another proof of the old saw that familiarity breeds contempt. In any case, most of the men and boys who came down to the sea had never seen salt water until they reached the training schools or the ships themselves.

It was these "Ninety-day Wonders," as well as their more

seasoned professional shipmates, of whom General MacArthur was speaking when he said this at the conclusion of hostilities:

They have brought us our lifeblood and they have paid for it with some of their own. I saw them bombed off the Philippines and in New Guinea ports. When it was humanly possible, when their ships were not blown out from under them by bombs or torpedoes, they have delivered their cargoes to us who needed them so badly. In war it is performance that counts.

23

AFTERMATH

In the purser's office of the Matson Navigation Company's ex-luxury liner *Lurline,* still painted battleship gray in the spring of 1946, sat a harried ship's officer poring over one of the strangest supply lists ever to come his way in a long and varied career at sea:

Bottles, nursing	each	300
Nipples, bottle	each	300
Baby oil	bottles	600
Safety pins	each	2,000
Absorbent cotton	pounds	750
Talcum powder	cans	600
Castile soap	cakes	600
Washcloths	each	600

Baby forks and spoons will be supplied on request.
The ship will also provide baby toilet seats.

On the bulletin board, tacked over the yellowing pages of rules and regulations for troops in transport, was a fresh, new announcement:

There will be a beauty contest held some time after we leave
Suva. Sun suits, shorts, or anything within reason can be worn.
The rumor is that the captain's decision will be final.

And alongside that announcement yet another:

The captain wishes to state that he is *not* seasick. We have
not said anything to this effect, but he insists on this denial being
printed.

If Captain Berndtson, in charge of this shipload of some eight
hundred unescorted women and their babies, was not seasick
he had every right to be. In his day he had seen troopships,
prison ships, blood boats and suicide ships. But now he was
caught up in the largest mass migration of war brides known
to history, and his gallant vessel, veteran of the Pacific campaign, was being hailed as a brideship, for it was currently
engaged in what was known in the lingo of the hour as Operation Diaper.

Before this romantic voyaging the *Lurline* had been part of
a vast armada of converted troop carriers engaged in Operation
Reverse—the job of bringing home the army and a mountain of
supplies from battle areas. Within a year from the time the
United States Army was pouring across the Rhine and the
Navy was bombarding Okinawa, six million overseas veterans
were home again. In the holds of other homeward-bound ships
were unused and unwanted war materials, as well as such cargoes as badly wanted rubber, bananas and, in one ship at least,
two kangaroos, all symbolic of a disorganized nation trying to
pick up the pieces of a disordered world. But in the order of
human values brides came before Spam, jeeps and army shoes,
and with returning troop movements nearing completion for-

eign wives of service men were given a civilian priority. As near as any bold calculator of matrimonial statistics could come, it was estimated that some sixty thousand brides and their babies—and there was more than one baby to every three brides—were impatiently waiting to cross the Atlantic. Another twelve thousand were waiting on the far shores of the Pacific.

Functioning with the team play that war had made routine, the army, the navy, the War Shipping Administration and the merchant marine combined forces to bring them to their new homes. The brides were placed under army jurisdiction. The Army Transport Service did the processing and other legal work. Wives did not come under the immigration quota system; they could become naturalized citizens in two years instead of the usual five. The shipping companies acted as agents for the War Shipping Administration as they had in wartime, and merchant ships supplemented by a few army and navy transports brought them over on a schedule geared to complete the migration by the summer of 1946 in the Pacific and by the end of the year in the Atlantic.

If One World was ever to become a reality, Operation Diaper was well on the way to forming a substantial link in the chain of events binding it closer together.

There were less-heartening phases in the return to the ways of peace. One overwhelming fact was that, in spite of losing over a thousand merchant ships in the war at sea, the nation now possessed a merchant fleet of nearly six thousand vessels for which its citizens had paid over seventeen billion dollars. What was to be done with this two thirds of the world's ships?

Confusion was abroad in the land. The abrupt end of hostilities had caught both the government and the ship operators flat-footed. Nobody was ready for an orderly conversion to peace. In the wake of the natural letdown and disorganization that inevitably follows the tensions of war it became apparent that there was no concrete, generally accepted plan for throwing the colossal war machine into reverse.

In the midst of all the arguments, overage, damaged or unwanted ships were being "sent up the river" by the hundreds to join the laid-up fleets. Libertys, Victorys, "C" ships, refrigerator ships, cable ships, tankers—all joined the retreat to sanctuaries in the James River, Virginia, and to half a dozen others scattered from Gulf ports to Puget Sound. There, under government ownership, stores, equipment and fuel were removed, lifeboats and cargo-handling gear were stored in the holds, preservatives were applied to machinery which was then sealed up, with dehumidifiers installed to prevent deterioration.

Meanwhile, the growing reserve fleet solved few problems—except for another war. For ship operators in those early months of peace the biggest problem was lack of a definite proposition by the government for selling its surplus ships. A ship sales act was the key to the whole problem of re-establishing the peacetime merchant marine. Thus far there was no such act.

With no over-all policy, and no channel of single authority for doing business, some of the ships were being sold to all takers for scrap; others were being swapped by shipping companies for new government-owned ones on generous turn-in allowances; still others were being returned to their former owners, regardless of what their plans might be, if any. Even a fleet of tugboats was caught up in the mad whirl of reconversion and thrown into the breach to relieve the housing shortage. Scores of them were dismantled and their cabins set up on college campuses for the use of veterans studying under the G.I. Bill of Rights. It seems to have been a good idea at that, since the tug cabins were fully equipped with built-in cabinets, kerosene galley stoves, self-contained refrigerators operated by small gasoline engines, toilets, lavatories, tables and two lower and upper bunks in each with springs and mattresses.

Still another piece in the jigsaw puzzle of reconversion was the fate of a considerable chunk of the merchant fleet which had come to be known in the spring of 1946 as "The Forgotten Ships." These were the ships, some empty, some hull down with unwanted cargoes, that were gathering barnacles in home ports as well as in distant seas. Symptomatic of this particular element of confusion was the case of the *Edwin Markham,* which sailed from San Francisco for Okinawa with a war cargo several days after the war was over. It was the start of an aimless cruise in the Pacific, with a cargo nobody wanted, which was to last nearly two hundred days. At sea the *Markham* was diverted to Ulithi, where she rode her hook for forty-two days. Then her skipper, Captain Wright, received orders to put to sea again and dump all ammunition. "My gunnery officer," he later reported, "put forty thousand dollars' worth over the side. There were about seventy-five other ships there that did the same thing. Most of that stuff had lots of salvageable brass, which is one of the United States' scarce metals."

From Ulithi the *Markham* was ordered to Saipan, then to Buckner Bay in Okinawa, up to Naha and back to Buckner Bay again, where Captain Wright found twenty-five other ships in the same plight as his own. "At Okinawa," he stated, "we were all ordered from one side of the island to the other for no other purpose than to hoodwink a Congressional committee into thinking we had just arrived." Finally the vessel was ordered to Luzon. At Manila her wandering was given some purpose, at least, when she loaded a shipment of desks, chairs, filing cabinets, a few generals' automobiles and some rattan furniture destined for the Officers' Club at Tokyo. From Tokyo, over six months after sailing from San Francisco, the *Edwin Markham* returned at last to the honest ways of her calling.

And there is the daffy odyssey of the Liberty ship *Ada Rehan,* brought to light in informal discussions in the bars of Blood

Alley at Shanghai, where the crew reported a nine-month round-the-world voyage during which a drunken baboon went berserk in the Persian Gulf, a floating mine field was mistaken for a herd of turtles, three Persian women stowaways caused a near breakdown of discipline at sea, the ship got lost because a seaman's magnet in his pocket swung the compass off, and the skipper suffered a nervous breakdown.

But perhaps this is laboring the point.

One postwar fact was crystal clear to American ship operators: other nations were speedily rebuilding their merchant fleets. In England and Norway, where ships are recognized as a means of national survival and shipping amounts to an export like any other commodity, a shipbuilding boom was on. Not only that, but England, to the surprise of many people, had come out of the war with about the same size merchant fleet as she had entered it with—twenty million tons. Already hard at work to regain her supremacy on the seas, her shipyards in 1946 were building new merchantmen at the rate of a ship every two days. Other traditional maritime countries also had transferred their comeback plans from the drawing boards to the shipways. Few nations were interested in acquiring America's war-built ships. Postwar-designed vessels in Britain, France and the Scandinavian countries were fast, economically operated, specially adapted carriers for specific trade routes and cargoes, and their construction costs were lower than prices were likely to be for American ships, when and if they were offered.

Meanwhile, in the United States special-interest groups were propounding the timeworn pros and cons of what to do about the merchant marine. Shipping men hoped that half the country's import-export trade would be carried in American vessels. The State Department argued for foreign ships to carry American overseas trade in order to earn dollars with which to buy American products. The navy beat the drum for a big merchant fleet, active as well as reserve, for national defense. Industry was simply interested in shipping as cheaply as possible, but with dependable service that would open and hold open foreign markets and sources of raw materials. And the average citizen, still preoccupied with swapping his old car for a new one and finding nylon stockings for his wife, liked to see the flag in every port but wondered if it was not an expensive luxury.

When President Truman signed into law the Merchant Ship Sales Act of 1946 American steamship companies were at last able to fix their sights for charting the course ahead. They could determine how many and what types of ships they could buy and how much they would cost. A Victory ship, for instance, which cost the government nearly two million dollars to build in 1941 and almost two and a half million by 1944, could be purchased for slightly under a million. The tailor-made "C" ships also were obtainable at below-cost prices. Few prospective purchasers were much interested in the million-and-a-half-dollar Libertys, even at the knockdown price of half a million dollars. Some people had hoped that the slow ponderous Liberty ships might be put out to pasture to roam the seas as tramps. But tramps must nose into obscure harbors and up unimproved rivers in their hunt for freight. A Liberty ship's size and draft bars her from thousands of shallow harbors all over the world.

American citizens were given first preference in the buying, then citizens of the Philippine Commonwealth, then noncitizens who had lost their ships in the interests of the Allied war effort, and, lastly, other noncitizens.

These were not necessarily giveaway prices, nor were they intended to be. With a weather eye, as always, on the mistakes of the First World War, a nice balance had to be struck between too high a price range, which would result in no buyers, and prices that were too low, which would dump ships by the hundreds on American operators who would then be surfeited with vessels rapidly growing obsolete while foreign competitors were building more efficient ships to capture world trade. More important still, too many ships too cheap would leave American shipyards idle, and a generation of craftsmen who had learned the know-how of shipbuilding would once again become a vanished race.

For the United States, more than any other nation, the problem of steaming to sea with a new revitalized merchant navy was more than an economic one. There were also the perils of statesmanship involved.

Since the first Panzer division had rolled into Poland in 1939 there was more food in the world than ever before and more people were starving than ever before. In wartime America there had been so much wheat that it was being stored in boarded-up schoolhouses, hotels, garages, any abandoned building that would hold the glut. In vacant lots behind the docks at San Pedro, California, Australian wheat was being dumped in mountainous piles as late as the summer of 1944, unprotected from the weather. Grain men complained that there was enough wheat to supply the entire country for two years without another planting.

An active male adult requires some 4,000 calories a day to keep him normally fit. In England the daily food ration permitted throughout most of the war was 2,800 calories. In wartime Germany it was 2,250; in Holland, 1,900; in Poland and Belgium, less than 1,000 calories a day. After the fighting stopped, the people of continental Europe had their food supply leveled off to a daily average of 1,500 calories.

Once again America's merchant fleet was charged with the responsibility of feeding the world's millions, of giving the peoples of the free world the will to fight, to live, to build again.

For food, the most elemental factor in morale, was the crucial weapon, the instrument of major strategy in peace as in war. After the war the side that had won the Battle of Food was ineluctably the side to head up the peace table. In the struggle to win the peace, that nation's ships which were still afloat would more than ever before be forceful instruments of its national policy.

24

LANDFALLS IN A NEW WORLD

God and our sailors we adore—
In time of danger, not before.

AT THE OUTBREAK of war in Korea in the summer of 1950 the nation's shipyards were building just two oceangoing cargo-carrying vessels to fly the American flag. The United States had dropped to ninth place in world shipbuilding. Even the conquered Japanese were building more ships than the Americans.

By the winter of 1951-1952 shipping needs, made acute by the growing armada engaged in the long haul across the Pacific, were so desperate that a 10,000-ton ship loaded with coal was leaving the United States every two hours, day and night. To fill the breach the best ships—some six hundred of them—were stripped from the laid-up reserve fleets and sent to sea by private shipping companies for government account. To most landsmen, preoccupied with the shrinking dollar and rising taxes, this was a reassuring demonstration of the readiness and strength of the "moth-balled" fleet, a sort of dividend resulting from the toil and treasure poured into the war-built merchant navy.

It was an unfortunate illusion. For although the nation still possessed over three thousand ships, active and reserve, their numbers were no longer a true measure of their strength. For one thing, the bulk of the fleet consisted of Liberty ships, obsolete before they were built. But the most significant and dangerous fact was that over four fifths of the entire merchant marine had been built for the Second World War. Within a six-year period beginning in 1961 most of this fleet would become obsolete in a block, if only by reason of overage, to say nothing of the sleek new designs coming off the drawing boards of other maritime nations. From the moment the A-bombs were dropped on Japan the urgent and continuing need had been for new modern tankers, ore carriers and freighters and for passenger ships that could be quickly and economically converted to troop transport. Even before the war ended, eleven of the nation's largest steamship companies had laid joint plans with the government to build a fleet of eighty-nine speedy new passenger and combination passenger-cargo vessels. Augmenting this program, the United States Maritime Commission planned a fleet of fifty efficient 12,900-ton freighters to be called "Mariner" class ships, capable of twenty knots.

Those were the plans. Actually twenty of the passenger ships, including the streamlined luxury liners, *Independence* and *Constitution,* were eventually built. Of the Maritime Commission's Mariners, thirty-five were finally under construction by 1952, led by the *Keystone Mariner,* which was ready for sea by the end of summer. An apathetic Congress slow to appropriate the necessary funds, an invisible national shipping policy, spiraling inflationary costs—these and other factors were blamed for the deflated dream. But underlying it all was the hard reality that American ships were being priced off the seas by foreign competitors with their lower construction costs and lower-paid crews. Without a new, practical system of government subsidies to offset this fatal disadvantage the alternative was to let the American merchant fleet go out of existence.

Once again the historic chain of events that had plagued the nation for six generations was being set in motion, to begin with the withering away of the postwar merchant fleet, followed by the timeworn rude awakening to find ourselves dependent on other nations' ships when war comes; then the paying through the nose for foreign ships' services when and if we can get them, and finally the frantic building of a vast armada of costly, inefficient, mass-produced tubs to carry our war cargoes.

But this time the miracle happened. In 1952, after seemingly endless Congressional balking and confusion, understandable, perhaps, in view of the seventeen billion dollars of the people's money spent to build the wartime merchant navy, a new, workable shipping-aid plan was at last put into law. By way of sugar-coating the pill for those disciples of private enterprise who found trouble in swallowing it, it was pointed out that all direct government subsidies to American shipping from 1938 to 1950, including both costs of building and sailing the ships, totaled 210 million dollars. By comparison, the United States had paid England about 100 million dollars during the Second World War to transport American soldiers on two ships alone—the *Queen Elizabeth* and *Queen Mary*—despite the fact neither of these great superliners could be registered under the American flag because they do not come up to the safety standards and requirements of United States laws.

Encouraged by the new shipping-aid law, two new programs were launched, one by the government, the other by private builders and shipowners. The government plan, an industry-government partnership, was essentially a rearmament program to produce war-worthy naval auxiliaries. Under its subsidy system a regular-service fleet of liners initiated by private capital but conforming to navy specifications would be built. Such ships would be designed for efficient peacetime use, with private shipyards, operators and the government participating in the costs to insure equality of competition with low-cost foreign shipbuilding and operation, and to guarantee maximum utility for defense purposes.

The private-capital program was to build tankers and ore ships to meet the rapidly growing demands for oil and minerals from overseas. These specialized vessels would continue to be built and operated on a strictly business basis without government aid. As for the balance of the fleet, perhaps a thousand ships—tramp freighters, coastal vessels and other types engaged in interterritorial trade—these, too, would get along without subsidies.

Facts, figures, plans . . . In the nerve-wearing atmosphere of the summer of 1952, superheated by two national political conventions and nagging concern for an American Army still fighting a holding action in Asia, there was not much in the confused shipping scene to win the attention, let alone the understanding, of ordinary people. But it is axiomatic that Americans like things big. And in New York City on July 3, at the foot of 46th Street on the Hudson River where a crowd of thirteen thousand visitors stood wildly waving farewell to an outbound ocean liner, a heart-lifting event had caught and held the fascinated attention of millions. There, as the mightiest ship of them all backed slowly out into the stream to begin her maiden voyage, an old dream was being revived, a dream that had been shattered on the stormy North Atlantic when the Collins liner *Pacific* had gone racing into oblivion on a grinding iceberg nearly a hundred years before.

There could have been no more fitting name for any ship than that of the *S.S. United States*. A dramatic symbol of the dual quality of the new merchant navy-to-be, she was a project in which thousands of Americans had pooled their imaginations and resources. The handicrafts of not only shipbuilders but also the skills of tens of thousands of workmen from 167 cities and twenty-eight states directly supplied the component parts for her construction. In a broader sense every state in the Union, through finished product or raw material, had a part in her building. Nor did it end there. For although William Francis Gibbs, the vessel's chief designer, had tested the first working model for his dream ship of the future in a towing tank as far back as 1913 and had nourished his dream with more advanced models down the years, in the end she was the product of many minds, with 1,200,000 blueprints required for her design. "I am very loath," said Gibbs on the occasion of her trial run, "to pose as the only designer or take any share that should go to so many other people."

And then there was the matter of her cost. There were all kinds of ways to figure the cost of the new ship and nobody liked any of them. One thing is certain: the American people had a very definite share in that element of her construction, too. Included in the final bill were about twenty-six million dollars for defense features the navy wanted built into the ship and twenty-two million dollars as a government subsidy to make up the difference in the cost of having her built in an American yard instead of a foreign one. The balance, thirty million dollars, was paid by the United States Lines Company, which bought the ship from the government. In other words, it cost the public forty-eight million dollars to build this seventy-eight-million-dollar vessel.

For its share of the money the navy got a ship that could be converted within a matter of hours to transport 14,000 troops in temperate-zone comfort to any war theater in the world. It got also a twin set of engine rooms in which were packed more power in less space than any liner ever built, together with an extra hull and watertight compartmentation for insurance against torpedoes, and a damage-control room in which the controls, annunciators, equipment and means of communication for complete safety were centralized—all radical departures from merchant shipbuilding. Not quite as large as the Queens, she was made as small as she could be to do the job set for her, and one of the jobs set for her was to be able to cruise 10,000 miles at high speed without stopping for fuel, water or supplies. And although she contained more interior hull space for passengers and crew than any other liner on the high seas, her 990-foot length and 101-foot, 6-inch beam enabled her to squeak through the Panama Canal.

As for the commercial features of the ship, the United States Lines, which had known moments of borrowed glory in operating the rechristened German liners *Leviathan* and *George Washington* during the years between the two world wars, rejoiced in a new superliner that embodied more advances in design, propulsion and hotel facilities for its two thousand peacetime passengers than any other great liner for the last half century. Not that she was built to be a fancy ship. Naval specifications had come first. The difference, as described by her designers, was similar to the difference between a modern efficient Pullman car and the old-fashioned ornate Pullmans of two generations ago. With a superstructure three city blocks long built entirely of aluminum to provide strength with a minimum of weight, she had great stability in rough seas by reason of her low center of gravity. And to make her completely fireproof, in addition to the standard precautions not only were such furnishings as the upholstery, bedding, draperies and similar items noninflammable, but even the paint used on the artists' decorations was fire retardant. The only wood permitted in her construction or fittings was that around parts of her propeller shafts, the butchers' chopping blocks, and the pianos in the public rooms.

Those are some of the things some of the people got for their money. Above all, to the great pride and satisfaction of everybody, an American shipyard had produced in the record time of thirty months the safest, fastest, most modern and efficient ocean liner and naval auxiliary in the world.

If it were possible to bring back a ghost of the past it is hard to imagine a more interested passenger aboard the *United States* as she steamed to sea on her maiden voyage than Mr. E. K. Collins, whose paddle wheeler *Baltic,* just a century before, had been the last American-built-and-owned ship to bring home the mythical blue ribbon for her record run from New York to Liverpool in nine days, thirteen and one-half hours at an average speed of 13.34 knots.

There is no guessing just which of the *United States*'s wonders would have struck Mr. Collins most deeply once he had recovered from the shock of her sheer size, which was sufficient to carry all four of his original steamships with room to spare. It is safe to say that after reaching his cabin, shut away from the noisy farewells of the thousands of passengers and visitors, he would have been fascinated by the air conditioning he could control by a flick of a switch and by the ship-to-shore telephone at his bedside, providing he had someone to explain the use of these miracles. As he wandered about the ship, perhaps venturing to use some of the nineteen elevators to get him up and down between the twelve decks, he would have found quite a few other additions to the luxuries of barber chairs, steam heat and electric-bell service of which the *Baltic* had boasted. Some he would recognize for what they were—the monel-metal swimming pool, the two theaters, the gymnasium and children's playrooms—but, making his way into the fore part of the ship, he might have wondered if the traditional fo'c'sle had been given over to passengers instead of the crew. For in addition to several well-equipped lounges with facilities for reading, writing, games and radio entertainment and separate dining rooms for various ratings, the crew had its own covered promenade deck and air-conditioned staterooms with individual thermo-static control, as well as a writing desk and over each berth a reading lamp.

Back amidships again in the main galley, where the ra-daranges were producing sizzling steaks in a matter of seconds and twelve-pound roasts were being cooked in thirty-five min-utes, there would have been even more explaining to do. As for trying to help him make sense of what he found on the navi-gation bridge where her officers were apparently guiding the ship without looking where they were going, he would have his ears filled with incomprehensible talk about loran, radar, gyro-compasses, echo depth sounders and a pitometer log; and in place of a burly helmsman fisting the traditional five-spoke wheel that frequently had to be lashed to hold a ship on its course during a storm he would observe a quartermaster toying with two little power-operated wheels no bigger than toys. To Mr. Collins such navigational wonders might well have brought back bitter memories, recalling to him the tragic night off Cape Race in 1854 when his liner *Arctic,* with no safety devices, no red and green running lights and only a seaman blowing his tin horn from the fo'c'sle head, was rammed by the French steamer *Vesta,* sending to the bottom, among the *Arctic*'s three hundred passengers and crew, his wife, son and daughter.

As a distinguished passenger Mr. Collins would undoubtedly have been invited to sit at the captain's table where Captain Manning's guests would be a-buzz with talk of the vessel's speed. At breakfast he would learn that on the first day out the ship had set a new record of 34.11 knots against 31.13 set by the *Queen Mary,* owned by his old rival, the Cunard Line. At breakfast following the second day's run he would have learned that the *United States,* operating through fog by the magic of radar, had covered the greatest distance any ship had ever made in one day—801 miles at 35.6 knots. And before breakfast fol-

lowing the third day's run he would have been roused from
sleep by a blast of the ship's horn announcing she had crossed
Bishop Rock, the official transatlantic finish line. She had made
the crossing in three days, ten hours, forty minutes at an average speed of 35.59 knots, beating the *Queen Mary*'s record set in
1938 by ten hours, two minutes.

Perhaps that would have given Mr. Collins enough to think
about for one voyage. But if he had been so minded he might
have made some calculations on what kind of a race his blue-
ribbon winner, the *Baltic,* would have made of it. In such a
mythical race the *Baltic* could have won it by a day or so, providing the handicap required the *United States* to land in England her first load of fourteen thousand troops with their light
equipment, return to New York for another division of fourteen thousand men and land them in England, all while the
Baltic was completing her first crossing.

American ship designers and builders had come a long way
from the day when a writer for the *Scientific American,* holding
a post mortem over the fate of the Collins Line, could justly observe: " . . . There is a science and genius among our nautical
engineers, but they want experience."

Today, in terms of ships and the men who build them, Americans have no peers. They can build them for any job at hand,
they can build them quickly and they can build them to last.
Any doubter of their durability would have done well to have a
look at an ancient tramp steamer bucketing her way up New
York harbor in the winter of 1945, flying the Red Duster of the
British merchant navy and sporting the name *Empire Falcon.*
To dockside bollard sitters she appeared to be just one more battered veteran of the war at sea still on the job. But a chipping
away of the layers of paint on her bow would have revealed a
name to stir old memories. She was the *Quistconck,* first of her

breed to be launched at Hog Island, where she was christened by President Wilson's wife. Too late for one war but able to fight through another, as had 113 of her sister Hogs, she was still snouting the sea lanes after twenty-six years on blue water.

In the creation of the superliner *United States,* as in the creation of any great ship, there is a dramatic expression of the potentials of the nation that built it. Whether or not these American potentials could be integrated and set in motion for the greatest good to the greatest number was a question to which the answer lay in the years immediately ahead.

Soon after the Second World War a hopeful sentiment had come from across the Atlantic when Lord Halifax, wartime British Ambassador to the United States, publicly told a group of American bankers:

We have two alternative policies from which to choose. We can turn the economic life of the world into a wild scramble, leaving the less fortunate to go to the wall in whatever way they choose. And we can spend some feverish years of jungle life in a cutthroat war for international trade ... until another dictator arises to exploit the miseries of the people and multiply them tenfold by another war. Or on the other hand, if we can handle these large matters with sufficient foresight, there will be enough on the plate for everybody.

On this side of the Atlantic there were signs that shipowners and others concerned were also broadening their vision. One leader in postwar thinking on the American shipping scene, Charles L. Wheeler, of the Pope & Talbot Lines, gave voice and direction to a new pattern of planning that must have turned old Elias Hasket Derby of Salem windship days over in his grave. Far from worrying about cutthroat competition and overlapping trade routes, Wheeler put forth the idea that the same rates and equal opportunities must prevail in passenger, express-cargo and freight space for all the inhabitants of the earth. Just as air, rail, water and truck systems now knit each separate nation, so could greater similar systems link the world with uniform tariffs by employing specialized fleets of ships to service the globe like a public utility. Such services, he contends, at rates equal for the lowliest person or the wealthiest cartel, would eliminate private and national advantage alike, leaving such advantages to the genius, initiative and ambition of the individual.

If some such plan were to succeed, the international contracts would have to be enforced by governments, yet be tempered by compromise to combine flexibility under private agreements. The inter-Allied shipping pool during the Second World War showed that such teamwork was possible. Without some kind of similar peacetime agreements for international team play the United States Treasury was destined to be burdened with bigger and better subsidies for years to come, leading to the mounting ill will of other nations. It was ever more apparent that the alternative to working with our friends across the seas for the common good would be a tragically wasteful world-wide scramble for trade. America could win such a struggle but the victory would be empty.

If food, having won two world wars, were also to write an enduring peace in the years to come, the meaning to Americans of the freedom of the seas would have to extend beyond these shores. For on the freedom of the seas now depended the freedom of the world.

INDEX

INDEX